THE TRIAL ON TRIAL
VOLUME 1

TRUTH AND DUE PROCESS

The trial is central to the institutional framework of criminal justice. It provides the procedural link between crime and punishment, and is the forum in which both guilt/innocence and sentence are determined. Its continuing significance is evidenced by the heated responses drawn by recent government proposals to reform rules of criminal procedure and evidence so as to alter the status of the trial within the criminal justice process and to limit the role of the jury. Yet for all of the attachment to trial by jury and to principles safeguarding the right to a fair trial, there has been remarkably little theoretical reflection on the meaning of fairness in the trial and criminal procedure, the relationship between rules of evidence, procedure and substantive law, or the functions and normative foundations of the trial process. There is a need, in other words, to develop a normative understanding of the criminal trial.

The book is based on the proceedings of two workshops which took place in 2003, addressing the theme of Truth and Due Process in the Criminal Trial. The chapters in the book are concerned with the question of whether, and in what sense, we can take the discovery of truth to be the central aim of the procedural and evidential rules and practices of criminal investigation and trial. Dealing with distinct but inter-related issues, the essays address models of the trial, the meaning of due process, the meaning of truth and the nature of evidence, and legitimacy and rhetoric in the trial.

The Trial on Trial
Volume 1
Truth and Due Process

Edited by
ANTONY DUFF
LINDSAY FARMER
SANDRA MARSHALL
VICTOR TADROS

·HART·
PUBLISHING

OXFORD AND PORTLAND, OREGON
2004

Hart Publishing
Oxford and Portland, Oregon

Published in North America (US and Canada) by
Hart Publishing c/o
International Specialized Book Services
5804 NE Hassalo Street
Portland, Oregon
97213-3644
USA

Hart Publishing is a specialist legal publisher based in Oxford, England.
To order further copies of this book or to request a list of other
publications please write to:

Hart Publishing, Salter's Boatyard, Folly Bridge,
Abingdon Road, Oxford OX1 4LB
Telephone: +44 (0)1865 245533 or Fax: +44 (0)1865 794882
e-mail: mail@hartpub.co.uk
WEBSITE: http//www.hartpub.co.uk

British Library Cataloguing in Publication Data
Data Available
ISBN 1–84113–442–2 (hardback)

Typeset by Hope Services (Abingdon) Ltd.
Printed and bound in Great Britain on acid-free paper by
MPG Books Ltd, Bodmin, Cornwall

Preface

This collection of chapters is the first published outcome of a three-year project, *The Trial on Trial*, which is funded by a grant from the Arts and Humanities Research Board. The specific aim of the project, which is explained in more detail in the Introduction, is to work towards a normative theory of the criminal trial; its further, larger aim is to explore the potential of such collaborative, interdisciplinary work between lawyers and philosophers.

Central to the project are two sets of workshops: one on *Truth and Due Process*, held in 2003, which produced the papers for this collection; the other on *Judgement and Calling to Account*, to be held in 2004, which will produce a matching collection of papers. Finally, the four editors will produce their own book at the end of the project.

Our grateful thanks are due to the Arts and Humanities Research Board, for the grant that made this project possible; to our universities (Edinburgh, Glasgow, Stirling) for the further financial and other kinds of support that they have provided; to those who have come to our monthly meetings and helped us to clarify different aspects of the project (Peter Duff, Scott Veitch, Mike Redmayne, William Wilson, Michael Brady, Gerry Maher); but above all to the participants in the workshops—to those who wrote papers, whose names appear in the Table of Contents, and to those whose commentaries and contributions made the workshops such a stimulating enterprise: Zenon Bankowski, Michael Brady, Rowan Cruft, Stuart Green, Klaus Günther, Tatjana Hörnle, Dudley Knowles, Gerry Maher, Paul Roberts, Sarah Summers, and Scott Veitch.

RAD/LF/SEM/VT

Contents

Notes on Contributors

Robert P Burns is Professor of Law at Northwestern University in Chicago, where he teaches courses in evidence, procedure, jurisprudence, and legal ethics. He is the author of *A Theory of the Trial* (1999) and other books and articles in the philosophy of law, evidence, ethics, and alternative dispute resolution.

Emilios Christodoulidis is Reader in Law at the University of Edinburgh. He teaches jurisprudence and sociology of law, and his research interests include the philosophy of public law, the study of transititional justice, systems theory, etc. His book, *Law and Reflexive Politics* (1998) won the European Award in Legal Theory and the 1998 SPTL Award for Outstanding Legal Scholarship and has been translated into Japanese.

Markus Dirk Dubber is Professor of Law and Director of the Buffalo Criminal Law Center at SUNY Buffalo. He edits the *Buffalo Criminal Law Review* and writes on criminal law, comparative law, and legal history. His books include *Victims in the War on Crime: The Use and Abuse of Victims' Rights* (2002), *Criminal Law: Model Penal Code* (2002), and *The Police Power: Patriarchy and the Foundations of Criminal Law* (forthcoming 2005).

Antony Duff is a professor in the Department of Philosophy at the University of Stirling. He works mainly in penal theory and in the philosophy of criminal law; apart from the project on the criminal trial, his main current project is on structures of criminal liability. He has published *Trials and Punishments* (1986), *Intention, Agency and Criminal Liability* (1990), *Criminal Attempts* (1996), and *Punishment, Communication, and Community* (2000).

Peter Duff is Professor of Criminal Justice in the law school at Aberdeen University. He has published widely in the area of criminal justice, often writing from a Scottish perspective, and has carried out several empirical studies for the Scottish executive designed to evaluate reforms to the criminal justice process. In addition, he is a member of the Scottish Criminal Cases Review Commission.

Lindsay Farmer is Professor of Law at the University of Glasgow. He is the author of *Criminal Law, Tradition and Legal Order* (1997), and co-editor (with S Veitch) of *The State of Scots Law* (2001). He has written a number of articles on the theory and history of criminal law and is currently working on a history of the criminal trial in the late nineteenth century.

x *Notes on Contributors*

John Jackson is Professor of Public Law and Director of the Institute of Criminology and Criminal Justice at Queen's University Belfast. He has written books and articles on evidence and criminal justice and is on the editorial board of the *International Journal of Evidence and Proof*. In 1998–2000 he was an independent assessor on the Northern Ireland Criminal Justice Review which was established under the Belfast Agreement to review the Northern Ireland criminal justice system.

Heike Jung is a professor in the Faculty of Law and Economics, Universität des Saarlandes. He has published widely on criminal law, criminal process and criminal policy, as well as on medical law, European law and comparative law; he also served for fourteen years as a judge in the Landgericht and the Oberlandesgericht in Saarbrücken.

Sandra Marshall is a professor in the Department of Philosophy at the University of Stirling and a deputy principal of the university. She has published on a range of topics in legal, political and social philosophy, and is currently working on issues concerning the status of victims in the criminal process. She is co-editor of the *Journal of Applied Philosophy*.

Matt Matravers teaches political philosophy and is Director of the Morrell Studies in Toleration Programme at the University of York. He is the author of *Justice and Punishment* (2000) and the editor of *Punishment and Political Theory* (1999), *Scanlon and Contractualism* (2003), and *Managing Modernity: Politics and the Culture of Control* (forthcoming). He is currently working on a book, *Responsibility Within Justice* to be published by Polity Press in 2005.

Jenny McEwan is Professor of Criminal Law at Exeter University. She has published widely on issues related to the function and efficacy of the criminal trial. This has led to involvement in some campaigning BBC television programmes. Her books include *Evidence and the Adversarial Process: the Modern Law* (1998) and *The Verdict of the Court: Passing Judgment in Law and Psychology* (2003).

Duncan Pritchard is Lecturer and Leverhulme Special Research Fellow in the Department of Philosophy at the University of Stirling. He has published widely in epistemology, including recent articles in *American Philosophical Quarterly*, *Synthese*, and *The European Journal of Philosophy*. He is the editor (with Michael Brady) of *Moral and Epistemic Virtues* (Blackwell, 2003) and is currently in the process of completing a book entitled *Epistemic Luck*.

Victor Tadros is Lecturer in Law at the University of Edinburgh. He teaches and researches in criminal law and legal theory. He was educated at the universities of Oxford and London and has previously held a lectureship at the University of Aberdeen. He is currently writing a book entitled *Criminal Responsibility*.

1

Introduction: Towards a Normative Theory of the Criminal Trial

ANTONY DUFF, LINDSAY FARMER,
SANDRA MARSHALL, VICTOR TADROS

T HE BASIC QUESTION addressed by this project may be briefly
stated: if someone is accused of committing a crime, how should they be
treated by the State? Yet the very simplicity of the question conceals a
complex range of issues that an answer to it might address. Even once we focus
on the criminal trial in particular, rather than the processes of criminal justice
more generally, a broad range of questions presents itself.

First, there are questions about the normative significance of criminal trials.
Is the criminal trial, or something like it, a necessary response by the State when
it accuses someone of criminal offending? Is it necessary in all cases, or only in
some? But this question cannot be answered without an understanding of what
the criminal trial is, which gives rise to a second set of questions. What are the
central features of the criminal trial, distinguishing it from other institutional
practices within the criminal justice system, and from other kinds of social institution? When, if ever, does a procedure for processing those accused of committing crimes stop being something that we would recognise as being a trial
and become something else? Given the range of procedures that have at different times and in different jurisdictions been described as trials, are there features
that we should take to be essential to a trial? Or are there merely a number of
different institutional arrangements, each of which might be considered an
example of a criminal trial?

This then gives rise to a further set of questions about the proper structure
and organisation of trials. Must the State bear the burden of establishing the
guilt of the accused? What should be the role of the judge? Should there be a
jury? These in turn lead into questions about the proper nature and aims of the
criminal trial that can be seen to be of fundamental political, moral and social
concern. What are the limits of state action in the criminal process? How
significant are the values of openness or public participation in the criminal

process? What is the meaning of 'fairness' in this context? Is the central aim of the criminal trial to discover the truth, and if so the truth about what? Or does the trial have other aims which either supplement or supplant this aim?

Given the importance of the trial to Western legal culture, it comes as something of a surprise to discover that there have been few published attempts to engage systematically with questions such as these. Our project thus aims to address, and provide tentative answers to, some of these questions.

At least in the contemporary rhetoric and debate, the importance of the criminal trial is perceived to rest on the State's fundamental obligation to protect the rights of the accused. Denial of the right to a fair trial is seen as a fundamental breach of the rights of the individual, and this protection is indeed enshrined in such key human rights charters as the European Convention on Human Rights (ECHR).[1] Trials are seen as important to the protection of the innocent against wrongful conviction. A public or open trial is seen as a means for the community both to call an accused to account for their actions, and to act as a check on state powers. The prosecution must present the case against the accused person in open court, and the accused must be given the opportunity to challenge the evidence and to present their own case, participating in a process rather than merely being the object of proceedings. If found guilty the sentence must be communicated to the accused in open court, both as an act of individual censure and as a symbolic restatement of legal and moral values to the broader community. By thus protecting the rights of the accused, the criminal trial is said to protect the accused against the abuse of power by the State and state officials.

These central features of criminal trials, or at least of criminal trials as they are perceived in contemporary Western debates, are bound up with particular rules of procedure or evidence and institutional practices that differ between legal systems. The project of producing a normative theory of the trial cannot be completely dissociated—and nor should it be—from the legal, sociological or historical study of particular institutions and social practices. Yet it must also reach beyond this. It is not uncommon for lawyers to claim that a certain feature of their legal system, such as the participation of a jury or the role of an investigating magistrate, is a necessary feature of any fair trial. Indeed, one of the particular difficulties faced—if not altogether successfully—by the European Court of Human Rights in the interpretation of Article 6 of the ECHR is precisely that of evaluating specific elements of the criminal trial in the light of the more general normative standards laid down in the Convention. Equally, while the sociologist or historian can point to the social functions of trials in a particular society or period, or identify patterns or trends in the development of

---

[1] Art 6 (1) In the determination of his civil rights and obligations or of any criminal charge against him, everyone is entitled to a fair and public hearing within a reasonable time and by an independent and impartial tribunal established by law . . .

(2) Everyone charged with a criminal offence shall be presumed innocent until proved guilty according to law.

(3) Everyone charged with a criminal offence has the following minimum rights . . .

procedures or standards, this leaves open the question of the importance that these functions or procedures might have to a normative account of the institution. The aim of our project, and we hope also its timeliness, consists precisely in this attempt to draw on diverse practices of criminal trials past and present with the aim of developing a normative theory of the trial that goes beyond an evaluation of the features of any particular system.

Of course it may be argued that such a project is misplaced. Every student of the criminal justice process is aware of the relative insignificance of trials in the disposal of those charged with crimes, as people are diverted away from criminal proceedings by a combination of formal and informal initiatives. In these circumstances it might be argued that the action is elsewhere: that trials are too expensive and can no longer be considered as a model or paradigm case for those charged with crimes, and that the focus should be on criminal process or procedure more generally. In short, if trials are so important, then how come there are so few of them? This is the claim that such an exercise runs the risk of distracting attention from the real issues in criminal justice and of legitimating procedures that are of only marginal importance. This is an important charge and one that we shall address in some detail below, for as we have already suggested a normative account should begin from criminal trials as they feature in our existing penal systems—even if it must at the same time challenge these systems' view of themselves. While a normative account is in some ways an ideal model of proceedings, it should neither provide a comforting rationalisation of existing procedures nor be presented in terms that are abstracted to too great a degree from existing debates about the criminal justice system. A theory of the criminal trial must not only be normatively acceptable, it must also be relevant. Furthermore, notwithstanding the declining frequency of trials, they are at least still of great symbolic importance for the criminal justice system—and so we shall start with an examination of recent debates about the reform of the criminal trial.

1 THE TRIAL UNDER ATTACK

One of the best reasons for taking the trial as an object of study is that the question of the trial and its place in the criminal justice system is something that is itself vigorously contested at the present time. These attacks can take one of two forms (though these are often conflated): those whose aim or effect is to do away with trials altogether; and those which are aimed at central features of a particular institutional instantiation of the trial, whose aim or effect would be radically to transform trials in that jurisdiction. The former might include initiatives to deal with offenders administratively (such as prosecutor fines and various forms of diversion) or alternatively developments such as restorative justice which seek to replace trial procedures with forms of mediation and reconciliation between victim and offender. These are highly significant in their

4 *Antony Duff, Lindsay Farmer, Sandra Marshall, Victor Tadros*

different ways, not least because they force us to focus on those aspects or features of the trial process that are important and worth defending. We will consider these issues in the next section. More significant for our present purposes are those initiatives which, in seeking to transform elements of the trial, are often taken by critics to be attacking the institution as whole. In these initiatives and the often intemperate responses that they generate the continuing centrality of the trial to the criminal justice system is revealed. After all, if nothing was at stake in the nature and aims of the adversarial trial, we might expect proposals for change, which are often specifically presented as technical or managerial in character, to be met with indifference. However, this is not what happens: proposals for changes in the management of trials or the law of procedure and evidence have encountered a great deal of resistance (even if the level of debate has not always been very high). Some commentators have gone so far as to argue that certain recent proposals put the very future of the adversarial jury trial at stake, and that this is a threat to democracy and the fundamental values of our society. Something, therefore, seems to be at stake in these debates about the criminal trial, which suggests that we should take as a starting point a review of some of the developments that have fed contemporary debate about the trial.

These recent 'attacks' on the trial have taken a variety of forms. The most recent, and perhaps most significant, proposal has concerned judicial case management. Reports by Lord Justice Auld in England,[2] and Lord Bonomy in Scotland,[3] have proposed changes to criminal procedure that would require the establishment of timetables for cases, under judicial supervision, at an early stage in the process. Though the proposals obviously differ in their precise form, their aim is to prevent the delays and adjournments in criminal proceedings that are seen to arise from leaving too much control over the conduct of the case in the hands of the parties. It is hoped that changing the judicial role to become more interventionist and directive will make trials more efficient and effective.[4]

The use of juries in criminal trials has also been hotly contested. A series of government initiatives from the late 1990s has sought to restrict the right to elect

[2] Lord Justice Auld, *Review of the Criminal Courts of England and Wales* (hereafter Auld report; London, HMSO, 2001; http://www.criminal-courts-review.org.uk). This has led to a White Paper setting out the Government's proposals for the reform of the criminal courts: *Justice for All* (London, Home Office, 2002; http://www.homeoffice.gov.uk). Cf Lord Woolf, *Access to Justice* (London, Department for Constitutional Affairs, 1996; http://www.dca.gov.uk/civil/final), which made comparable proposals concerning case management in the area of civil justice.
[3] Lord Bonomy, *Improving Practice. 2002 Review of the Practices and Procedure of the High Court of Justiciary* (Edinburgh, Scottish Executive, 2002; http://www.scotland.gov.uk/library5/justice/rppj-00.asp). This was more narrowly focused than the Auld Report, considering only the High Court, and concentrating largely on managerial issues. This led to a White Paper: *Modernising Justice in Scotland* (Edinburgh, Scottish Executive, 2003; http://www.scotland.gov.uk/library5/justice/mjis-00.asp). Legislation based on the report (the Criminal Procedure (Amendment) (Scotland) Bill) is currently before the Scottish Parliament.
[4] Aspects of the changing judicial role are reviewed in the contributions to S Doran and J Jackson (eds), *The Judicial Role in Criminal Proceedings* (Oxford, Hart Publishing, 2000).

for a jury trial in England and Wales.[5] It has been argued at different times that the right of election has favoured professional criminals, that juries are vulnerable to threats and 'nobbling' more generally, that jurors are unable to understand complex trials, and that they are in general an unreliable institution. These various criticisms were brought together in the Auld Report, which, in addition to recommending the abolition of the right to elect for jury trial in 'either-way cases',[6] proposed abolition of the 'right' of the jury to return verdicts in defiance of the law or evidence—so-called jury nullification—and the use of special verdicts so as to make juries more accountable for their decisions.[7]

Another controversial area is the law of evidence, where a number of diverse proposals has been seen as undermining the criminal trial. Measures taken for the protection of vulnerable witnesses through the use of video technology and screens have limited the possibilities for direct confrontation and cross-examination.[8] Requirements for the disclosure and agreement of non-controversial evidence prior to the trial are viewed as part of a shift from primarily oral (and adversarial) proceedings to written proceedings.[9] Proposals to allow the jury to be made aware of the previous convictions of an accused person have been attacked as undermining the presumption of innocence and the very possibility of a fair trial.[10]

In criminal procedure, the proposed abolition of the double jeopardy rule, following the Macpherson report,[11] has been accused of undermining the principle of finality in criminal proceedings and of opening up new possibilities for the abuse of state power.[12] The principle of finality has further been affected by the establishment of review commissions both in Scotland and in England and Wales to deal with alleged miscarriages of justice. Finally, a variety of proposed reforms of sentencing, from the codification of law to the establishment of

---

[5] The most recent proposals were by the Conservative Government in 1997, then Labour in 2000 and again in 2003. A modified form of the proposals was enacted by the Criminal Justice Act 2003, p VII. The longer history is reviewed in the Auld Report, ch 5, paras 123–49, 173–80. See also S Doran, 'Trial by Jury' in M McConville and G Wilson (eds), *The Handbook of the Criminal Justice Process* (Oxford, Oxford University Press, 2002). It is worth noting that Scottish defendants have never had the right to choose their mode of trial; the prosecutor decides the mode of trial for 'either-way' offences: see P Duff, 'The Defendant's Right to Trial by Jury: A Neighbour's View' [2000] *Criminal Law Review* 85.

[6] Auld report, ch 5.

[7] Auld report, ch 5, paras 99–107; ch 11, paras 25–55. See also Matravers in this volume.

[8] See generally L Ellison, *The Adversarial Process and the Vulnerable Witness* (Oxford, Oxford University Press, 2001); J McEwan, 'Special Measures for Witnesses and Victims' in M McConville & G Wilson (eds), n 5 above.

[9] See Duff in this volume.

[10] Auld report, ch 11, paras 112–20. For a critical review of the issues see M Redmayne, 'The Relevance of Bad Character' (2002) 61 *Cambridge Law Journal* 684.

[11] *Report of the Stephen Lawrence Inquiry*, Cmnd 4262–1 (London, HMSO, 1999). See also Law Commission, *Double Jeopardy and Prosecution Appeals* (No 267; London, HMSO, 2001); Auld report, ch 12, paras 47–65.

[12] See http://politics.guardian.co.uk/queensspeech2002/story/0,12595,837252,00.html for the joint statement by Liberty, Legal Action Group, the Criminal Bar Association and the Bar Council in response to the Queen's Speech of November 2002.

sentencing commissions, has been attacked on the grounds of their potential for undermining the independence of the judiciary.[13]

This list is far from exhaustive, but it gives an idea both of the types of reforms that are being proposed and of the type of response that is generated. What is notable about this list is that although all the proposed reforms are obviously linked by their connection to the trial and criminal procedure, the grounds on which the trial is being defended (by either the proponents or opponents of the reforms) may vary greatly—making it hard to tell exactly what is at stake in these debates. Thus, we see variously, the importance of adversarial procedure, the orality of proceedings, the presumption of innocence, the liberty of the individual, the independence of the judiciary and the ancient right to trial by one's peers all being invoked in defence of the institution. Even if it is not clear that there is any single principle or set of principles that links all of these issues, it should be clear by now that there is a pressing need to develop our normative theoretical understanding of the criminal trial in a way that can help to illuminate these issues, both individually and in relation to each other.

One place that we might expect to find such a normative framework is in the Auld Report.[14] Although the Auld Report has been perceived to be concerned largely with the issue of effective case management, the terms of reference and the scope of the final report go far beyond this to include criminal justice personnel, evidence and criminal procedure, and it attempts to present the proposals in these diverse areas as part of a coherent package of reforms. However, the coherence, such as it is, does not derive from any clearly expressed or articulated normative principles, since this is an area in which Auld is notably equivocal. Auld refers to the importance of convicting the guilty and acquitting the innocent, yet considers it 'obvious' that the purpose and function of the trial cannot be limited to that.[15] The right to a fair trial is identified as a longstanding feature of English criminal justice, but qualified as being 'near absolute'.[16] The broad framework of the report is then provided by the idea of a need to balance various interests, burdens, agencies and individuals within the criminal justice system. He described his project as, a broad inquiry into how the criminal courts should do their job so as to combine fairness with efficiency, while also having regard to the interests of all involved in or exposed to their process.[17]

There are two important contexts to this balancing.[18] First, there is the role of the courts in the determination of guilt or innocence and in the sentencing of

[13] The Sentencing Advisory Panel for England and Wales was established under the Crime and Disorder Act 1998. The Sentencing Guidelines Council for England and Wales was established by the Criminal Justice Act 2003 to take over the role of the Court of Appeal in issuing sentencing guidelines. In Scotland, the executive announced the establishment of a sentencing commission in 2003.

[14] See n 2 above. For a sympathetic review see J Jackson, 'Modes of Trial: Shifting the Balance towards the Professional Judge' [2002] *Criminal Law Review* 249.

[15] Auld report, ch 1, para 4.

[16] Ibid, ch 1, para 13.

[17] Ibid, Foreword, para 5.

[18] Ibid, Introduction, para 4.

convicted defendants. Here there is need to ensure that procedures are 'fair' with respect to the various individuals and interests involved (including victims, witnesses and jurors), as well as to ensure that the mode of trial is appropriate to the alleged crime. Yet the content of this fairness is not made clear. This is in part because certain features of the criteria of fairness are not fully articulated (what, for example, is the measure of seriousness or appropriateness?), but more importantly because too much rests on the idea of balance as a worthwhile end in itself, without fully considering whether or why certain rights or interests might weigh more heavily in this balance, or indeed whether certain rights or interests ought to be balanced at all.[19] Secondly, Auld asserts that the courts must be 'considered in the context of the criminal justice system as a whole, including the community at large and the various agencies and others involved in the process'.[20] The meaning of this is uncertain. While it appears to invite consideration of the role of courts as political institutions, the scope and difficulty of this issue is quickly limited to ensuring that the various participants in the criminal justice system are satisfied with their role and the outcomes that the system produces. The general justifying aim of the system is reduced to that of efficient crime control, and legitimation is reduced to the need to ensure public confidence in the system[21]—concepts with little determinate normative content.

It is perhaps unfair to criticise Auld for failing to articulate a clear normative framework where others, from royal commissions to politicians and academics, have also failed. However, it is surely worth pointing out that while he significantly advances the debate in terms of the breadth of his approach and his willingness to see connections between diverse proposals, there is less of an obvious coherence to some of his proposed reforms. Thus it is hard, for example, to see what if anything links the continuing prohibition of research into juries' actual deliberations and the proposals to make juries more accountable, or the defence of adversarial procedure and the advocacy of judicial case management. The balance seems to be drawn in an ad hoc way, driven by considerations of expediency or tradition rather than by any more fundamental principles.

An area where we might we might look for greater theoretical coherence is that of human rights, incorporated into UK law since 2000.[22] Much of the early litigation arising under the Act has been brought under Article 6, the right to a fair trial.[23] This has not only forced the courts to reflect, if only at a basic level,

---

[19] For scepticism about the balancing approach to human rights in the context of criminal justice, see A J Ashworth, *Human Rights, Serious Crime and Criminal Procedure* (London, Sweet & Maxwell, 2002).

[20] Ibid.

[21] See Auld report, eg Introduction, paras 31–32, 34.

[22] Human Rights Act 1998. The Act came into force in Scotland one year earlier as a consequence of the Scotland Act 1998 s 57(2).

[23] Much of this litigation concerns delays in bringing cases to trial, though there have also been challenges based on the presumption of innocence and the use of temporary judges.

on the fairness of their own procedures, it has also opened British courts and law out towards a wider European jurisprudence and debate about the meaning of fairness in trial proceedings. Of particular importance here are questions about the relationship between pre-trial and trial procedure, and the integration (or balancing) of the protections contained in adversarial and inquisitorial proceedings. Yet it is striking here that there remains a great deal of uncertainty and disagreement over the scope and impact of the provisions of the ECHR. For some, the rights contained in the Convention are (nearly) absolute, and states must bear a heavy burden of justification if they are to derogate from these provisions, while others argue that Article 6 merely gives new expression to rights that have long existed in UK law.[24] More importantly, the explosion of jurisprudence on this question in both domestic and European law has not led to any notable developments in the normative understanding of the principles involved. As the right to a fair trial becomes of increasing legal and political significance—an issue that is yet more obvious in the context of the detention of terror suspects without trial and the international row over the fate of the detainees at Guantanamo Bay—it is yet more important that we develop our normative understanding in this area.

2 THE SIGNIFICANCE OF THE CRIMINAL TRIAL

Despite the continuing debates surrounding the criminal trial and its procedures, many of those who study the criminal justice system empirically might be inclined to think that our project is an irrelevance. A normative theory of the criminal trial, they might argue, may be interesting in theory, but it would be too detached from the reality of the criminal justice process to have any significant normative implications for that process as it currently operates. Focusing on the criminal trial in particular, it may be argued, shows that we are too much in our ivory tower, the only place in which it is still plausible to think that criminal trials are a significant part of the way in which the State responds to criminal offending.

One argument, which we think does not have significant implications for our project, concerns the frequency of jury trials in particular. It has often been noted that jury trials are relatively infrequent, and it has been argued, for that reason, that they ought not to be considered the central focus of criminal justice scholarship.[25] In attempting to develop a normative theory of the criminal trial, however, we do not assume that jury trial ought to be of central concern, either as the object of study, or in its outcome. Our project, at this stage at least, leaves open the possibilities that juries should not be a necessary feature of criminal tri-

---

[24] Compare G Maher, 'Human Rights and the Criminal Process' in T Campbell, D Goldberg, S McLean and T Mullen (eds), *Human Rights. From Rhetoric to Reality* (Oxford, Blackwell, 1986), 197, with R Buxton, 'The Human Rights Act and the Substantive Criminal Law' [2000] *Criminal Law Review* 331. See also Auld report, ch 1, para 12.

[25] See P Darbyshire 'The Lamp that Shows that Freedom Lives' [1991] *Criminal Law Review* 740.

als, or that their use need not be frequent or systematic, or even that they should never be used at all.

More significant is the argument that the central focus of criminal justice scholarship should be neither jury trials *nor any form of contested trial*. When considering the question of how the State ought to deal with those who are suspected of committing criminal offences, the trial, the argument goes, is the least significant aspect of the process. The disposal of suspects, in the vast majority of cases, occurs without recourse to a contested trial, or at least a trial where the contest concerns the guilt or innocence of the accused (as opposed to the sentence that she ought to receive).

There are a number of reasons why this might be the case. First, there are cases in which a citizen is suspected of committing a criminal offence, but where nothing further occurs. There may not be enough evidence to proceed with a prosecution, or prosecution may not be in the public interest. If that is the case, the criminal trial does not occur, and the question of whether the suspect committed the criminal offence is left open.[26]

Secondly, cases might not be contested at trial because they are disposed of, with either an admission or a finding of guilt, without recourse to a trial. The suspect might be formally cautioned, for instance—a process that involves an admission of guilt, but no court process.[27] Or a sanction such as a 'fiscal fine' might be imposed—a sanction that can be administered without a court hearing.[28]

Thirdly, the defendant may be diverted to a different kind of process. This might occur because the defendant suffers from a mental disorder, which allows diversion to a psychiatric institution without recourse to the criminal trial;[29] or because the defendant is a child, who can be dealt with in the juvenile justice system rather than through a full contested trial.[30] It might also occur because special kinds of processes exist as alternatives to the criminal justice process for dealing with particular kinds of offence. For example, there exist drug courts to deal with offenders who are addicted to proscribed drugs,[31] and domestic

---

[26] For a good introduction to this problem, see A J Ashworth, *The Criminal Process: An Evaluative Study* (2nd edn, Oxford, Oxford University Press, 1998) ch 5.

[27] See Ashworth, ibid; R Allen 'Alternatives to Prosecution' in M McConville and G Wilson, n 5 above.

[28] P Duff, 'The Prosecutor Fine' (1994) 14 *Oxford Journal of Legal Studies* 565–87.

[29] Normally under the rubric of the Mental Health Act 1983. See G Richardson, *Law, Process and Custody: Prisoners and Patients* (London, Weidenfeld & Nicolson, 1993) ch 9; R D Mackay, 'Mentally Abnormal Offenders: Disposal and Criminal Responsibility Issues' in McConville and Wilson, n 5 above; and, for an overview of practice in Scotland, Scottish Executive, *Serious Violence and Sexual Offenders: Criminal Justice Recommendations of the MacLean Committee* (www.scoland.gov.uk) ch 3.

[30] See the essays in J Winterdyk (ed), *Juvenile Justice Systems: International Perspectives* (2nd edn, Toronto, Canadian Scholars Press, 2002), and I Weijers and R A Duff (eds), *Punishing Juveniles: Principle and Critique* (Oxford, Hart Publishing, 2002).

[31] For a brief introduction, see P Bean, 'America's Drug Courts: A New Development in Criminal Justice' [1996] *Criminal Law Review* 718. As Bean notes, such courts are sometimes adopted after the accused has been sentenced, but they are also sometimes adopted as a substitute to prosecution, where criminal charges are dropped if the process is deemed successful.

violence courts to respond to instances of domestic abuse.[32] Theoretical work on restorative justice has had an obvious impact in the development of some alternatives to the criminal justice process.[33]

Fourthly, disposal of the case might involve a court process, but one which is not fully contested. This will be the case if the defendant pleads guilty to the offence with which he is charged. In 'adversarial' systems at least, this commonly occurs after 'plea-bargaining'. There is an inducement for the defendant to plead guilty. Either he pleads guilty to a lesser crime, or a different crime, from the one which he is suspected of perpetrating, or he pleads guilty in the hope or expectation that this will result in a lesser sentence.[34] Often where a guilty plea is achieved, it is the result of pressure from defence counsel who commonly 'negotiate' cases with the prosecution.[35]

In short, the argument is that the contested trial, which is sometimes portrayed as a fundamental keystone of criminal justice in a democratic and free society, is mere ideology. The contested trial is only the presentational surface of the criminal justice system, a surface which masks the reality of the criminal justice process. That reality is the administrative processing of cases through relatively informal methods to control the 'criminal population', usually using relatively minor offences.[36] Providing a normative theory of the trial only helps to secure this ideology in its place, while the reality of the criminal justice system operates beneath this surface. And for this reason, the argument goes, normative discussion of the contested trial is irrelevant.

This argument is certainly significant to our project. If the contested trial is as infrequent as is claimed, there is good reason at least to consider whether focusing on the criminal trial is worthwhile, or whether it is indeed possible to focus on the criminal trial without investigating the whole criminal justice process. However, in our view, these facts about the criminal justice system help to establish rather than undermine the significance of developing a proper normative theory of the criminal trial.

Let us address the argument that the criminal trial cannot properly be approached in isolation. The criminal trial is only one part of the criminal justice process, it is claimed, and a theory of the trial can only be developed within the context of a theory of the criminal process more generally. This may be

---

[32] See the essays in H Strang and J Braithwaite, *Restorative Justice and Family Violence* (Cambridge, Cambridge University Press, 2002).

[33] For a good overview of the literature, see G Johnstone, *A Restorative Justice Reader: Texts, sources, context* (Cullompton, Willan, 2003).

[34] See J Baldwin and M McConville, *Negotiated Justice* (London, Martin Robertson, 1977); M McConville, 'Plea Bargaining' in McConville and Wilson, n 5 above. But it has been reported that there is little evidence of the practice of sentence discounting in magistrates' courts: see M McConville, L Bridges, J Hodgson and A Pavlovic *Standing Accused* (Oxford, Clarendon Press, 1994) 188.

[35] Baldwin and McConville, ibid; McConville, Bridges, Hodgson & Pavolivic, ibid.

[36] See M McConville, 'Plea Bargaining: Ethics and Politics' (1998) 25 *Journal of Law & Society* 562.

thought particularly true given that the way in which a case is investigated and presented by the police will clearly have a significant impact upon its outcome.[37]

It is undoubtedly important that any theory of the criminal trial is sufficiently connected to other aspects of the criminal justice process to be achievable and fair. In understanding the criminal trial, it is clearly important to understand its relationship to other aspects of the criminal justice process. However, we think that the criminal trial is central to understanding at least some of these other processes, and that for this reason it makes theoretical sense to begin with a theory of the criminal trial. Exactly what kind of investigative and pre-trial process is acceptable, it seems to us, depends upon the nature of the criminal trial and what it attempts to achieve rather than the other way around.

It is well understood that rules of the admissibility of evidence cast a long shadow over the operation of other aspects of the criminal justice process. Admissibility will affect the way in which the police investigate an offence, the decision to prosecute, the decision of the accused whether to plead guilty, and to what offence. The same kind of argument holds true with regard to a normative theory of the criminal trial. The norms that govern the trial process will determine the appropriate way in which the accused is to be treated pre-trial. If it is central to the criminal trial to respect the autonomy of the accused, as is claimed by some of the authors in this collection,[38] for example, the way in which this is elaborated is likely to have implications not only for the way in which the criminal trial ought to be conducted, but for the way in which other limbs of the criminal justice process ought to function. Even if the criminal trial does not always occur when an individual is accused of a criminal offence, it does provide fundamental background to the operation of the criminal justice process as a whole. Let us outline these claims in a little more detail.

First, the point of many of the practices outlined must be understood, in terms of their meaning and their value, principally in the light of the criminal trial. And for that reason, our evaluation of those practices will depend on the principles that ground the criminal trial. For example, the meaning of a caution is plausibly that the defendant is put on notice that, if her behaviour recurs, she will be prosecuted. The caution, as with other forms of diversion from prosecution, depends on the possibility of the trial whether for the present offence or for future offences. Similarly, it is at least plausible to argue that the practice of pleading guilty is simply a foreshortened version of the contested trial. The contest is over from the beginning, as the defendant concedes at the outset. The practice of pleading guilty supposes that the defendant has the opportunity to contest her guilt if she so wishes.

Secondly, normative evaluation of other elements of the criminal justice system arguably rests on their relationship to the criminal trial. Suppose, for

---

[37] See M McConville, A Sanders and R Leng, *The Case for the Prosecution* (London, Routledge, 1991); D McBarnet, *Conviction* (London, Macmillan, 1981). For a recent overview, see A Sanders, 'Prosecution Systems' in McConville and Wilson, n 5 above.

[38] See particularly the chs by McEwan and Dubber in this volume.

example, as we suggested in section 1, that the value of the criminal trial is that it protects certain rights of the accused against state power. That might leave open the possibility that there are cases in which the criminal trial is not necessary, for there are other protections against the abuse of state power against the accused. But that is not to say that the criminal trial is marginal in the criminal justice process. For it may still be the case that there is a broad range of circumstances in which the criminal trial is the only effective way of protecting the rights of the accused. In order to understand whether there are cases in which the rights of the accused can be protected adequately without recourse to the contested trial, it is important to know in some detail what those rights are, and how the trial might serve to protect them. Given that the trial is one of the central ways in which the rights of the accused are adequately protected, there is at least good reason to consider other aspects of the criminal justice process against the standards set by the criminal trial, properly understood and properly theorised.

Once we begin to consider some of the other values that the criminal trial might properly aim to promote and protect, the reasons for studying the criminal trial become even more powerful. For example, as we noted in section 1, it is considered centrally important in debates about criminal justice that the trial is a public forum, which operates with public participation. Clearly, other aspects of the criminal justice process do not meet the standards of publicity achieved by the criminal trial. Once we understand whether and why it is important for the criminal trial to be public, we are likely to be in a better position to evaluate whether there are problems with other aspects of the criminal justice process given their failure to achieve this level of publicity. A normative investigation into the criminal trial will aim to scrutinise publicity as a value in relation to the treatment of those accused of criminal offences. There is good reason to suppose that such an investigation will also help to establish the *scope* of the principle of publicity, if indeed it is a principle at all. That will help us to evaluate whether the lack of publicity in other elements of the criminal justice process is problematic.

This shows that investigating the values of the criminal trial will be relevant to establishing the values that ought to underpin the process more generally. Now, it might be objected that this only strengthens the argument that we should be investigating the values of the process more generally. However, there is a further set of reasons why the criminal trial ought to be the starting point for this investigation. Just as the meaning of pre-trial investigation and procedure is determined by the nature of the criminal trial, so normative evaluation of pre-trial investigation and procedure is determined by a normative theory of the criminal trial.

Consider, for example, hearsay evidence. There is a question about whether hearsay evidence ought to be admitted during the trial. This might turn on whether hearsay evidence is probative. But it might also turn on other values that the criminal trial will want to protect. For example, hearsay evidence may be inadmissible because the accused ought to be provided with a proper opportunity to contest the evidence of witnesses, and this might be thought to be a particular instance of the more general value of autonomy that the trial ought to promote and protect. But whether hearsay evidence is admissible in court will clearly have an impact upon pre-trial investigation and procedure. It will have an impact on how crime is investigated, which cases are taken to court, when the accused is likely to plead guilty and so on.

Furthermore, our normative understanding of hearsay evidence will have an impact on how crime *ought* to be investigated. The mode of investigation ought not to undermine the central values that are to be protected at trial. If the criminal trial requires that evidence is not only probative, but also capable of contestation, the investigation must be directed to providing not merely material that proves that the accused has committed the offence, but material that provides the accused with a proper opportunity to defend himself in open court. This means that criminal justice agencies must not only provide transcripts of evidence by others, or even video recording of the evidence of others; they must persuade those others to give evidence in open court. The investigation, as a result, is not merely about finding the facts; it is about persuading witnesses to engage in the trial process if that process goes ahead. And that may involve reminding those witnesses of any obligations that they might have to participate in the criminal trial.[39] That may be important even if the contested trial does not ultimately go ahead.

But the idea of permitting the accused to have a proper opportunity to contest the account that others provide of her conduct cannot be fully explicated without focusing on the criminal trial. For providing such an opportunity, at least on one account, *is* to provide the accused with a trial. Hence, how we understand the nature of the investigation itself is determined by how we understand the criminal trial. The investigation may, on the one hand, merely be a process for finding the truth. It may also be a process which involves encouragement of citizens to participate in the criminal trial. Which way we evaluate the process of investigation depends upon a normative understanding of the criminal trial.

We can see the potential impact of a normative theory of the criminal trial in more depth if we consider in a little more detail sentence reduction through plea bargaining. Sentence reduction through plea bargaining is, as we have noted, a common way in which the full criminal trial is avoided. This practice, it is sometimes rather unconvincingly claimed, is motivated by the fact that the defendant deserves a lesser penalty if she has shown contrition for committing the offence by pleading guilty to it. There can be little doubt that the prime motivations for allowing plea bargaining are in reality the cost of the full blown criminal trial, including the cost in time, and the improvement in the proportion of crimes that

[39] See S E Marshall, 'Victims of Crime: Their Station and its Duties' in M Matravers (ed), *Managing Modernity: Politics and the Culture of Control* (Routledge, forthcoming).

are 'cleared up'.[40] The prime motivations for the defendant, on the other hand, are almost certainly the reduction in sentence itself, and the desire to circumvent the time, effort and cost involved in defending oneself rather than any feeling of penance for what she has done. And, as noted above, this is often a result of 'advice' from defence counsel.[41]

Now, a normative theory of the criminal trial should help us to become clearer about the extent to which, or the conditions under which, such a practice is acceptable. On the one hand, there is a question about whether a full trial, more or less in the form that captures popular imagination with a thoroughly contested process concerning the guilt or innocence of the accused, must be held in order to justify any conviction for any offence. Such a requirement would clearly render our current criminal justice system unworkable, but it might be the conclusion of the search for an acceptable normative theory. If that was the conclusion, normative theory would provide a powerful critique of current practices: only those convictions that resulted from a full, contested criminal trial could, on this account, be considered justified; all other convictions ought to be quashed.

On the other hand, a normative theory of the criminal trial might help to establish that the full criminal trial is necessary only under some conditions, or not necessary at all. For example, it might be necessary only if the defendant wishes to contest the evidence against her. Now, there is a question about whether this is compatible with, or undermined by, the provision of inducements, in terms of sentence reduction, to plead guilty rather than contesting the evidence. It is widely noted that sentence reduction provides an inducement to the innocent as well as the guilty to plead guilty to the charge,[42] and this might be thought to be inconsistent with the requirement that the State must have proved beyond reasonable doubt that the defendant is criminally responsible if a conviction is to be justified.

But there may be further normative reasons that can be stacked against plea bargaining. If the criminal justice process is understood as normatively driven by communication with the accused about his conduct, rather than solely by the instrumental goal of establishing guilt or innocence, for example, plea bargaining may be seen as illegitimate not because it undermines proof beyond reasonable doubt, but rather because it undermines the kind of communicative enterprise that the criminal justice process ought to be: the criminal justice process, it may be argued, is precisely to be distinguished from a bargaining process.[43] In that case, even if it could be shown that plea-bargaining very rarely provides inducements to the innocent who is accused of a criminal offence, it

---

[40] See McConville, 'Plea Bargaining', n 34 above.
[41] See Baldwin and McConville, n 34 above; McConville, Bridges, Hodgson and Pavlovic, n 34 above.
[42] See McConville, 'Plea Bargaining', n 34 above, at 369–72.
[43] See further s 3 below.

may be considered illegitimate.[44] That depends upon a more general normative account of the criminal trial, an account that we hope to provide.

Relatedly, there may be a question about whether the legitimacy of a criminal conviction depends on actually holding a full criminal trial, on the one hand, or merely on the defendant having the opportunity to have her case tried in full on the other. For example, the significance of the criminal trial may be that the defendant, if charged with an offence, must have a proper opportunity to answer that charge. And if the trial is merely an opportunity that must be provided to defendants, we must ask about the conditions that might undermine that opportunity. Plea bargaining may be seen in that light: does the inducement of a reduction in sentence effectively deny the defendant a proper opportunity to defend herself against the criminal charge? Is there any difference between an inducement to plead guilty and a disincentive to go to trial? And if there is not, do all such disincentives constitute illegitimate denials of the opportunity to defend oneself against a criminal charge? If an actual, full criminal trial is required, on the other hand, there is no question about the legitimacy of plea bargaining. Where such a bargain is used to avoid the trial, on that account, it must be illegitimate.[45]

Finally, there is a question about the significance of the offence and the relationship between that and the criminal trial. Should all offences be tried in full, or is it legitimate to distinguish between different kinds of offence in terms of criminal procedure? For example, it may be that a full criminal trial is necessary to justify a conviction for some serious offences, but not for lesser offences. Some systems distinguish between crimes and misdemeanours, and only the former must be prosecuted through the full criminal trial.[46] Other systems do not distinguish between kinds of offence in that way. Perhaps, given the infrequency of full trials in their current form, a normative theory ought to begin with a general account of the trial that is plausible for trying the majority of offences, an account that might need bolstering when serious offences are charged.

But those questions can only be answered in the light of a normative theory of the criminal trial. It is only once the purposes of the trial are established that we can hope to become clear about the significance of jury trial, for example.

[44] This may be compatible with some sophisticated consequentialist accounts of the criminal justice process, for example that developed in P Pettit and J Braithwaite, *Not Just Deserts: a Republican Theory of Criminal Justice* (Oxford, Oxford University Press, 1990). See s 3 below.

[45] This kind of theory may, at least in part, motivate the scepticism with which plea-bargaining has been viewed by German theorists. For discussion see J H Langbein, 'Controlling Prosecutorial Discretion in Germany', (1974) 41 *University of Chicago Law Review* 439; M Dubber, 'American Plea Bargains, German Lay Judges, and the Crisis of Criminal Procedure' (1997) 49 *Stanford Law Review* 547.

[46] For discussions of the impact that this distinction has had in the German criminal procedure, see Langbein, ibid; J Herrmann, 'The Rule of Compulsory Prosecution and the Scope of Prosecutorial Discretion in Germany' (1974) 41 *University of Chicago Law Review* 468. Andrew Ashworth argues that there may be good reason to create a separate category of 'civil' offences, whose boundaries should be carefully policed, which would have less human rights protection: *Human Rights, Serious Crime and Criminal Procedure*, n 19 above, at 118.

That depends upon the nature of the public trial: whether the central value of criminal trials is accuracy, or whether it performs functions beyond the accurate determination of guilt. Furthermore, such a theory will help us to determine whether the trial is best seen as a requirement or a mere opportunity. And hence it will shed significant light on the circumstances, if any, in which some kind of plea bargaining is acceptable.

Similar points can be made about other ways in which the contested trial is avoided. The acceptability of using an alternative forum to resolve a dispute that is criminal in nature depends upon the purposes of the criminal trial. If the criminal trial is merely a forum for the effective resolution of disputes, some such alternative forum might be an acceptable locus to deal with criminal conduct. But perhaps the criminal trial ought to be more ambitious than that: more ambitious in terms of impartiality, democratic accountability and openness. If that is the case, alternative modes of dispute settlement might be found wanting in two ways. First, in terms of legitimacy: alternative forms of dispute settlement might be insufficiently public and representative both in their nature *qua* fora, and in terms of the norms that they use. Secondly, in terms of the protections they provide: alternative forms of dispute settlement, through being less public, might not properly protect the rights, including the human rights, of the accused.[47] Whether this is indeed the case can only properly be understood if we understand something further about the proper nature of the criminal trial within its institutional and political context; and that is what a normative theory of the trial should provide.

Finally, a normative theory of the criminal trial should help us to understand the use of prosecutorial discretion. Do those who have suffered as victims of a criminal offence have a right to see the (alleged) perpetrator brought to trial when possible? And if so, under what conditions is this right enforceable? What follows from the fact that criminal law is an aspect of public rather than private law, where the victim is sometimes accorded no more standing than a witness; should this status of the victim survive in the light of a properly defended theory of the criminal trial? It is only once we understand this that we can properly understand how prosecutorial discretion should operate, and in relation to whose interests.

Far from showing the irrelevance of our project, the fact that criminal trials are relatively rare in our system, despite political and public attachment to the criminal trial, shows precisely the relevance of our project. For it is only in the light of a general theory of the criminal trial that the acceptability of the current practices of criminal justice can properly be assessed, or proposals about changing those practices properly be made.

That is not to say that the criminal trial is the proper place to begin when thinking about criminal justice. There is good reason to suppose that the crim-

---

[47] See A J Ashworth, 'Responsibilities, Rights and Restorative Justice' (2002) 42 *British Journal of Criminology* 578.

inal trial must build upon theories of criminal law and theories of punishment, and to a degree a theory of the criminal trial can only be developed in the light of those theories. However, theoretical work on criminal law and punishment is very well developed in the literature, sufficiently so that those resources are available to us in developing a theory of the criminal trial. Whilst theoretical work on other areas of the criminal process, such as the criminal investigation, is rather underdeveloped, we do not think that such theoretical work is essential to the development of a normative theory of the criminal trial. On the contrary, it is the theory of the criminal trial that ought to guide theoretical work on the rest of the criminal process.

3 A NORMATIVE THEORY OF THE CRIMINAL TRIAL?

A normative theory of the criminal trial must include some account of what it is a theory of—of what a criminal trial is. This is not to say that it must begin with a precise definition of the concept of a criminal trial, for instance one that specifies necessary and sufficient conditions for something to count as a trial. There is good reason to suppose that the search for such a definition, in advance of normative theoretical work, is likely to be futile. Any account of the central or essential features of criminal trials must be partly determined by an account of the proper purposes of the criminal trial. Whatever kind of 'definition' we might produce must reflect, rather than being logically prior to, a normative theory of the trial.[48] To indicate the kind of familiar process that we are concerned to theorise, all we need say at this stage is that the criminal trial is a formal, legal process through which it is to be determined whether someone is guilty of committing a criminal offence, and thus whether he is liable to punishment for it.

This leaves open various questions that certainly should be left open at this preliminary stage: what kind of determination should result from the trial (what a verdict of 'guilty' or 'not guilty' should mean, if, indeed, those are appropriate verdicts); whether trials should always be contested (whether it is appropriate sometimes to accept pleas of 'guilty'); whether they should be 'inquisitorial' or 'adversarial' in form (in so far as that distinction can be clearly drawn); whether sentencing is part of the trial, or should be seen as a separate process; whether trials should be 'public', not just in that they are conducted by public officials, and deal with 'public' rather than 'private' wrongs (with crimes rather than with civil wrongs), but in that they are conducted in public. These and other questions about the proper structure and procedures of criminal trials should be answered, in so far as they can be given determinate answers, by a normative theory of the aims and values by which criminal trials should be structured.

[48] But see J Jaconelli, 'What is a Trial?' in M Mulholland and B Pullan (eds), *Judicial Tribunals in England and Europe, 1200–1700: the Trial in History*, vol I (Manchester, Manchester University Press, 2003) 18.

To talk of 'a normative theory of the criminal trial' might suggest that we aim to establish an account of those aims and values that will be universally applicable across all times and all places—a theory that will apply to anything that counts as a criminal trial, whatever its legal, political or historical context. But that is not our aim, since we share the suspicions that many theorists have voiced at such attempts at ahistorical, a-contextual normative theorising. Our aim is rather, more modestly, to develop a normative theory that is appropriate to the context in which it is formed and will be applied—the context of a twenty-first century state that purports to be democratic, and to respect the set of roughly liberal values that, whatever the controversies about their precise meaning and application, are the common currency of contemporary legal and political debate. We will need (in the end, but not in this introduction) to explicate some of those values and their implications for the criminal trial, and in doing so we will be able to show how they can ground a normative theory that has real critical bite: but we will not seek to justify those values themselves. We will also need, in the end, to ask how ambitious even a relatively modest, localised normative theory can aim to be. Should we, for instance, aim to decide between 'adversarial' and 'inquisitorial' models of the trial? Or should we instead recognise that somewhat different normative theories will be appropriate to each type of trial process—or, perhaps, recognise that a normative theory of the trial might leave significant aspects of its structure and procedures underdetermined, rendering either process acceptable? Or should we abandon these two models in favour of some other model of the trial?

Normative theorising about the criminal trial might begin with the question of what this particular institution, this process through which it is formally established whether someone is guilty of a criminal offence, could be for: what function or purpose could it properly serve within a system of criminal law, or within a polity? If we ask that question, a simple answer at once presents itself: that a trial's proper purpose is to establish the truth about whether the person being tried committed an offence. If we then ask why that should be worth doing, the simple answer is that it enables the identification of those who, having committed a criminal offence, should be punished: criminal trials connect the substantive criminal law to the penal law, and enable the State to apply the sanctions for which the law provides to those on whom they should be imposed. These simple answers are certainly not wrong: a trial culminates in a verdict that must surely be understood as asserting (or purporting to assert) a truth about the defendant's guilt or innocence; and the most obvious practical effect of that verdict is that the defendant is either (if found 'guilty') sentenced to a punishment, or (if found 'not guilty') freed from the threat of punishment. But they are much too simple, since they leave many crucial questions unanswered. Three sets of such questions can be distinguished.

What Truth?

The first set of questions concerns the truth that the trial is supposed to establish: what should a verdict of 'guilty' or 'not guilty' mean or say? Though proof of a defendant's guilt obviously involves proof of various relevant facts (facts about what she did, what she intended or believed, and so on), we cannot plausibly read the verdict as simply asserting some factual proposition: the trial involves the application of legal norms and standards to the defendant; a 'guilty' verdict expresses the judgment that she violated those norms, or did not meet those standards, a violation that warrants her condemnation and punishment. We must then face some familiar questions about this normative dimension of the criminal process. Can we read the verdict as involving no more than a 'detached normative statement' about the bearing of the law's norms and standards on this defendant's conduct,[49] or should it involve the committed application of those norms and standards by a court that accepts them? Are those norms autonomous—can their meaning and authority be found within the law; or do they depend on deeper moral or political norms, which are therefore implicated in the court's verdict? How far are those norms determinately given in advance of the trial; how far are they interpreted, determined or constructed in the trial process itself? Can those norms be applied without some commitment to the values underlying them? Whose norms are they, or should they be?

We also need to ask whether a 'guilty' verdict should be read simply as asserting that the defendant *is* guilty, or rather as asserting that he has been *proved* guilty by an appropriate (or 'due') process. The latter reading might be especially appropriate for 'not guilty' verdicts in systems that place the burden of proof on the prosecution, and that do not allow (as Scottish trials allow) for a verdict of 'not proven': surely 'not guilty' cannot amount to an assertion of the defendant's innocence, but must rather be read as asserting that he has not been proved to be guilty. On that point, we might instead say that if we take the presumption of innocence seriously, the prosecution's failure to prove the defendant's guilt leaves the presumption that he is innocent undefeated, so that the 'not guilty' verdict constitutes a proper reaffirmation of his innocence. But there remains a question about the relationship between the verdict and the process that leads to it.

Consider a defendant who is indeed guilty, and who is convicted through a process that is in some serious way unsatisfactory or inappropriate. Should we say that the 'right' (the accurate, or even just) outcome has been reached, albeit by a procedure that was unjust or in some other way defective, thus distinguishing 'accuracy of outcome' from 'fair procedures' as distinct aims of the

---

[49] On 'detached normative statements', see J Raz, *The Authority of Law* (Oxford, Oxford University Press, 1979) 153–59.

criminal process;[50] or that the verdict itself is tainted by the injustice or impropriety of the procedures by which it was reached, in which case we should perhaps read the verdict as making some implicit reference to those procedures? This question connects to those discussed below about the role of truth within the criminal trial; we will say more about it shortly.

Does Truth Matter?

The second set of questions concerns the value of the truth-finding that is, on the simple view, the main, or even sole, aim of the criminal trial: why is it important to establish such truths as these—important enough to justify the costs incurred by maintaining a system of criminal trials?

One obvious answer is that such truth-finding assists the 'general justifying aim' of the criminal justice system as a whole: that aim is to control crime by detecting, convicting and punishing the guilty,[51] and the criminal trial formally identifies the guilty. This is to give truth, and the criminal process as a whole, an instrumental rationale, as serving the social good of crime reduction, and thus serving those further social goods that crime reduction serves. Nor, once we begin to think through an instrumentalist perspective, need we see crime control, by the identification and punishment of the guilty, as the only end that criminal trials can serve: they can also, for instance, provide satisfaction, or closure, for victims and others affected or disturbed by crime; they can (depending on how the verdict is understood) provide those who assert their innocence with a chance to have their names publicly cleared; they can provide a powerful symbolic reassertion of the power and authority of the law and the State. But it is as what at least purports to be a search for the truth that the trial serves such other ends as these.

A plausible instrumentalist, or consequentialist, theory of the trial would be complex in at least two respects: it would include a rich account of both the intermediate and the final ends that a criminal trial, as part of a system of criminal justice, should serve, and of their relative importance as compared to other ends that make claims on the State's resources; and it would provide arguments, including substantial empirical evidence, to support its claims that criminal trials, or a particular kind of criminal trial, will efficiently serve those ends.[52] The question is, however, whether a *purely* consequentialist theory, however rich and complex, can be normatively plausible: that is, can we understand the

---

[50] See, eg Law Commission, *Double Jeopardy and Prosecution Appeals* (No 267; London, HMSO, 2001) para 7.12; quoted (and criticised) in Auld report, ch 12, para 58; see also Auld report, ch 1, para 7, on the Government's objectives of 'just processes and just and effective outcomes.'

[51] A J Ashworth, 'Concepts of Criminal Justice' [1979] *Criminal Law Review* 412 at 412, quoted approvingly in *Auld Report*, ch 1, para 8, ch 12, para 51; Ashworth n 26 above offers a much richer, more nuanced discussion.

[52] For an outline of an ambitiously consequentialist account of criminal justice, see Braithwaite and Pettit, note 44 above.

normative significance of criminal trials, the values by which they should be structured, purely in terms of their instrumental contribution to some set of further ends? This question gains force when we realise that the justifying aims cited in the previous paragraph may require only the *appearance* of truth or truth-seeking as means to them. What satisfies victims and provides a sense of closure, what assures citizens of the State's authority and power, what deters crime, is the persuasive appearance that the guilty are being formally detected and punished; and while the best way to bring about the appearance of X will often be to bring about X itself, sometimes appearances are most efficiently produced by deception or illusion. The simplest illustration of this point is the all too familiar charge against purely consequentialist theories of criminal punishment: that they would sanction, or at least regard as a morally open option, the punishment of those known to be innocent if this would serve the further aims of the system.

Some consequentialists admit that charge, and argue that if the deliberate conviction of the innocent would be beneficial, it would be justified;[53] others argue that a properly sophisticated consequentialist account would preclude such injustice.[54] But the core of the objection is not that consequentialists would in fact sanction such injustices; it is, rather, that by portraying them as only contingently wrong, in virtue of their harmful effects, consequentialists fail to capture the character of the wrong that they involve. The point is not that consequentialists would justify a system of criminal trials that would sometimes convict the innocent: for any human system of criminal justice will sometimes do this (if it convicts anyone), since any such system will be fallible. The point is that the falsehood involved in the conviction of an innocent could in principle, if it appeared to be the truth, be warranted by consequentialism. If crime control and reduction is the general justifying aim of the criminal justice system, which criminal trials must serve, conviction of the innocent will be considered wrong only if and because it would probably not be an efficient means to those ends. To this critics object that what is wrong with the conviction of an innocent is not that it is unlikely efficiently to serve the crime-preventive or other consequentialist aims of the penal system, but that it constitutes an intrinsic and serious injustice to that defendant. Hence, even if the consequentialist account can provide good reason why the innocent should not be convicted, it cannot provide *the proper moral explanation* of what is wrong with such convictions.

There are two different ways in which truth might be of intrinsic rather than mere instrumental value. First, the demand of truth might set negative side-constraints on the criminal process: a trial might not establish the truth about the defendant's guilt or innocence, but it must avoid establishing falsehood as

---

[53] See, eg J J C Smart, 'An Outline of a System of Utilitarian Ethics' in Smart and B Williams, *Utilitarianism: For and Against* (Cambridge, Cambridge University Press, 1973) 1, 69–72.

[54] For two of the more plausible arguments, see R M Hare, *Moral Thinking: Its Levels, Methods and Point* (Oxford, Oxford University Press, 1981), chs 3, 9.7; Braithwaite and Pettit, note 44 above, at 71–76.

truth by convicting an innocent.[55] This constraint might naturally be expressed in the language of rights—a right that protects citizens against wrong convictions. That right cannot be or generate a right to a criminal process that guarantees acquittals for all the innocent; but it could be taken to generate a right to a process that provides fair and equal protection against mistaken convictions—protections more secure than would be provided by a purely consequentialist theory.[56] This exemplifies another familiar type of normative theory: instead of offering a purely consequentialist account, we accept a consequentialist account of the 'general justifying aim' of the system, but recognise non-consequentialist side-constraints on the means that we may use in pursuit of that aim.[57] If we pursued this kind of account, we would then need to ask what other values set what other side-constraints on the criminal trial, which would lead us into one way of understanding the demands of 'due process'; we return to this in the next subsection.

Secondly, however, truth might be not a mere negative side-constraint on the criminal process, but a positive goal: we should have a system of criminal trials that aims to establish the truth, not (not merely) because this will serve certain further ends, but because establishing the truth is intrinsically important. Furthermore, we should aim at true answers to the appropriate questions. We might now invert the relationship between some of those further ends and the value of truth: victims and others, we might now say, will be appropriately satisfied by a trial because it marked a genuine attempt to establish the truth; rather than seeing the truth as valuable because it satisfies them, we see their satisfaction as worth pursuing because it reflects the value of the truth. But why should the truth be important, if not as a means to further ends?

In answer to this question, we might talk of the importance of recognising, and ascribing responsibility for, the wrongs that citizens have done and suffered, by calling wrongdoers to account for the wrongs they have done. We might argue, that is, that a polity should take due public notice of the public wrongs that its citizens commit (the kinds of wrong that properly concern the criminal law); that if it is to accord its citizens (both victims and offenders) the respect due to them as responsible agents, it should take such notice by a public process of ascribing responsibility for those wrongs, which calls the alleged wrongdoer, as a responsible citizen, to answer the charge of wrongdoing, and to

---

[55] If we read an acquittal as asserting that the defendant is innocent, the acquittal of the guilty also establishes a falsehood as truth, and the claim (if we are to justify a system that operates the presumption of innocence) must be that it is even more important to avoid false convictions than it is to avoid false acquittals. But if we instead take an acquittal to mean that the defendant has not been proven guilty, this at least reduces the tension between the demand to convict the (provably) guilty and the demand not to convict the innocent.

[56] See, eg R M Dworkin, 'Principle, Policy, Procedure' in C F H Tapper (ed), *Crime, Proof, and Punishment* (London, Butterworths, 1981) 193.

[57] See H L A Hart, *Punishment and Responsibility* (Oxford, Oxford University Press, 1968) 1–27. On side-constraints generally, see R Nozick, *Philosophical Explanations* (Oxford, Oxford University Press, 1981) 28–29; see also Braithwaite and Pettit, n 44 above, at 26–36.

answer for the wrongdoing if it is proved against him. This would suggest a different conception of the criminal trial, as a process not merely of establishing the truth *about* a defendant and his conduct, but of engaging *with* the defendant in a procedure that calls him to answer to a charge of wrongdoing—a procedure that aims to communicate with the defendant as a responsible agent. We cannot explicate the character, foundations and implications of this conception here (it will be more prominent in later publications from this project), but it will clearly also make a significant difference to how we answer the third set of questions about truth and the criminal trial.

Truth in the Trial

Suppose we accept that trials aim to establish the truth, in answer to an appropriately formulated question about whether a defendant committed a criminal offence. Should we understand the various procedures and rules that structure the trial in instrumental terms, as serving the aim of truth?

If we are to determine how far criminal trials should be 'adversarial' in their structure, or how far 'inquisitorial'—in so far as that distinction still has any useful role to play;[58] or what the rules of evidence should be; or what role (if any) lay people should play in the trial—for instance in reaching the verdict; or any of a host of other questions about the structure of the trial: should we simply ask which procedures will make it most likely that the court will find the truth? The answer to that question must be 'no', since there are other values in play: the point is not merely that there are other, in particular symbolic, ends that trials may serve, and to which some of their procedures are properly oriented (think, for instance, of the symbolic significance of the very architecture of the court room, and the clothing of the participants), but also that there are obvious constraints on the means by which the truth is to be pursued, which can be plausibly rationalised as non-consequentialist constraints. To take an extreme example, if we ask why a confession secured by torture should not be admitted as evidence, the answer is surely not just or primarily that such a confession would be unreliable; it is that it would be simply wrong to use such means, however reliable their results might be. While many of the trial's rules and procedures are indeed to be explained wholly or at least largely as instrumental to the aim of truth-finding (and are to be normatively criticised from that perspective), others cannot be thus understood.

How should they be understood? One familiar possibility is to apply the model of a side-constrained consequentialism to the trial's internal structure, and to rationalise some rules as reflecting, not judgments about how the truth can be most efficiently and reliably pursued, but side-constraints on the pursuit of that truth. This is one way to interpret the idea of 'due process', and the

---

[58] See Auld report, ch 11, para 3; and the chs by Duff, Jung and McEwan in this volume.

values that can be collected under that (increasingly vague) heading.[59] To identify the values that should figure in such a conception of due process, we might
then look to the idea of citizenship, and (especially in contexts in which certain
rights are entrenched in a constitution, as in the United States, or in a convention, as in Europe) to an account of the fundamental rights that citizens have
against the State: a trial should pursue the truth, but not through procedures or
on the basis of investigations that violate the citizens' rights—rights of, for
instance, autonomy, freedom and privacy.

There is clearly much work to be done (and much has been done by theorists
of criminal process) in identifying the values that ground such side-constraints,
and in working out what rules they might justify. A further important feature of
this approach is that, unless we take an implausibly absolutist view of every
such constraint, it builds a fundamental kind of conflict, tension or compromise
into the very structure of the criminal trial: to use a metaphor that is much used
and much abused in English debates, we will face a constant need to 'balance'
the consequential demands of the efficient pursuit of truth against the non-
consequentialist side-constraints that we recognise on that pursuit.[60] The question we want to raise here, however, is whether this approach can generate a
normatively adequate conception of the trial.

It suggests that there are two quite distinct and separate sets of normative
demands on the trial: one set concerns the reliability of the trial as a truth-
seeking process; the other concerns the extent to which that process respects the
rights of those affected by it—especially but not only defendants. If we accept
this distinction, we must ask what the implications should be of a breach of one
of the side-constraints. If a breach of the truth-related procedural rules makes a
conviction unsafe, it must of course be overturned on appeal; but what if the
trial violated a requirement of due process in a way that did not cast doubt on
the truth of the verdict? Should we count the conviction as 'unsatisfactory', to
be overturned on appeal; or should we say that only 'unsafe' convictions, whose
truth is cast into doubt, should be overturned, and look for other remedies for
other breaches of due process?[61] What if a breach of due process occurred before

---

[59] So one could read Packer's well-known contrast between the 'Crime Control' model and the
'Due Process' model of the criminal process as portraying crime control as the justifying aim and due
process as the set of values that constrain the pursuit of that aim: see H Packer, *The Limits of the
Criminal Sanction* (Stanford, Stanford University Press, 1968); Ashworth, *The Criminal Process*,
n 26 above, at 26–28. On constitutional due process see W R LaFave, J H Israel, N J King, *Criminal
Procedure* (3rd edn, St Paul Minnesota, West Publishing, 2000).

[60] On 'balance', see Ashworth, *The Criminal Process* n 26 above, at 30–40; Auld report, ch 1,
paras 12–18; G Maher, 'Balancing Rights and Interests in the Criminal Process' in R A Duff
and N E Simmonds (eds), *Philosophy and the Criminal Law* (Stuttgart, Franz Steiner, 1984) 99. An
analogous insecurity affects the Hartian justification of punishment in terms of a consequentialist
'general justifying aim' whose pursuit is constrained by various non-consequentialist values (see
Hart, n 57 above): for useful critiques, see N Lacey, *State Punishment* (London, Routledge, 1988)
46–56; J Morison, 'Hart's Excuses' in P Leith and P Ingram (eds), *The Jurisprudence of Orthodoxy*
(London, Routledge, 1988) 117.

[61] On the controversial (in English law) distinction between 'unsafe' and 'unsatisfactory', see
Auld report, ch 12, paras 5–10.

the trial—suppose, for instance, that a defendant is present to stand trial only because the police or prosecuting authority arranged for him to be kidnapped from abroad: should that be taken to undermine the legitimacy of the trial and the verdict—or only if it casts doubt on the truth of the verdict?[62] On a 'consequentialism with side-constraints' model, it is not clear that or why such breaches of side-constraints should undermine the validity of the verdict: we must of course condemn them and find some remedy for them, but if the verdict's correctness is not undermined, why should it not stand? Other theorists, however, talk of the 'integrity' of the trial—an integrity that depends both on what happens during the trial, and on the criminal process that precedes it, and that is undermined by serious breaches of due process whether or not they cast doubt on the accuracy of the verdict.[63] This suggests that due process values bear on the very ends of the trial process, rather than just setting side-constraints on our pursuit of ends that can be adequately characterised without reference to due process.

The same suggestion emerges if we attend more carefully to the idea that the trial process must be consistent with (or perhaps even expressive of) respect for the rights of citizens who are subject to it. If to be treated as a citizen is to be treated as a responsible agent (for this is a central feature of the ideology of liberal democracy), we must ask what kind of trial process could treat those subjected to it as responsible agents; an intuitively plausible answer, which draws on the close connection between being responsible and being answerable, is that what is required is not merely a process that seeks to establish a relevant truth about a suspected offender, but one that calls a citizen to answer a charge of wrongdoing. If we think of trials in these terms, the truth about whether this defendant committed the crime charged is still obviously crucial to the trial's rationale: the trial aims to determine whether that charge is well founded. What matters now, however, is not just that the truth be established, but that it be established by an appropriate process of calling the defendant to answer the charge—by a process that addresses the defendant as a responsible citizen. This is not just a side-constraint on a system whose positive aim is the discovery of the truth; it is integral to the very aims of the criminal trial. On such a view, serious breaches of due process, serious failures to address the defendant as a responsible citizen, undermine the legitimacy of the trial as a process that calls citizens to answer charges of wrongdoing, and thus also undermine the legitimacy of the verdict as a judgment that is to emerge from such a process.[64]

---

[62] Contrast *R v Horseferry Road Magistrates' Court, ex parte Bennett* [1994] 1 AC 42 with *US v Alvarez-Machain* 504 US 655 (1992).

[63] See A J Ashworth, 'Exploring the Integrity Principle in Evidence and Procedure' in P Mirfield and R Smith (eds), *Essays for Colin Tapper* (London, Butterworths, 2003), 107; I H Dennis, 'Reconstructing the Law of Criminal Evidence' (1989) 42 *Current Legal Problems* 21, on the idea of the 'legitimacy' of the verdict.

[64] For a development of this idea, see R A Duff, *Trials and Punishments* (Cambridge, Cambridge University Press, 1986) ch 4.

We will have more to say in later publications about this conception of the criminal trial as a process of calling to account, and about its role in structuring a normative theory of the trial,[65] but we cannot pursue the issues raised in this section—about the role of truth in the criminal trial, and about the relationship between truth and due process—in more detail here. They are, however, all addressed, in different ways, by the contributors to this collection, to whose chapters we now turn.

4 WHICH TRIAL, WHOSE TRUTH?

What truth (if any) does the trial aim to establish? As Matt Matravers points out in his chapter it is at least a common lay assumption that 'the purpose of the trial is to get to the right answer'. Or, as John Jackson puts it, 'to determine whether there has been a breach of the law'. However, we can see straight away that these two might not amount to quite the same thing, a fact developed by Matravers in his discussion and interpretation of jury nullification: a seemingly paradoxical power that the jury has, since it appears to involve the jury in deliberately acquitting against what is clearly required by law and, crucially, against the facts as the jurors believe them to be. This seems entirely at odds with the idea that the trial aims at truth. In trying to resolve this paradox, Matravers emphasises the way in which actions are not mere 'brute facts' but come under evaluative descriptions which will form the juror's understanding of the events in dispute and thus provides an account of nullification which makes it rational and defensible. Similarly Robert Burns, in developing the argument for the trial as narrative, argues for a conception of truth in trials that takes into account a context of values which lie outside the trial itself, and for a coherence account of truth. This he wishes to contrast quite starkly with any account of the trial process of a mechanistic kind. Any such 'mechanical jurisprudence' of the trial simply cannot capture the phenomenon of the common law trial but serves only to distort it. Heike Jung argues that 'truth in adjudication' is not merely found but has to be reconstructed within its distinctive institutional context, which will include procedural aims that are not necessarily simply those of arriving at the truth. Sometimes indeed, he argues, there are situations in which the truth is not paramount: plea bargaining for example cannot be aimed at truth but might nonetheless be justified.

---

[65] One important question will be whether we should look for a unitary, coherent theory of the trial that posits, if not one single aim, at least a coherently integrated set of aims that can be pursued together; or should we rather recognise that any system of criminal trials, set within the complex set of practices that constitute the criminal law, will be answerable to a number of distinct aims and values that are all too likely to conflict? Even if we should ultimately recognise the impossibility of producing a single, coherent normative theory, however, this does not render the enterprise of normative theorising any less important, as an exercise both in identifying, articulating and justifying the various aims and values to which the trial should answer, and in helping us to see how we should respond to the conflicts between them.

The trial, then, might seem to be a forum where contested versions of events struggle to be given the status of truth—a struggle out of which a resolution of the dispute will emerge. How far this is either a necessary or even a desirable way of dealing with breaches of the law forms at least one of the topics of debate in these essays. There are, after all, many other ways in which truth might be established, and the trial as a forum for establishing truth may conflict with values such as efficiency, while efficiency may conflict with other values fundamental to justice. Thus, as Peter Duff argues in his chapter, recent developments in Scotland which increasingly place a duty on the parties, prosecution and defence, to agree undisputed evidence, and require courts to rely more on written evidence and less on oral testimony, all of which are intended to increase efficiency, result in subtle changes to the adversarial nature of the trial in Scotland which are not necessarily benign. They raise, he argues, important questions, for instance about the presumption of innocence and the right not to co-operate.

The criminal trial, then, is not simply a neutral, entirely open space in which the pursuit of truth goes on: the rules of evidence themselves structure the pursuit of truth in a particular way, and the requirement to achieve finality itself might seem to place a constraint on the pursuit of truth. John Jackson, in responding to the claims that the adversarial process is not oriented towards truth, argues that within certain constraints on truth, imposed for example by the demand for finality, we can nevertheless see how the adversarial process can provide rational procedures which are truth-serving. Nor is the criminal trial a static enterprise; changes in the way we test and justify claims to truth have influenced its history and spring from a demand for finality as well as truth. So, for example, as Jackson points out, we need to pay attention to the use of scientific evidence and expert witnesses, and to the ways in which they may influence the conception of truth at play in the criminal trial.

The account of the trial as a truth-determining institution in the form implied above might be thought to reflect a concentration on the adversarial form of trial familiar in roughly Anglo-Saxon jurisdictions. Can we draw a clear distinction between adversarial and inquisitorial forms either in theory or in practice? Is either better suited to the pursuit of truth? Does the introduction of more inquisitorial modes of judicial activity, as outlined by Peter Duff, also require judges to have a more active role in assessing evidence at the expense of the jury? If so, why would that matter? Possible answers to these kinds of question are to be found in the discussions of the structure of other rights and values which must underpin the trial, and which will need to come into the argument here. Markus Dubber's paper sets out the way in which autonomy must function as a fundamental value in the criminal process, insofar as that itself is characterised as one aspect of *law*, and law is understood as a mode of governance that is to be distinguished from what Dubber calls *police*—a quite different mode of governance. Citizens, on this account, are to be understood as self-governing agents, from which it follows that citizens brought to trial for alleged of crimes must be participants in their trials (confession being the ultimate case of applying the norms of law to oneself). This focus on autonomy will clearly have implications for the way truth might be pursued, and Jenny McEwan's chapter explores the issues that arise here for the two different models of the trial: adversarial and inquisitorial. If we suppose that the parties to the trial have a right to the truth, then there have to be ways of exercising that right which respect the rights of all parties: McEwan's discussion of the rules of evidence with respect to rape, for example, bring out the difficulties that we encounter here. We might also wonder who is to count as a party to the trial: the adversarial model may seem overly individualistic, the inquisitorial model on the other hand may seem to give too much of a role to the judges and thus to the State; as McEwan notes, the rights of victims and witnesses are also increasingly a feature of debate in this context. We might wonder too why a guilty plea should obviate the necessity for a trial: why should such a plea not itself be subjected to some kind of testing if it is the truth we are after? As we consider such questions as these, we might be led to wonder whether the trial is not merely, or even at all, a forum for discovering the truth, but rather a forum for displaying or demonstrating it.

On whichever model of the trial we favour in theory, or adopt in practice, there will be a requirement for someone, judges, juries or both, to come to a judgment about the truth of what they are told. That is to say, they will need to make judgments on the basis not of first person observation or experience but of the testimony of others. This is, of course, something that we do all the time in everyday life, and it is quite fundamental to the general structure of human social life. How are we to understand the epistemological status of the beliefs that we arrive at in this way, and how are we to view the role of testimony in the trial? Duncan Pritchard draws on the philosophical debates in epistemology and the pragmatics of assertion to show how the legal context is 'more epistemologically demanding than non-legal contexts' and to lend weight to the idea that an inferentialist model best captures the way in which justified beliefs are formed in the trial context.

Even if we take it that the criminal trial aims at truth, while recognising the need both to balance the demand for truth against the other demands of justice, and to see the trial as an important part of the process of applying the law to citizens, we need to consider more generally the question of what it means to be a citizen to whom the law speaks. In his discussion of the rebel on trial Emilios Christodoulidis raises the quite fundamental question of the legitimation of the trial process. How far does a normative theory require coincidence between the addressor and addressee of norms for its legitimacy? Is there, as he argues, a dramatic paradox at the heart of discourse theory in particular, but also of liberal theory (perhaps of the kind argued for in Dubber's paper), in the way that it deals with those citizens who do not accept the norms instantiated in the law but from whom it demands acceptance? Back, full circle we might say, to the question of whose view of the truth is or can be in play in the criminal trial.

2

Changing Conceptions of the Scottish Criminal Trial: The Duty to Agree Uncontroversial Evidence

PETER DUFF

1 INTRODUCTION

I T IS CLEAR that, in many modern Western jurisdictions, the conception of the criminal trial is changing, albeit often slowly and sometimes almost imperceptibly. Among the main factors contributing to this change, many of which are interlinked, are: the rise in managerialist ideology in the criminal justice system, reflecting broader social developments; rises in reported crime (until recently) and the resulting inability of criminal courts to cope with the resulting workloads timeously; an increasing sensitivity to the rights of the accused, most recently represented in Scotland (and the rest of the UK) by the incorporation of the European Convention on Human Rights (ECHR) into domestic law; and an increased concern for victims and witnesses. In this chapter, I wish to examine one particular aspect of the way in which the nature of the criminal trial in Scotland is slowly being transformed, namely through the creation and strengthening of a duty upon the parties to agree uncontroversial evidence in advance of trial. When this measure was first introduced, I argued that it had the potential to alter the ideology upon which the Scottish criminal trial is founded,[1] representing a move away from an adversarial model of the criminal justice process in an inquisitorial direction,[2] and subsequent developments are beginning, I think, to bear out this prognostication. The purpose of this chapter, therefore, is to assess what the introduction and evolution of a duty

---

[1] P Duff, 'Intermediate Diets and the Agreement of Evidence' [1998] *Juridical Review* 349.

[2] In this context, it is interesting to note that a similar trend has recently been identified in the English criminal trial by inter alia J McEwan, in the present volume and J Jackson in 'The Adversary Trial and Trial by Judge Alone' in M McConville and G Wilson (eds), *The Handbook of the Criminal Justice Process* (Oxford, Oxford University Press, 2002). Jolowicz has argued that the same process is far advanced as regards the English civil trial in 'Adversarial and Inquisitorial Models of Civil Procedure' (2003) 52 *International Comparative Law Quarterly* 281.

to agree uncontroversial evidence tells us about the basic conception of the criminal trial in Scotland.

It is useful at the outset to describe very briefly what is meant by the 'adversarial' and 'inquisitorial' models and what purpose is served by citing such concepts.[3] Damaska, perhaps the doyen of comparative criminal proceduralists, summarises the difference between adversarial and inquisitorial systems as that between a 'party contest' and an 'official inquiry'. The adversarial model implies: the parties are partisan and have sole control over the presentation of their case; there are complex and restrictive evidentiary rules; the prosecution must prove its case without compelling the assistance of the defence; the judge is a passive umpire with no prior knowledge of the case; and the outcome is determined by a single hearing held in public at which there is a heavy emphasis on the oral presentation of evidence. This, of course, is broadly the approach adopted by the common law jurisdictions as well as in Scotland.[4] In contrast, the non-adversarial model implies: there is an official investigation to establish the truth; the parties do not control the presentation of the evidence; there are few restrictive evidentiary rules; the defence is expected to assist in the discovery of the truth; the judge plays an active part in the gathering and selection of evidence; and the outcome results from a cumulative administrative process which has built up a case file, or '*dossier*', of largely written evidence. This, of course, is the approach adopted by the 'inquisitorial' systems of continental Europe.

These two models are of course over-simplifications or 'suggestive caricatures'.[5] It is unlikely that any real system of criminal procedure is purely adversarial or inquisitorial; in practice, most systems fall somewhere between the two extremes and combine aspects of each model. For precisely this reason, it has been suggested recently that these models are not particularly useful and, more specifically, that they represent an 'outmoded . . . polarity'[6] at a time when modern criminal justice processes are increasingly coming together.[7] In my opinion,

---

[3] For the classic exposition of these two models of criminal procedure, see M Damaska, 'Evidentiary Barriers to Conviction and Two Models of Criminal Procedure: A Comparative Study' (1973) 121 *University of Pennsylvania Law Review* 506. See also M Damaska, 'Structures of Authority and Comparative Criminal Procedure' (1975) 84 *Yale Law Journal* 480, and J H Merryman, *The Civil Law Tradition* (2nd edn, Stanford, Stanford University Press, 1985), ch XVII.

[4] The Scottish system does contain some elements which owe more to the inquisitorial approach—for instance, the hierarchical system of public prosecution and the mechanism of judicial examination—but both in overall terms and at the court stages of the process, the approach adopted is clearly adversarial (see C Gane, 'Classifying Scottish Criminal Procedure' in P Duff and N Hutton (eds), *Criminal Justice in Scotland*, (Dartmouth, Aldershot, Ashgate 1999). Such models are always simplifications and more clear-cut than reality. See below.

[5] Damaska, 'Evidentiary Barriers to Conviction', n 3 above, at 577.

[6] J Hatchard, B Huber and R Vogler, *Comparative Criminal Procedure* (London, BIICL, 1996) 6.

[7] See N Jorg, S Field and C Brants, 'Are Inquisitorial and Adversarial Systems Converging' in P Fennel, C Harding, N Jorg and B Swart (eds), Criminal Justice in Europe: A Comparative Study (Oxford, Clarendon, 1995); J F Nijboer, 'Common Law Tradition in Evidence Scholarship Observed from a Continental Perspective', (1993) 41 *American Journal of Comparative Law* 299; T Weigend, 'Is the Criminal Process about Truth?: A German Perspective', (2003) 26 *Harvard Journal of Law and Public Policy* 157; and H Jung, this volume.

however, they were, and are, useful for the purposes of this analysis of the introduction of the duty to agree uncontroversial evidence to Scots law for three
related reasons. First, I would have been unlikely to pay much attention to an
apparently uninteresting and technical series of amendments to the Scottish criminal justice process had I not been sensitised to their significance by my (rudimentary—at that stage) knowledge of the literature on the adversarial/inquisitorial
divide. Secondly, the models provided useful analytical tools for locating these
changes to the criminal justice process within a broader context of reform, rather
than leaving them to be perceived as an isolated initiative. Thirdly, the adversar-
ial/inquisitorial polarity can help to anticipate, identify and explain possible tensions with other elements of the process that might be created by such reforms. I
hope to illustrate the latter two points below. It is significant, I think, that other
commentators too have recently found these models still of use in analysing shifts
in policy in criminal procedure systems.[8]

At the outset, it should be noted that the story I shall tell is complicated by
the fact that the duty to agree uncontroversial evidence emerged largely as a
by-product of the introduction of compulsory intermediate or first diets[9] in
response to managerialist demands that the criminal justice process should
become more efficient and cost-effective. In essence, an intermediate diet is a
court hearing which takes place shortly before a trial diet in order to confirm
that all preliminary matters have been dealt with, that the accused is still intending to plead not guilty, that all the witnesses are available and that the trial is
likely to go ahead on the scheduled date. The duty to agree uncontroversial evidence is also operated through this procedure. Thus in this introductory part of
the chapter, I shall simply describe as briefly as possible, the interlinked history
of this duty and intermediate diets in order to provide the necessary background
for what is to follow.

It has long been possible in Scots law for the prosecution and defence to agree
particular facts in advance of trial. These are recorded in a 'minute of admission' or 'minute of agreement', which is lodged with the court papers in the case
and then placed before the court at trial. As far as I am aware, the question of
attempting actively to encourage the agreement of evidence first surfaced during
a major review of the Scottish criminal justice process by the Thomson committee in the 1970s.[10] While it is clear that the main concern of the committee
was the large number of late changes of plea to guilty, some anxiety was
expressed about the time wasted during trials in proving uncontroversial evidence.[11] The committee had few ideas about how to increase the agreement of

---

[8] Fennell et al, n 7 above, adopt this framework for their book. L Ellison has recently defended
the value of this framework of analysis in *The Adversarial Process and the Vulnerable Witness*
(Oxford, Oxford University Press, 2001) ch 7.
[9] A diet is simply the Scottish term for a court appearance. Henceforth, the term 'intermediate'
diets should be read as including 'first' diets, which are the equivalent of intermediate diets in solemn
procedure, unless each is expressly dealt with.
[10] *Criminal Procedure in Scotland (Second Report)* (Cmnd 6218, HMSO, 1975) para 36.01.
[11] Chs 20, 30 and 36.

uncontroversial evidence and made no specific proposals to address the perceived problem. Following this report, the Criminal Justice (Scotland) Act 1980 introduced discretionary intermediate diets, in summary cases, a completely new departure and very much in 'in the nature of an experiment.'[12] These were intended mainly to enable the court to check that the accused still intended to plead not guilty but also to enquire into the state of preparation of both parties, including whether there was any progress towards the agreement of evidence.

In the early 1990s, in the course of a wider review of the efficiency and cost-effectiveness of the criminal justice process, the issue of the agreement of uncontroversial evidence was raised again. One of a series of Scottish Office papers which emerged from this scrutiny was concerned primarily with three related issues: (1) cancelled trials; (2) adjourned trials; and (3) the increasing length of trials.[13] The authors of the paper (henceforth 'the review group') suggested that the solution to the first two problems was the introduction of compulsory, as opposed to discretionary, intermediate and first diets in summary and solemn procedure respectively.[14] The difficulty posed by longer trials was seen as the 'least serious'[15] of the three problems but there was concern that the existing procedures for agreeing uncontested evidence were used 'only patchily and with varying degrees of success.'[16] Thus, there was considerable discussion of various measures which might reduce the amount of evidence led during a trial or speed up its presentation, all of which essentially involved the agreement of more evidence in advance of the trial.[17] The review group noted that the introduction of compulsory pre-trial diets might well help, observing that any increase in the agreement of evidence would be 'a bonus' stemming from the need to alleviate the problem of abortive trials.[18] It stated also that it would be beneficial if the judge were to engage in 'specific efforts to ensure that both parties make reasonable efforts to agree evidence,'[19] further arguing that the court's efforts in this direction would be aided if the parties were put under a statutory duty to make the requisite attempt.[20]

In the White Paper *Firm and Fair*, which emerged from the scrutiny of the criminal justice process, the Government ratified without comment the review group's proposal that a statutory duty to attempt to agree evidence should be

---

[12] Solicitor General, Parliamentary Debates 1979–80, Standing Committees, vol 12, First Scottish Standing Committee, 5th June, col 948. See also: cols 927–28; and Lord Advocate, Parliamentary Debates (HL) 1979–80, vol 404, col 1196.

[13] Scottish Office, *1993 Review of Criminal Evidence and Criminal Procedure* (Edinburgh, The Scottish Office, 1993).

[14] The discretionary intermediate diets introduced in 1980 had quickly fallen into disuse in most courts, according to the review group, n 13 above, para 77.

[15] Para 11. Very little evidence was cited to substantiate the review group's perception that trials had lengthened (see paras 44–48).

[16] Para 50.

[17] Paras 49–53, 58–61, 89–97.

[18] Para 76.

[19] Para 54.

[20] Para 78.

created and the relevant provision is now contained in section 257 of the Criminal Procedure (Scotland) Act 1995. This requires the prosecutor and the accused each to identify any facts which 'he considers unlikely to be disputed ... and in proof of which he does not wish to lead oral evidence' and to 'take all reasonable steps to secure the agreement of the other party'. It further stipulates that 'the other party shall take all reasonable steps to reach such agreement.' The duty to agree uncontroversial evidence applies both to summary and solemn procedure.[21] An unrepresented accused is exempted from this duty because he is thought to lack sufficient expertise to assess the evidence with a view to possible agreement.[22] It should also be noted that the Government approved the proposal to introduce mandatory intermediate and first diets[23] and legislation duly followed,[24] although, as regards solemn procedure, first diets were made compulsory only in the Sheriff Court.[25] Thus, in the vast majority of cases, the judge has the opportunity provided by a pre-trial hearing to check whether the parties have complied with section 257.

Despite these initiatives, it is generally accepted that the creation of a statutory duty to agree evidence has made very little difference in practice. What research evidence there is indicates that it is still fairly rare for the parties to agree evidence in advance of trial.[26] Worries about the efficiency of the criminal justice system have recently come to a head yet again, resulting in the setting up in 2001 of two official reviews, first, by Lord Bonomy of the procedures used in the High Court and, second, of summary criminal justice, by a committee under the chairmanship of Sheriff Principal McInnes. In his report, Lord Bonomy observed that at present the duty to agree evidence is 'more honoured in the breach than the observance.'[27] He recommended that first diets, to be renamed

---

[21] In High Court cases, where of course there is no mandatory first diet, either of the parties may apply to the Court to fix a preliminary diet on the basis inter alia that there are documents or 'any other matter which in his view ought to be agreed' (s 72(1)(c)). The Court has a discretion whether to hold such a diet and, where it does, the procedure resembles that of a first/intermediate diet in that the judge is expected to enquire into the state of preparation of the parties and the extent to which the parties have complied with their duty to take reasonable steps to agree evidence (s 73).

[22] This implemented a suggestion by the Law Society in 'Briefing on Criminal Justice (Scotland) Bill (HL): Amendments to be Moved in Committee' (Edinburgh, Law Society, Dec 1994 and Feb 1995) 9.

[23] *Firm and Fair* (Cmnd 2600, HMSO, 1994), para 2.19.

[24] Criminal Justice (Scotland) Act 1995, which was swiftly consolidated into the Criminal Procedure (Scotland) Act 1995.

[25] It was thought that because the High Court does not sit permanently anywhere but Edinburgh and Glasgow, simply going 'on circuit' to the other major towns on an intermittent basis, it would be administratively too complicated to schedule first diets in the High Court (*Firm and Fair*, n 23 above, para 2.20). In the interests of accuracy, I should note that, in theory, the High Court is also 'on circuit' when sitting in Glasgow but, in practice, as a result of the volume of business, it sits there continuously.

[26] F McCallum and P Duff, *Intermediate Diets, First Diets and Agreement of Evidence in Criminal Cases: An Evaluation* (Edinburgh, Scottish Executive Central Research Unit, 2000) ch 6. One can exclude from this scientific or forensic reports—known as 'routine' evidence—which is often agreed. This will be discussed further below.

[27] Lord Bonomy, *Improving Practice: 2002 Review of the Practices and Procedure of the High Court of Judiciary* (Edinburgh, HMSO, 2002) paras 8.9, 8.12.

'preliminary diets', should be made compulsory in the High Court, as they are in solemn procedure in the Sheriff Court, primarily to avoid problems of adjournments and delays,[28] but he observed that these would provide an opportunity to determine which matters were in dispute and on what issues witnesses were required because their evidence was disputed.[29] In similar vein, the McInnes committee in a consultation paper canvassed the strengthening of intermediate diets in summary procedure, primarily in order to increase the prospect of pre-trial pleas but also to enhance the agreement of non-contested evidence.[30]

In the rest of this chapter, I shall argue that the birth and subsequent development of the duty to agree uncontroversial evidence represents a significant shift in the conception of the criminal trial in Scotland. This I shall do by examining three important ramifications of the duty that I think illustrate the move in an inquisitorial direction. Thus, in the second part of the chapter, I shall demonstrate the way in which the role of the judge might alter as a result of being given responsibility for overseeing the agreement of uncontroversial evidence. In the third section, the increasing emphasis on written evidence at the expense of oral testimony will be examined. Finally, I shall discuss the problem raised for defence agents, traditionally operating on the basis of adversarial ideology, by the existence of a duty to agree uncontroversial evidence. In looking at these three substantive issues, I am concerned primarily with developments at an ideological level. In other words, whether the duty to agree uncontroversial evidence actually brings about the changes envisaged by its architects matters less than what it implies about the conception of the criminal trial upon which they are basing their arguments.

2 THE JUDGE AS INQUISITOR?

In my view, the introduction of experimental intermediate diets in summary procedure in 1980 marks the start of a process which is beginning slowly to move the judge[31] away from the traditional adversarial model of a purely passive adjudicator with no previous knowledge of the case.[32] Certainly, opponents

[28] Paras 6.21–6.28, 8.3–8.7.

[29] Paras 8.3–8.5.

[30] The review has produced a number of consultation papers, including 'Review of Summary Justice—Practitioner Workshops: Background Paper' (2003) which gives some indications of the committee's thinking (henceforth 'McInnes').

[31] For convenience, I shall use the word 'judge' to cover, High Court judges, sheriffs, and justices and magistrates in the district court.

[32] The Thomson committee, n 10 above, in recommending preliminary diets in solemn cases, had envisaged that the judge would play a purely passive role: while the court should be informed of all matters agreed and these would be formally recorded, it was emphasised that 'in no circumstances should the court be informed of the tenor of fruitless discussion' (para 30.05). Its recommendation was that the judge conducting this diet would also be the trial judge, thus presumably it was important, in terms of the adversarial ideology it clearly adopted, that trial judges should have no prior knowledge of the substance of the case.

of this change expressed disquiet that the introduction of intermediate diets, while looking 'dry, dusty, technical and uninteresting,' might begin to alter the nature of the Scottish criminal justice process.[33] They were particularly concerned about the potential for judicial activism inherent in the legislation, worrying that it might shift the judicial role in an 'inquisitorial direction'.[34] There was uncertainty as to what might be entailed in allowing the judge to check on the parties' 'state of preparation' at the intermediate diet, and the Law Society and others were worried that this provision would enable the judiciary to 'root around' into what constituted the defence, perhaps demanding to see the precognitions[35] and acting as an 'inquisitor'.[36]

   This slowly changing perception of the appropriate role for the judiciary became much more explicit with the review group's proposals in the early 1990s.[37] The review group argued that previous experience demonstrated that it was not enough simply to schedule a pre-trial hearing to check on the progress of the case and that what was required was more 'active management' of intermediate diets by the judiciary. It was convinced that recent experiments indicated that if intermediate diets were handled correctly they could be made to work and, consequently, it suggested following up with legislation various recommendations which had emerged from these experiments.[38] Having noted the rather restricted and vague definition of the judicial role in the Criminal Justice (Scotland) Act 1980 and criticised judges for not questioning the parties about their state of preparation, the review group canvassed the idea of setting out in the new statute a list of 'specific duties' for the judge which would encourage a more 'pro-active approach'.[39] In *Firm and Fair,* the Government agreed with this proposal and adopted the list of judicial duties suggested by the review group.[40] Thus, the Criminal Procedure (Scotland) Act 1995 requires the judge to establish whether the trial is likely to go ahead on the scheduled date and, in particular, to ascertain: (1) the state of preparation of the parties; (2) whether the accused is adhering to a plea of not guilty; and (3) the extent to which the parties have attempted to agree evidence. The court is explicitly empowered to ask the parties any question for these purposes.[41]

---

[33] Donald Dewar, Parliamentary Debates 1979–80, Standing Committees, vol 12, First Scottish Standing Committee, 5 June 1980, col 926.

[34] Norman Buchan, col 941.

[35] A precognition is a summary of an interview of a witness conducted by the procurator fiscal or a defence solicitor, indicating what evidence he is likely to give. It is very similar to a statement by the witness given to the police but the distinction between the two is crucial in the Scots law of evidence.

[36] Dewar, n 33 above, col 936.

[37] Review group, n 13 above, paras 73, 75–81, 105–8.

[38] Paras 76–78. The experiments had been conducted by court programming groups set up by the Scottish Office in 1991.

[39] Paras 78, 106.

[40] *Firm and Fair*, n 23 above, para 2.18.

[41] S 148 deals with intermediate diets; s 71 with first diets; and s 73 with preliminary diets.

The main objection to the review group's proposals in this area had come from the Scottish Law Commission (henceforth, the 'SLC') which expressed concern that the introduction of compulsory intermediate and first diets, along with the duty to agree uncontroversial evidence, represented 'a silent drift from traditional principles.'[42] In essence, the SLC's main complaint was that the proposals were based upon narrow 'managerial' considerations rather than being worked out in terms of more general values. This meant that, in the SLC's view, they did not integrate particularly comfortably into the existing adversarial framework of Scottish criminal justice.[43] While the SLC was not necessarily opposed to moving in the direction desired by the review group, it wanted such reform to be 'securely founded on principle,' even if this required an 'articulate statement of new principles' to shape the Scottish criminal justice process.[44] The Government was certainly sensitive to such concerns: in the parliamentary debates over the Criminal Procedure (Scotland) Act 1995, the Lord Advocate denied the allegation that the Government was simply 'tinkering' unreflectively with the criminal justice system, but did accept that the Government had not addressed 'such fundamental issues' as whether there should be a move towards an inquisitorial approach, an idea which he 'vigorously resist(ed)'.[45]

It is significant in terms of the thesis I am advancing here that the SLC's criticisms appear to be directed mainly at the provisions for the agreement of evidence, rather than intermediate diets per se.[46] In particular, the SLC was worried by the review group's 'ideal' of the 'interventionist' and 'domineering' judge, who would make strenuous efforts to secure the agreement of evidence.[47] It took issue with the view of the latter that it was unnecessary for judges to consider the substance of the evidence in order to encourage and secure the agreement of evidence.[48] Instead, the SLC claimed that the judge cannot ascertain whether the parties have made reasonable efforts in this direction without knowing more about the nature of the evidence, and that this information would have to be obtained through 'rigorous' questioning of the parties. Thus, the SLC thought that the pressure which the review group's proposals would place on judges actively to identify the disputed issues jeopardised the judicial role as 'a trial umpire who knows little or nothing of the pre-trial background of the case'.[49] This criticism assumes, of course, that the same judge will

---

[42] Scottish Law Commission, *Responses to 1993 Review of Criminal Evidence and Criminal Procedure (and) Programming of Business in the Sheriff Courts* (Edinburgh, SLC, 1993), para 8.
[43] Paras 1–3. On a more practical level, the SLC also argued that insufficient research had been done on either the dimension of the problems or the likely efficacy of the suggested reforms (para 9).
[44] Paras 4–8, 25.
[45] Parliamentary Debates (HL) 1994–95, vol 559, col 575.
[46] The SLC's focus is somewhat ironic, given that the review group saw the agreement of evidence as a comparatively unimportant by-product of intermediate diets (see above).
[47] SLC, note 42 above, paras 12–13.
[48] Review group, n 13 above, para 107.
[49] SLC, n 42 above, paras 12–16.

conduct the intermediate or first diet and trial diet, which clearly was the intention of the review group and the assumption of the SLC.[50]

One might respond to the SLC that the review group's view does have some validity because the judge can often tell simply from the list of witnesses what their evidence is likely to be and whether it is likely to be controversial. For instance, it is easy to predict the nature of the evidence of forensic scientists in a drugs case or of a string of householders in a case involving multiple burglaries. In these situations, the judge can probably query any failure to agree such evidence without going into much in the way of detail. On the other hand, as the SLC fear, the relevant provisions do create an implicit pressure on the judiciary to find out more about the substance of the evidence in advance of the trial. After all, it cannot realistically be denied that the more information acquired by the judge, the easier it will be for him to assess what the issue(s) in dispute are and what could reasonably be agreed as being uncontroversial. In brief, it is this implicit shift in ideology—it being a hallmark of the inquisitorial, as opposed to the adversarial, system that the judge plays an active role in the identification of the issues to be determined and has foreknowledge of the evidence to be led at trial—that worried the SLC. As Jolowicz argues, in his recent discussion of developments in English civil procedure, the 'informed' judge, armed with increased powers, will lead to the 'evisceration of the basic notions of the adversary system.'[51] In any event, the Government brushed aside the SLC's concerns, observing in rather sweeping terms that '(t)he whole tradition of Scottish justice suggests that the judiciary are well able to distinguish management of these procedural issues from interference in the substance of the case before them.'[52]

Subsequent developments are bearing out the SLC's analysis, although one caveat must be mentioned before looking at these. It is that the practicalities of court scheduling have meant that the trial judge usually is not the judge who conducted the intermediate or first diet and little effort is made to ensure that she is.[53] Thus, the fear that judges would come to cases with foreknowledge of the facts and issues has not been borne out, although in the smaller, less busy courts, it might well be the same judge who normally hears the case at both stages. Other developments in an inquisitorial direction, however, outweigh this purely practical point. Principally, in his recent report, Lord Bonomy proposed that in order to forestall the present practice whereby there is an 'automatic challenge' by the defence to any notice of uncontroversial evidence served on it by the prosecution under section 258 of the Criminal Procedure (Scotland) Act 1995, 'it would not be unreasonable to require the defence to give a reason for

---

[50] Review group, n 13 above, para 81. SLC, n 42 above, para 27. Similarly, the Thomson committee, n 10 above, had recommended that the first diet in solemn procedure should take place before the same judge as would conduct the trial (para 30.05). The review group accepted that this would not always be possible in practice.

[51] Jolowicz, n 2 above, at 286–87.

[52] *Firm and Fair*, n 23 above, para 2.36.

[53] See McCallum and Duff, n 26 above, ch 6.

contesting the notice.' If the Crown was not convinced by the reason, it could raise this matter at the preliminary diet 'with a view to the presiding judge determining whether the Crown should be required to prove the points in issue or may rely on the terms of the notice.'[54] This is a radical proposal in that it envisages the judge at a pre-trial hearing being empowered to focus the issues for trial, determining those which give rise to room for genuine debate and restricting the list of witnesses accordingly. Clearly, this would inevitably involve the judge in 'rooting around'[55] to a considerable extent into what exactly constitutes the accused's defence and, of course, the evidence itself in order to ascertain whether the latter is relevant to the former.

Similarly, the McInnes committee called for a change of 'court culture' in the summary courts, with a more proactive judiciary and better preparation by the parties prior to the intermediate diet. The committee envisaged intermediate diets being 'properly managed' by the bench, which would 'scrutinise' and 'question' the activities of both parties. As regards agreement of evidence, the committee noted that the evidence of some witnesses is of a purely formal nature, unlikely to be subject to cross-examination. In such cases, it thought it 'arguable' that the onus should be on the defence at the intermediate diet to explain why it cannot agree such evidence. The committee's view was that if the defence were unable to persuade the court that the interests of justice required the presence of a witness at trial, the police statement of that witness would be taken as evidence.[56] Thus, like Lord Bonomy, the committee appeared to accept that the adversarial model of an entirely passive bench was no longer appropriate and that, to some extent, the judge would have to enquire actively during pre-trial proceedings into the nature of the evidence. Further, both sets of proposals weaken the right of the parties to be the sole determinants of what evidence to present at trial, a right which is integral to adversarial ideology.[57] Instead, Lord Bonomy and the McInnes committee clearly envisage that the judiciary would be able to over-ride that right and determine which witnesses are relevant, a procedure much more familiar under an inquisitorial model of the criminal justice process. For instance, in the Netherlands the court may refuse to call a witness if no apparent reason for the presence of the witness can be given by the defence[58] and in Belgium the judge can refuse to hear a witness

---

[54] Bonomy, n 27 above, para 8.9. He also suggested that the defence could be obliged to reply to this notice and that such a defence notice could also identify any uncontroversial (from its point of view) evidence (para 8.10).

[55] To use Dewar's phrase: see n 33 above.

[56] McInnes committee, n 30 above, at 6.

[57] Indeed, the SLC had emphasised precisely this point in a report published a year prior to their response to the review group's proposals: Report No 137, *Evidence: Report on Documentary Evidence and Proof of Undisputed Facts in Criminal Proceedings* (Edinburgh, SLC, 1992), paras 4.15, 4.19–21.

[58] A Beijer C Cobley, A Kip, 'Witness Evidence, Article 6 of the European Convention on Human Rights and the Principle of Open Justice' in Fennell, n 7 above, at 287.

whose pre-trial statement is in the dossier despite the defence's wish to question that witness.[59]

3 THE PRINCIPLE OF ORALITY

It is clear that if an increasing amount of uncontroversial evidence is agreed by the parties prior to trial, this will change to an extent the nature of the Scottish criminal trial. The predominant emphasis on the oral testimony of the witnesses, selected solely by each party, will be reduced and more importance will be attached to the submission of written documentation, negotiated and agreed in advance of trial with some active involvement in the process by the judiciary. This represents a significant shift from the idealised conception of an adversarial trial, based purely on an examination and cross-examination of the prosecution and defence witnesses, towards a more inquisitorial or non-adversarial type of proceedings which relies heavily on a dossier, which is produced with the co-operation of the parties, sometimes under the supervision of a judge, during pre-trial proceedings, and extracts of which, summarising witness testimony, are often read out at trial.[60] Thus, it is worth looking at this change of focus in a little more detail, particularly as regards the form in which uncontroversial evidence might be presented to the trial court.

Returning to the work of the review group in the early 1990s, it examined the possible forms non-contested evidence might take, the explicit aim being to substitute agreed written evidence for oral evidence.[61] First, it judged that the existing joint minute of agreement or admission would be 'quite satisfactory' once backed up by the proposed introduction of a pre-trial hearing 'at which the parties were explicitly questioned about the agreement of evidence,' and the imposition of a statutory duty to agree evidence.[62] The Government agreed that the joint minute would remain useful[63] and section 256 of the Criminal Procedure (Scotland) Act 1995 restates the necessary procedure. It is worth pointing out that this is immediately followed by the provision which creates the duty to agree uncontroversial evidence (section 257), thus indicating the close link between the two provisions. Clearly, the optimism of the review group was unfounded as it is now generally accepted that there has not been any great increase in the number of joint minutes of agreement or admission.[64] Neither of the more recent reviews of criminal justice—ie Lord Bonomy's review of High

---

[59] C Van den Wyngaert, 'Belgium' in Van den Wyngaert (ed), *Criminal Procedure Systems in the European Community* (London, Butterworths, 1993) 23.

[60] Jolowicz, n 2 above, makes the same point in relation to the recent changes in English civil procedure. See also Beijer, n 58 above, and J R Spencer, 'Orality and the Evidence of Absent Witnesses', [1994] *Criminal Law Review* 628.

[61] Review group, n 13 above, para 57.

[62] Paras 49–52, 97.

[63] *Firm and Fair*, n 23 above, para 2.30.

[64] McCallum and Duff, n 26 above, ch 6; Bonomy, n 27 above, para 8.9.

Court procedure and the McInnes committee's review of summary procedure—had much to say about the use of this particular form of agreed evidence.

Secondly, the review group proposed widening the scope of the existing mechanisms for the certification of 'routine' and other similar types of evidence—such as forensic reports—to further areas, primarily evidence of previous convictions and of the transmission by a police officer of a production to a laboratory.[65] The Government agreed with this and also suggested that the legislation should enable new categories of routine evidence to be added by statutory instrument as necessary.[66] The 1995 Act duly reflected these suggestions[67] and, significantly, extended the procedure for the certification of routine evidence to solemn procedure.[68] Thus, for instance, in cases where video evidence is to be used in court, section 283 allows certification by the person responsible for operating the system of the location of the camera, the nature of their responsibility for it and that the film is a record of events occurring at a specified time and place. That person is not needed as a witness in court. In all situations, it should be remembered the defence has the right not to accept the written evidence and to insist upon the relevant witnesses providing oral testimony at trial.[69]

Thirdly, the review group also considered a proposal advanced earlier by the SLC that the prosecution could serve on the defence a 'Statement of Facts Not in Dispute' which would be held to be conclusively proved unless the defence objected, thus avoiding the need for the relevant witnesses to attend court. Despite the review group's opposition to this suggestion,[70] the Government favoured it.[71] Thus, section 258 of the 1995 Act introduced a new procedure as regards 'uncontroversial evidence' whereby, in essence, if one party thinks that facts are 'unlikely to be disputed', he may serve a notice on the other party either specifying the facts or referring to an annexed document (for example, a witness statement).[72] As with routine evidence, this may be done up to fourteen days before trial and, if the other party does not challenge some or all these facts within seven days, the relevant facts will be deemed to be conclusively proved. In practice, like the joint minute, this procedure is little used. Initially prosecutors devoted quite a lot of time in solemn cases to drafting such notices but these were invariably met with a 'blanket' challenge by the defence.[73] Consequently,

---

[65] Review Group, n 13 above, paras 58–61.

[66] *Firm and Fair*, n 23 above, paras 2.24–25.

[67] Ss 280–84, sch 3.

[68] S 280(4).

[69] The Act allows such certificates to be served on the defence up to 14 days before trial, and the defence has a right to challenge such a certificate, within 7 days of it being served.

[70] Review Group, n 13 above, paras 98–101. In its response to the review group, the SLC, n 42 above, reiterated its view that the serving of a statement of undisputed facts upon the defence would be useful, although it suggested that this procedure might be restricted to solem procedure at first instance (paras 32–36).

[71] *Firm and Fair*, note 23 above, paras 2.32–34.

[72] The court has a discretion to allow a challenge outwith the time limit in 'special circumstances'.

[73] McCallum and Duff, n 26 above, ch 6.

the prosecution soon ceased to issue such notices as a matter of routine and now only do so on rare occasions. More recently, Lord Bonomy thought that the notice of uncontroversial evidence represented the best means of increasing the agreement of evidence and, as we saw above, suggested that the bench should be permitted effectively to impose such a notice upon the defence.[74]

Finally, the review group discussed the 'more radical step', also considered by the SLC in its earlier paper, of rendering signed witness statements admissible as evidence where they had been served on the other party and had not been met by a counter-notice requiring the attendance of the witness.[75] The SLC had not favoured this approach but the review group was impressed by the fact that a similar procedure in England appeared to work very well.[76] It accepted that Scottish police practice as regards the taking of statements would have to change but concluded that this option should be made available in Scotland. In response, the Government argued that witness statements would often not be a suitable basis for agreement on their own because they might contain too much extraneous material or because the facts in them might have to be related to pro- ductions (for example, where there is a police statement describing no more than the discovery of a knife found in a dustbin outside a night club and this has to be linked to the accused and a prior attack within the club). Thus, while they thought that witness statements might sometimes be suitable as they stood, it would usually be more effective to use them as a basis for a minute of agreement or append them to the statement of uncontroversial facts which made reference to their contents.[77] In the event, the legislation makes no specific reference to witness statements.

As noted above, both Lord Bonomy's review and the McInnes committee's paper recommended that more use should be made of witness statements and, if unchallenged, they should simply constitute evidence at trial which would be read to the judge or jury. Lord Bonomy added that there was also no reason why a notice of uncontroversial evidence should not be accompanied by the relevant witness statements, both sets of papers again to be read out at trial.[78] Again, this represents a significant shift from adversarial ideology which sets great store on the oral testimony of witnesses and has traditionally been highly reluctant to grant this sort of material evidential status, unlike inquisitorial ideology which has long utilised this type of procedure. As Wiegend observes, adversarial sys- tems tend to keep the pre-trial and trial phases of the process 'strictly separate', whereas inquisitorial systems 'allow (more or less liberally) information to be imported from the pre-trial investigation into the trial.'[79] For example,

---

[74] Bonomy, n 27 above, paras 8.8–8.9.
[75] Review group, n 13 above, paras 62–66.
[76] For a recent summary of the position in England, see R Leng, 'The Exchange of Information and Disclosure' in McConville and Wilson (eds), n 2 above, 205, at 208–9.
[77] *Firm and Fair*, note 23 above, paras 2.32 and 2.34.
[78] Bonomy, n 27 above, para 8.9.
[79] Weigend, n 7 above, at 164.

Hatchard informs us that in the German trial, 'substantial sections of uncontroversial material may simply be read out aloud by the president from the
dossier'[80] and Wyngaert observes that in The Netherlands 'the trial is very often
restricted to discussing the value of data in files compiled long beforehand.'[81]
Indeed, from an adversarial perspective, it is quite astonishing how far some
inquisitorial systems will go in routinely dispensing with the need for oral testimony at trial and relying instead upon prior statements by the witnesses.[82]

In this context, it is important to note that it has always been agreed that one
of the keys to facilitating the agreement of evidence is greater disclosure of the
prosecution case to the defence prior to trial.[83] Thus, the review group suggested that in summary cases the prosecution should provide the defence with
copies of all witness statements but it acknowledged that the question of
confidentiality, previously raised by the Thomson committee,[84] would have to
be overcome. The review group did not think that this problem was insupera-
ble, observing that police witness statements had been available to the defence
since 1991 and, further, that an experiment was being carried out in Paisley
whereby some civilian statements were being supplied to the defence.[85] In the
ensuing White Paper, the Government indicated that most consultees were in
favour of the routine supply of witness statements to the defence and that the
experiments in this area would continue but made no further commitment on
this topic.[86] In his report, Lord Bonomy observed that it was increasingly common for the defence to be provided with 'some statements' in a case but that
there was still no standard practice largely because statements are taken in a
variety of ways and circumstances and because 'their quality is variable'. [87] This
helps to confirm an impression that the real difficulty in routinely supplying witness statements to the defence is not that of confidentiality but the poor quality
of many statements recorded by the police.[88]

---

[80] Hatchard et al, n 6 above, at 52.

[81] Van Den Wyngaert, n 59 above, at 298.

[82] In this context, it is illuminating to read some of the judgments of the European Court of
Human Rights (ECtHR) on the practices adopted in some inquisitorial jurisdictions. Particularly
good examples are *Kostovski v Netherlands* (1989) 12 EHHR 140; *Saidi v France* (1995) 17 EHHR
251; *Van Mechelen v Netherlands* (1997) 25 EHRR 647, and *A M v Italy* 14 December 1999 (application no 37109/97). In all these cases, the ECtHR held that the refusal to hear the witnesses at trial
amounted to a breach of Art 6 but the significance here lies in the insight into the procedures
routinely adopted in the relevant jurisdictions.

[83] The review group, n 13 above, for instance, argued that this would increase both the number
of early pleas and the agreement of evidence (paras 27, 89–95). For discussion of the development of
the reciprocal disclosure scheme in England, see Leng, n 76 above.

[84] The Thomson committee, n 10 above, took the view that precognitions and statements made
to the police should not be made available to the defence because of the need for confidentiality
(paras 17.10–12,15), a view supported by the Government in the debate over the 1980 Act (Solicitor
General, n 12 above, col 930).

[85] Review group, n 13 above, paras 92–93.

[86] *Firm and Fair*, n 23 above, para 2.22.

[87] Bonomy, n 27 above, para 7.4.

[88] I have been told this on several occasions by senior functionaries connected with the criminal
justice system.

Lord Bonomy went on to observe that discussions had been taking place for more than twenty-five years about the way statements are taken, their standard and the question of their being made available to the defence and suggested that 'a concerted effort should now be made to resolve this issue once and for all.' Thus, he recommended that a working party should be set up, including representatives of the various interested bodies, 'to try to devise a scheme for the taking of witness statements that would enable them to be given to the defence routinely,' although he accepted that there might be 'sound reasons' for an inability to create a comprehensive scheme.[89] The latter point is perhaps overly pessimistic given that this type of regime has operated successfully for years in England and that he did not give any examples of what might constitute 'sound' reasons. The McInnes committee also favoured greater disclosure by the prosecution to the defence of civilian witness statements in order to encourage the agreement of evidence.[90] Again, it is normal in inquisitorial systems that the defence have early access to the dossier and the witness statements contained therein.[91]

In summary, prior to the 1980s there was an unquestioned assumption that virtually all of the evidence at a Scottish criminal trial would take the form of oral testimony from witnesses selected and presented solely by the two parties. During the 1980s and 1990s, there was increasing pressure on the parties to reach agreement upon uncontroversial evidence which would be presented in written form. More recently, two official reviews have recommended that the bench should have the power to determine, contrary to the will of the parties, that certain evidence should be presented in written form, rather than through oral testimony. The increased use of written evidence, particularly the statements of witnesses, and the judicial supervision of the selection of the evidence to be presented at trial, are both hallmarks of an inquisitorial type process and represent a shift from the classic adversarial ideal. Further, the increased emphasis on the disclosure of the prosecution case to the defence bears some resemblance to the availability of the dossier compiled by the prosecutor or, occasionally, an investigating magistrate to the defence at all times. In short, in Scotland, there has been continuing pressure, reflected in the introduction of new mechanisms, to place more reliance at trial on written evidence, available to and agreed by both parties, and a corresponding desire to reduce the importance of the oral testimony of witnesses selected solely by the competing parties.

---

[89] Bonomy, n 27 above, para 7.5.
[90] McInnes, n 30 above, at 5. Like Lord Bonomy, it thought that this would also enhance the possibility of early guilty pleas.
[91] For instance, see Ellison, note 8 above, at 142–44.

4 AN ADVERSARIAL DEFENCE?

This section concentrates upon the role of the defence solicitor or advocate.[92] In particular, I will demonstrate that the responsibilities of the defence in an adversarial process sit uneasily with the duty to agree uncontroversial evidence and I will argue that this clash again illustrates that there has been a departure from traditional adversarial principles in an inquisitorial direction. Returning to the origins of the debate, the Thomson committee made one or two suggestions which might indirectly increase the agreement of uncontroversial evidence but essentially it took the view that the presumption of innocence meant that the parties could not be compelled to do this and that, 'as a matter of principle, an accused person is entitled to put the Crown to proof of its case against him.'[93] These opinions clearly stem from the committee's implicit adherence to adversarial ideology. It does not matter that the evidence is unlikely to be contested at trial; it is a fundamental right of the accused in an adversarial system of criminal justice to insist that the prosecution prove every aspect of its case. In the view of the Thomson committee, this meant that little could be done to further the agreement of evidence and, ultimately, it simply expressed a 'hope' that solicitors would consider it their 'duty' to admit facts which were certain to be proved at the trial.[94]

In the early 1990s, the review group took a somewhat similar view. It acknowledged that the success of its recommendations to improve intermediate and first diets would be dependent on increased co-operation by the defence. As regards the agreement of evidence, it considered the question of sanctions where the defence 'deliberately and resolutely' refused to agree any evidence, despite the proposed statutory duty to do so.[95] Its view, however, was that the defence's right to adopt this stance 'flows from our adversarial system' and thus that it was not practical within this framework to devise effective sanctions without running the risk of prejudicing the rights of the accused. Nevertheless, it did observe, rather ominously, that the existence of the intermediate diet would ensure that the parties could be questioned about their willingness to agree evidence and the reasons for the failure to agree uncontroversial facts would be 'exposed' in open court.[96] It concluded that there would be 'hopefully few' cases where the defence refused to agree any evidence in advance but gave no reasons for this view, which was presumably based, like that of the Thomson commit-

---

[92] I have dealt at length elsewhere with the consequences for the accused of the move towards the agreement of evidence, in particular discussing critically the debate over this issue which took place between the review group, n 13 above, and the SLC, n 42 above. See P Duff, 'The Agreement of Evidence and the Presumption of Innocence: An Insoluble Dilemma?' (2002) 6 *Edinburgh Law Review* 25.

[93] Thomson committee, n 10 above, paras 20.05–20.06. See also paras 36.03–36.06.

[94] Paras 30.06 and 36.04.

[95] Review group, n 13 above, para 82.

[96] Para 79.

tee, on the premise that defence agents have responsibilities to the courts as well as their clients.[97]

The SLC took issue with the review group's rather optimistic views on this matter and pointed out that the defence may have 'sound' reasons for refusing to co-operate in the agreement of uncontroversial evidence, although it gave no examples.[98] It went on to resist the review group's implied criticism of the defence agent who 'deliberately and resolutely' refuses to agree evidence in order that he can put the Crown's case to the test, pointing out that it was in fact the 'duty' of the defence agent to act in this way. Furthermore, the SLC deplored the possibility that any perceived lack of co-operation at the intermediate diet might be met with the 'interrogation' of the defence agent by the judge or judicial disapproval of his behaviour being expressed in open court: 'We would find it particularly offensive if a responsible advocate or solicitor for an accused person who was in fact innocent was obliged to undergo hostile judicial interrogation, with the threat of judicial disapproval, if he declined to agree evidence.'[99] In support of this position, the SLC cited the following quotation from the Guide to the Professional Conduct of Advocates: 'He must . . . do his best for the client and . . . be fearless in defending his client's interests, regardless of the consequences to himself (including, if necessary, incurring the displeasure of the bench).' In essence, it seems to me that the SLC were identifying a potential tension between the position of a defence agent operating under adversarial values being subjected to a new mechanism which is more consistent with inquisitorial ideology.

On the one hand, the defence lawyer has a duty to his client to do his utmost to ensure that the latter is not convicted. Discussions of the responsibility of the defence agent in adversarial ideology often open with the observation of Lord Reid in *Rondel v Worsley* that 'the role of the defence lawyer is to promote fearlessly and by all lawful and proper means the lay client's interests.'[100] In his book about the values which ought to be embodied within the criminal process, Ashworth argues that it is 'perfectly proper' for the defence lawyer to take advantage of a 'technical' legal point and 'to advise the defendant on the best tactical means of pursuing the line of defence . . .'. In summary, '(t)he defence lawyer's role is essentially partisan . . .'.[101] If this is so, it is surely the defence lawyer's professional duty to refuse to agree any evidence in advance of trial, particularly since no adverse consequences arise for his client from the failure to agree evidence. And there is always the possibility that his client may accrue some benefit from such a refusal. After all, there is the chance that the witness

---

[97] Para 82.

[98] SLC, n 42 above, para 21.

[99] The SLC's anxiety should also have applied equally to the situation where the accused was in fact guilty because the present structure allows—and indeed adversarial ideology encourages—the accused to hear all the evidence against him in open court.

[100] [1969] 1 AC 191, at 227–28.

[101] A J Ashworth, *The Criminal Process: An Evaluative Study* (2nd edn, Oxford, Oxford University Press, 1998) 69.

who was to provide the evidence in question fails to turn up on the day of the trial or proves thoroughly unconvincing in the witness box. The SLC certainly recognised the force of this argument in an earlier report on the evidence of vulnerable witnesses:

> Defence lawyers are understandably reluctant to enter into joint minutes of admissions, particularly in respect of matters which, though non-controversial, are crucial for proof of the prosecution case: a witness might die, or disappear, or fail to give evidence on the crucial matter, and, by signing the minute, the defence lawyer would have denied his client the benefit of the fortuitous event.[102]

On the other hand, the defence lawyer has a duty to agree evidence which is unlikely to be contested at trial.[103] The tension between these competing duties, towards the client and the court, can be disguised, as other tensions arising in the defence role often are, by the device of claiming that the defence agent is 'an officer of the court', which brings with it certain ethical responsibilities, but, on any kind of detailed examination, this concept is almost entirely without substance.[104] In reality, of course, any pressure on defence agents to co-operate over uncontroversial evidence stems not primarily from any ethical position or any notional duty as an officer of the court, but mainly from lawyers' working culture and defence agents' need to retain good relationships with the prosecution and the court. It has often been observed that these latter influences tend to act as a countervailing force to the values or ethics implied by adversarial ideology.[105] In any event, what the SLC correctly identified was that the review group's proposals were implicitly attempting to curtail the duty of the legal agent to do his utmost for his client, arising from an adversarial ideology which places an emphasis on competition between the parties whereby the defence should never co-operate with the prosecution unless it is in his client's interests. Instead, the review group were seeking to increase the extent to which a common version of events could be agreed before trial through the co-operation of the parties, a practice that sits more comfortably with inquisitorial ideology which encourages the disinterested pursuit of the truth to be presented to the trial court in the dossier.

---

[102] SLC, *Report on the Evidence of Children and Other Potentially Vulnerable Witnesses*, Report No 125, (Edinburgh, SLC, 1990) para 3.13. It repeated this point in its subsequent report on documentary evidence and undisputed facts, n 57 above, para 4.8.

[103] In a recent article entitled 'Lawyers' Duties to the Courts' (1998) 114 *Law Quarterly Review* 63, D Ipp identifies a recently emerging 'general duty to conduct cases efficiently and expeditiously.' Obviously, it could be argued that this encompasses a duty to agree uncontroversial evidence.

[104] See the seminal article: M H Freedman, 'Professional Responsibility of the Criminal Defence Lawyer: The Three Hardest Questions' (1966) 64 *Michigan Law Review* 1469 in which he illustrates the unresolved tensions between the defence agent's duties to his client and to the court. See also M Damaska, *The Faces of Justice and State Authority* (New Haven, Yale University Press, 1986) 142–44, and M Blake and A J Ashworth, 'Some Ethical Issues in Prosecuting and Defending Criminal Cases' [1998] *Criminal Law Review* 16.

[105] See, for instance, M McConville, L Bridges, J Hodgson and A Pavlovic, *Standing Accused* (Oxford, Clarendon, 1994). This is argued to be particularly so in the case of plea-bargaining: M McConville, 'Plea Bargaining: Ethics and Politics' (1998) 25 *Journal of Law and Society* 562.

As noted above, the Government simply ratified the proposal to create a statutory duty to agree evidence without comment.[106] Thus, it did not address the SLC's concern about the invidious position in which defence agents might be placed. Ironically, the proposals now advanced by Lord Bonomy and the McInnes committee might inadvertently resolve, or at least reduce, the potential for conflict in the duties of defence agents. As explained above, both reviews recommended that if the prosecution suggests at the intermediate or first diet that the defence is behaving unreasonably in refusing to agree uncontroversial evidence, the court may require the defence to show why it is necessary to its case to dispute the evidence of the relevant witnesses at trial. If the arguments of the defence do not convince the court, the judge may rule that the statements of these witnesses will suffice as evidence and excuse the witnesses from attendance at the trial. This procedure might have the effect of reducing the tension in the role of defence agent caused by the conflicting demands of his duty to his client and his duty as an officer of the court. If these proposals are implemented, the defence agent would be able 'resolutely' to refuse to agree any evidence and yet be confident that the judge would simply overrule him as regards truly uncontentious evidence, thus freeing the relevant witnesses from the need to attend the trial. The irony in this is that the aim of the recommendations was not to make it easier for the defence to refuse to agree any evidence but precisely the opposite.

In summary, the creation of the duty to agree uncontroversial evidence brought about a tension between the adversarial ideology underpinning the role of the defence agent and the inquisitorial ideology which lay behind the thrust to secure the agreement of evidence before trial. This is particularly apparent from the fact that under the 1995 Act there is no sanction for a breach of this duty because of concerns that any such sanction would infringe upon the traditional rights of an accused in an adversarial system. The tension inherent in the role of the defence agent as regards the agreement of evidence was simply disguised by an empty reference to his role as an 'officer of the court'. The most recent proposals are very radical in that, for the first time in Scotland, we might see the parties losing control over decisions about the substance of the (admissible) evidence to be led at trial, another hallmark of the adversarial model of justice. In contrast, we saw above that in some inquisitorial jurisdictions, the judge can simply refuse to hear a witness if he thinks that witness's testimony would not be helpful. Further, and even more pertinently in this context, the judge may choose to rely on a previous statement if there is no apparent reason to hear the oral evidence of the witness. Thus, in The Netherlands, for instance, the judge will often refuse to call a rape victim and instead rely upon the account given by the victim to the examining magistrate at a pre-trial hearing.[107] It seems that in Scotland we are seeing movement, albeit perhaps in its infancy, towards

[106] *Firm and Fair*, n 23 above, paras 2.17–19.
[107] Ellison, n 8 above, at 148–49. See also Beijer et al, n 58 above, at 287.

a similar position whereby the judiciary, rather than the two competing adversaries, determines the issues and evidence around which the trial is to revolve.

5 CONCLUSION

To recap, the traditional conception of a criminal trial in Scotland conforms very closely to the adversarial model of the criminal justice process. The trial is the centrepiece of criminal proceedings, rendering any pre-trial proceedings of secondary importance. The judge, whether sitting with a jury or alone, comes to court on the day of trial with no prior knowledge of the case. He plays a passive role throughout proceedings, the two parties having determined what evidence to present. The trial involves oral testimony from witnesses selected by the parties, each side presenting its own witnesses whose testimony is tested in cross-examination by the other party. The prosecution is required to prove all aspects of the case against the accused and there will have been little co-operation between the parties prior to trial. In contrast, the conception of a trial under an idealised inquisitorial model of criminal justice is rather different. The trial is simply one stage, albeit an important one, in the criminal proceedings against the accused. The presiding judge, often sitting as part of a panel, comes to court on the day of trial with considerable knowledge of the case, having read all the relevant papers which are contained in the dossier. The judge, rather than the parties, sometimes determines which witnesses should be heard and it is virtually always the judge who questions them. There will be great reliance on the written material in the dossier, witnesses only being called where there is some doubt or controversy over an issue. The defence will have had access to the dossier throughout proceedings and might well have played a part in its assembly.

Against this background, I have outlined the way in which the creation and evolution of the duty to agree uncontroversial evidence has begun to change the notion of a Scottish criminal trial. While the trial itself might not yet have changed very much in practice, the ideology which underlies it has begun to move in an inquisitorial direction. We started from a position where in the 1970s the Thomson committee thought that nothing could be done to encourage the agreement of evidence, primarily because of its adherence to adversarial ideology. It thus took the view that the accused had the right to insist that every witness against him should be obliged to testify at trial and that he should not be pressurised into making it easier to present the case against him. In the 1990s, we saw the creation of a statutory duty to agree uncontroversial evidence, the expansion of the forms such evidence could take, and greater importance placed on pre-trial proceedings. The Review Group certainly hoped that this would decrease the number of witnesses called to court and encourage the use of written evidence, agreed by the parties prior to trial. Nevertheless, it was unable to recommend any sanction for even a flagrant breach of the duty to agree uncontroversial evidence because of its view, firmly based in adversarial ideology, that the defence was entitled not to assist in the assembly of the case against the accused.

In 2002–03, we have seen two large-scale, official reviews of criminal justice recommend that, during pre-trial proceedings, the judge should be empowered to enquire into the need for witnesses to give oral testimony at trial and, by deciding that certain witnesses are unnecessary, effectively overrule the traditional right of the parties to have sole control over the presentation of their cases. This notion of the judge playing an active role in pre-trial proceedings, determining which witnesses should be heard at trial and assisting with the assembly of what might be loosely termed a 'dossier' of various pieces of written evidence for the trial, is more consistent with inquisitorial ideology than the traditional adversarial model. It remains to be seen, of course, whether these proposals find their way into future legislation and, if they do, whether they have much impact. My guess is that their effect will be minimal both because of the culture of adversarialism which, quite naturally, still permeates the Scottish criminal justice process and the requirement under Article 6(3)(d) of the ECHR that the accused has the right 'to examine or have examined witnesses against him.'[108]

As regards the latter point, inquisitorial systems possess various mechanisms to allow the accused to have witnesses examined prior to trial, for instance, through a pre-trial hearing before an examining magistrate at which the accused may put questions, through the magistrate, to the witnesses.[109] Consequently, such jurisdictions can utilise a written record of such interviews at trial without necessarily being in breach of Article 6(3)(d). In the absence of such procedures, which, for obvious reasons, have never been necessary in adversarial systems, it seems to me that judges will be extremely reluctant to overrule a request from the defence to have an opportunity to question a witness at trial. Unless the evidence of the witness is clearly irrelevant, a judge's refusal to accede to the defence's request is likely to constitute a breach of Article 6(3)(d). Thus, Scottish judges are likely to operate any procedure which allows them to insist that some form of written evidence, in place of the oral testimony of the witness, will suffice at trial with extreme caution.

In any event, as I noted at the outset, the effectiveness of these and other measures to encourage the agreement of uncontroversial evidence does not really matter in terms of my argument. The significant point is that such proposals can be made at all. Only thirty years ago, recommendations of this nature would have been unthinkable to the Thomson committee, thus illustrating the extent to which the notion of the criminal trial in Scotland has changed, largely, it has to be said, as a result of bureaucratic and financial pressures rather than any careful reconsideration of basic principles.

---

[108] For discussion of this and the jurisprudence of the ECHR, see Beijer et al, n 58 above; Nijboer, n 7 above, at 311–12; Ellison, n 8 above, at 67–71; R Reed and J Murdoch, *A Guide to Human Rights Law in Scotland* (London, Butterworths, 2001) 362–66.

[109] The ECtHR cases cited at n 82 above describe examples of such procedures.

[There have been two major developments since the time of writing this article in August 2003. First, the McInnes Committee, whose report was published in January 2004 (*The Summary Justice Review Committee: Report to Ministers*), recommended that, in summary cases, a judge should be granted the power, on the application of one party, to rule that certain evidence is uncontroversial and the statement of the witness should be admissible at trial, but this will be subject to the safeguard that the other party should still be able to cite the witness to the trial for oral examination (paras 20.23–33). Second, many of the Bonomy proposals have been enacted by the Criminal Procedure (Amendment) (Scotland) Act 2004, most provisions of which will be implemented in April 2005. Section 13C enables the court in solemn proceedings, on the application of any party, to direct that any challenge to a notice of uncontroversial evidence served by that party is to be 'disregarded . . . if the court considers the challenge to be unjustified'. This provision will be inserted into the relevant part of the Criminal Procedure (Scotland) Act (as s 258(4A)) and enables the judge to rule that certain evidence is uncontroversial and thus conclusively proved even if the party upon whom the notice was served disagrees and wishes the relevant witness to be called. It remains to be seen whether this more radical stance will also be applied to summary procedure or whether the more cautious approach envisaged by the McInnes Committee will prevail. I suspect the former is more likely simply because there would be little, if any, justfication for differing regimes governing summary and solemn procedure.]

3

Ritual, Fairness and Truth: The Adversarial and Inquisitorial Models of Criminal Trial

1 INTRODUCTION

THE CURRENT DEBATE on the reforms in the Criminal Justice Act[2] demonstrates the continued willingness of legal traditionalists to fight tooth and nail in defence of the adversarial features of the criminal trial in England and Wales.[3] The common law tradition has many influential adherents who believe that adversarial trial is the embodiment of procedural justice.[4] The Phillips commission of 1981 noted some of the shortcomings of adversarial procedures, but concluded that even if it were desirable to change over to a fully-fledged inquisitorial system, the effect would be so fundamental 'upon institutions that had taken centuries to build that it would be impossible on political and practical grounds.'[5] Nevertheless, legislative reforms chip away at the purity of the adversarial model across Britain.[6] Indeed, many jurisdictions find themselves with cause to reconsider the wisdom of retaining the harsher features of their adversarial inheritance; reforms in the pursuit of efficiency and reduced cost, the admission of reliable and relevant evidence and the humane treatment

---

[1] I am indebted to the editors and to participants at the AHRB-funded workshops, 'The Trial on Trial', for their perceptive and constructive comments on this chapter. They are not to any degree responsible for the weaknesses that remain.

[2] Extension of hearsay exceptions, admissibility of criminal record, disclosure by the defence of witness details.

[3] *Briefing on the Criminal Justice Bill* (Bar Council and the Criminal Bar Association), www.barcouncil.org.uk/documents/BriefingOnTheCriminalJusticeBill (March 2003).

[4] Legal historians Landsman, Beattie and Langbein have been accused of assuming the development of aggressive adversarial criminal justice to be a natural and welcome evolutionary process; D Cairns, *Advocacy and the Making of the Adversarial Criminal Trial 1800–1865* (Oxford, Clarendon Press, 1998) 32–36.

[5] Royal Commission on Criminal Procedure *Report* (Cmnd 8092; London, HMSO, 1981) para. 1.8

[6] See P Duff, 'Changing Conceptions of the Scottish Criminal Trial: the Duty to Agree Uncontroversial Evidence' (this volume).

of witnesses are being considered and implemented all over the world.[7] Yet, at about the same time, the criminal justice systems of continental Europe, never pure exemplars of the inquisitorial paradigm,[8] have shown some impatience with certain elements of their own structures.[9] Some have introduced more adversarial elements, so that now, anything resembling a truly inquisitorial system[10] is impossible to find. Germany abolished the examining magistrate in 1975, and Italy in 1988. Could it be the case that civil and common law jurisdictions are evolving simultaneously from their opposite ends of the spectrum to harmonise naturally into a uniform, 'mixed' system? Such a development would certainly be convenient in terms of inter-state cooperation in the detection and policing of international crime, but there may be practical difficulties. Against establishing a more inquisitorial procedure in common law jurisdictions, it has been argued that putting the burden of inquiry upon the judge is reasonable where the source of the law is a code plus academic commentaries. But Anglo-American law is more complicated, and it makes sense to impose the burdens of effort and expense upon the parties.[11]

If it were possible to start afresh, with a blank sheet of paper on which one could design the perfect adjudicative system for the administration of criminal justice, what would be the rational choice? The Chinese were effectively in that position recently. They consulted widely, considered the advantages and shortcomings of the kinds of criminal trial conducted in various modern states, and eventually opted for a system with many adversarial features.[12] The reasons for this decision may have been political and historical rather than philosophical; whether or not in a perfect society one system could be said to be superior to the

[7] Eg, Australian Law Reform Commission, *Evidence* (Sydney, Australia, 1987); Law Commission of New Zealand, *The Evidence of Children and Other Vulnerable Witnesses: a Discussion Paper*, Preliminary Paper 26 (Wellington, New Zealand, 1996); Law Commission of New Zealand, *Evidence: Reform of the Law*, Report 55 (Wellington, New Zealand, 1999); Law Reform (Miscellaneous Provisions) (Scotland) Act 1990, ss 56–60; Law Commission of England and Wales, *Evidence in Criminal Proceedings: Hearsay and Related Topics*, Report 245 (London, HMSO, 1997) ; Sir Robin Auld, *Criminal Courts Review* (London, HMSO, 2001; www.criminal-courts-review.org.uk).
[8] The classic exposition of the features 'pure' adversarial or inquisitorial criminal trials would contain is: M Damaska, 'Evidentiary Barriers to Conviction and Two Models of Criminal Procedure: A Comparative Study' (1973) 121 *University of Pennsylvania Law Review* 506.
[9] S C Thaman, 'The Jury as a Catalyst for the Reform of Criminal Proceedings in Continental Europe: the Cases of Russia and Spain' in J F Nijboer and J M Reijntjes (eds), *Proceedings of the First World Conference on New Trends in Criminal Investigation* (The Hague, Koninklijke Vermande bv/Open University of The Netherlands, 1997).
[10] It is acknowledged by the author that the terms 'adversarial' and 'inquisitorial' are imperfect and may even cause offence; M Cappelletti and B G Garth, *Civil Procedure: XVI International Encyclopaedia of Comparative Law* (Tübingen, JCB Mohr, 1996) 31–32. However, they remain useful shorthand to describe the different traditions of common law and civil law criminal justice, as long as it is recognised that each category contains significant variations in structure and procedure. O Chase, 'American Exceptionalism and Comparative Procedure' (2002) 50 *American Journal of Comparative Law* 277. See, also Duff, n 6 above.
[11] D Luban, *Lawyers and Justice: an Ethical Study* (Princeton, Princeton University Press, 1988).
[12] See M McConville and G Wilson, 'Preface', in M McConville and G Wilson (eds), *The Handbook of the Criminal Justice Process* (Oxford, Oxford University Press, 2002).

other is not a question this paper can address. But it would seem impossible to consider rationally the rival merits of the two models of criminal trial, unless it can be established what the purpose of the trial might be.

2 PURPOSE OF THE CRIMINAL TRIAL

Symbolic and Cathartic Function

When Peter Sutcliffe, the 'Yorkshire Ripper', was accused of the murders of thirteen women, prosecution lawyers were willing to accept a plea of guilty to manslaughter by way of diminished responsibility. They were aware that every psychiatrist who had examined him agreed that Sutcliffe suffered from severe mental illness. Yet when the manslaughter plea was offered to the trial judge, Mr Justice Boreham, he refused to accept it. He insisted that the prosecution ignore the medical opinion of their own expert witnesses and that the murder allegation be pursued on the basis that Sutcliffe was of sound mind.[13] The judge's action was praised by the popular press—a reaction partly due, it appears, to scepticism about the ability of psychiatrists to assess the 'supposedly mad'.[14] It is unlikely, however, that Boreham J similarly doubted the ability of a number of distinguished psychiatrists to diagnose a paranoid schizophrenic. It seems more likely that he thought a contested trial necessary to provide some kind of healing process following the fear and distress that Sutcliffe's terrible killings had engendered. The cathartic effect of a contested trial would not have been produced by the short sentencing hearing that follows the acceptance of a plea of guilty. In the same way, perhaps, Rosemary West was inevitably victimised when the suicide of her husband, Fred West, deprived the public of the spectacle of the trial of the perpetrator of England's most horrific serial killings. In any event, the Court of Appeal appeared untroubled by apparently irrelevant and outrageously prejudicial evidence being adduced to implicate her in the murders.[15]

The 'animal' trials of the sixteenth and seventeenth centuries could be seen as a ritualised response of a society, severely damaged by catastrophe, to its own helplessness. Evans[16] describes the trials of pigs and other animals, not only in respect of specific offences for which they were directly responsible, such as killing a child, but more generally to colonies of rats where crops had been eaten

---

[13] J Bennett-Levy, 'Psychiatric Diagnosis in the Witness Box: a Postscript on the "Yorkshire Ripper" Trial' (1981) 34 *Bulletin of the British Psychological Society* 305. The prosecution case, in the absence of any medical opinion evidence to suggest that Sutcliffe was not insane, rested principally on his calm demeanour in the witness-box.

[14] *News of the World*, 24 May 1981.

[15] This evidence included allegations of childbeating and promiscuity; *West* [1996] 2 Cr App R 374.

[16] E P Evans, *The Criminal Prosecution and Capital Punishment of Animals* (London, Heinemann, 1906) 18–21.

(the defendants famously being represented at trial by Bartholomew Chassenée), or where plague had been introduced into a community. Evans does not see these trials so much as symbolic rituals, rather as an attempt by the Church to demonstrate its power over all living things within its domain. However, he recounts a 'more recent event'[17] in China when fifteen wooden idols were tried and condemned to death by decapitation for causing the death of an important man upon whom they had fallen. The sentence was carried out in front of an excited and noisy crowd.[18] Evans provides other instances of objects, from cartwheels to fishing boats, being blamed and tried for causing harm.[19] Does this show a need for a ritual following a traumatic event, for catharsis? Certainly, it appears that there is a need for 'finality'; it has been argued that trial by ordeal was not the inevitable response of a crude and super-stitious people to harm caused. The ordeal was reserved for cases when the required number of oath-helpers was missing, or the dispute could not be settled in any other way.[20]

Obviously the particular nature of the ritual that serves this purpose will vary according to cultural norms. In England and Wales much is made of the import-ance of the defendant being tried by twelve of his or her peers. Haldar has noted[21] the legitimacy this is thought to give the trial, quoting Coke: 'The law delighteth herself in the number twelve . . . that number twelve is much respected in Holy Writ, as in twelve apostles, twelve stones, twelve tribes'.[22] However, in England and Wales, this romantic picture is misleading; most con-tested trials are conducted in the less formal atmosphere of the magistrates' courts, and the majority of trials are not fought at all.[23] And, if the need for spec-tacle is part of the raison d'être of criminal proceedings, it is curious that it is in the adversarial jurisdiction, where theatricality is at its most blatant, that a guilty plea closes down the case and deprives everyone of the show. Continental legal systems mistrust the guilty plea, and investigate the facts of the case irre-spective of the accused's admission of guilt. But Boreham J's decision to insist on a contested case with full examination of the gruesome evidence attached to the 'Ripper' murders may have been a recognition that in some extreme cases, at least, even members of a society well used to disposal of criminal cases by way of the guilty plea would feel that matters had not been brought to a proper close.

---

[17]   No date given.

[18]   Ibid, 174.

[19]   Ibid, 186–9.

[20]   M Damaska, 'Rational and Irrational Proof Revisited' (1997) 5 *Cardozo Journal of International and Comparative Law* 25; A Engelman, *A History of Continental Civil Procedure* (ed Robert Millar; Boston, Little Brown, 1927).

[21]   P Haldar, 'On the Sacrifice in Criminal Evidence', in P Rush, S McVeigh and A Young (eds), *Criminal Legal Doctrine* (Dartmouth, Ashgate, 1997).

[22]   E Coke, *First Part of the Institute of the Laws of England (his Commentary on Littleton)* (New York, Legal Classics, Gryphon, 1823) 154 (a).

[23]   The reforms recommended by Sir Robin Auld, n 7 above, and the provisions of the Criminal Justice Bill 2003 will make this even more marked.

A Fair Means of Settling a Dispute?

Lawyers in modern, sophisticated societies, do not see the trial as a savage means of seeking psychological 'closure'. Rather, they believe the trial to be civilised, impartial and fair:

> There are bodies or proceedings which, although ostensibly qualifying as 'courts' and 'trials', have procedures that are so aberrant that they come to be regarded as courts and trials in name only. Hence the use of such terms as 'kangaroo court', 'show trial' or 'Star Chamber trial' to describe travesties of due process.[24]

Notions of legality and due process are central to the very definition of a trial. In addition, Antony Duff[25] has shown that the criminal trial has a significance beyond the identification of offenders and the selection of measures to ensure that they do not damage society again. If the trial were purely 'instrumental' in that way, then participation by the defendant directly in the proceedings would not be afforded the central importance that all developed jurisdictions attach to it. A purely instrumental inquiry might be better informed when the defendant participates, but, Duff argues, this participation is seen as far more than a means to assist an accurate evaluation of the case; it is essential to justice:

> The aim of a criminal trial is not merely to reach an accurate judgment on the defendant's past conduct; it is to communicate and justify that judgment—to demonstrate its justice—to him and others.[26]

For a trial, as opposed to a diagnostic proceeding with entirely instrumental objectives, is a 'rational process of proof and argument which seeks to persuade the person whose conduct is under scrutiny of the truth and justice of its conclusions.'[27]

Duff's argument is supported by a recent decision of the Divisional Court. In *R v Thames Youth Court*,[28] a juvenile was to be tried for aggravated vehicle-taking. Just before the prosecution was due to open its case, the defendant was arrested in relation to another offence. A defence application to have the case adjourned was refused, although the district judge did offer to adjourn as soon as it was time for the defence case to begin. On an application for judicial review of the refusal, Pitchford J held that although there is a discretion to proceed with a criminal trial in the defendant's absence, particular care must be exercised in cases involving juveniles, because a young defendant may not have the same development and understanding as an adult. Thus, in this case, the defendant's vulnerability increased the State's obligation to guarantee his effective participation in the

[24] J Jaconelli, 'What is a Trial?' in M Mulholland and B Pullan (eds), *Judicial Tribunals in England and Europe, 1200–1700: the Trial in History*, vol 1 (Manchester, Manchester University Press, 2003), 22.

[25] R A Duff, *Trials and Punishments* (Cambridge, Cambridge University Press, 1986).

[26] Ibid, 115 (author's italics).

[27] Ibid, 116.

[28] [2002] *Criminal Law Review* 977.

trial,[29] suggesting that that the insistence upon defendant participation is based upon a more fundamental principle than the need to maximise procedural efficiency. For although an immature defendant might be less able than an adult to ensure or assist the accuracy of the verdict, it appears that his or her presence is more important than that of an adult. This is consistent with Duff's suggestion that the defendant must be made to appreciate how and why the verdict has been reached; a young person may need to learn what society considers justice to be.[30]

If the prerequisite of a fair trial is participation in it by the person accused, adversarial and inquisitorial methods are equally legitimate, but advocates of the adversarial trial also praise its emphasis on party participation and control. 'Current ideology extols the adversary system primarily as the best system for protecting individual dignity and autonomy.'[31] Whether or not this is the case, there is some evidence that lay people think that it is. In Thibaut and Walker's laboratory experiments, subjects were asked first to express a preference for adversarial or inquisitorial procedures, but were then randomly assigned to simulations that adopted either model. The cases in which they were involved might feature disputes where the evidence was evenly balanced, others where it was weighted to favour one party. Those who went through adversarial procedures were far happier with the verdicts and rated the proceedings as fairer than those who went through inquisitorial procedures, whether or not they were favoured by the result. This was true not only of American, but of French and German subjects. Parties apparently preferred adversarial proceedings because they had more control.[32] But the researchers omitted a feature characteristic of inquisitorial systems, that on appeal the facts may be and often are, considered *de novo*, thus providing for a second opinion on their merits. So the picture of inquisitorial process they provided was, arguably, unflattering and somewhat distorted, at least as far as complex cases likely to be appealed are concerned.[33]

According to Thibaut and Walker, the preference for adversarial procedures was heavily dependent upon the freedom of action of the parties to the dispute. A hallmark of the adversarial trial is that it is the parties who determine which issues will be tried and what evidence the court will hear. Procedural autonomy, argues Dubber,[34] would include the right to choose a lawyer or to represent oneself in court. Yet in England and Wales, we have recently become prepared to restrict the defendant's operation of these rights in certain circumstances. Under

---

[29] D Ormerod, 'Commentary' [2002] *Criminal Law Review* 978–79.

[30] It has been held that it is not unfair to hold a trial on the facts although the defendant is unfit to plead; the proceedings are not criminal because they are not followed by a penalty; *R v H* [2003] 1 All ER 497.

[31] E E Sward, 'Values, Ideology and the Evolution of the Adversary System' (1989) 64 *Indiana Law Journal* 301, 302. For exploration of the concept of autonomy in this context, see M Dubber, 'The Criminal Trial and the Legitimation of Punishment' (this volume).

[32] J Thibaut and L Walker, *Procedural Justice* (Hillside, New Jersey, Erlbaum, 1975); 'A Theory of Procedure' (1978) 66 *California Law Review* 541.

[33] H F M Crombag in P J van Koppen and S Penrod (eds), *Adversarial versus Inquisitorial Justice: Psychological Perspectives* (New York, Kluwer, 2003).

[34] N 31 above.

the 1999 Youth Justice and Criminal Evidence Act a defendant may not cross-examine in person a range of vulnerable witnesses including children and complainants in sexual cases.[35] Parliament decided that it would not be satisfactory for the trial judge to take over the cross-examination of the vulnerable witness,[36] and instead provided for a legal representative to act on the defendant's behalf, with or without the defendant's consent.[37] It has been claimed that a defendant who cross-examines in person 'does not do it in the hope of an acquittal; he does it in the hope of inflicting future pain.'[38] The accused must be given the opportunity to arrange for representation for the purpose of cross-examining the vulnerable witness in question,[39] but if he declines to do so, the court may appoint a legal representative to perform the task,[40] in which case payment will be made out of central funds.[41]

Can a trial be fair where a defendant is forced to accept a lawyer not of his or her choosing, particularly given that such an advocate 'shall not be responsible to the accused'?[42] Article 6 of the European Convention on Human Rights (ECHR) refers to the right to defend oneself in person or to have legal assistance of one's own choice. The British Government is confident that there is no contravention in the 1999 provisions. The European Court of Human Rights (ECtHR) has held that other rights have to be balanced against those conferred by Article 6,[43] for example the right of witnesses to protection from cruel and inhuman treatment, and from unwarranted intrusion into their private lives.[44] In *Croissant v Germany*[45] it was held that a requirement in German law that certain defendants would be forced to be legally represented was compatible with Article 6. However, to impose legal representation upon a defendant in inquisitorial proceedings raises different considerations from those posed by the 1999 Act. The importance of cross-examination in adversarial proceedings suggests that it may significantly prejudice a defendant to have a lawyer 'parachuted in' late in the day to take over the cross-examination of a particular witness without having heard earlier parts of the trial. Some defendants distrust lawyers, and may refuse to communicate with advocates imposed on them. Trial judges who in the past took over the cross-examination of child witnesses from unrepresented defendants at least had the advantage of having heard the evidence and arguments so far during the trial.

---

[35] Set out in sub-s (3).
[36] As happened in *De Oleivera* [1997] *Criminal Law Review* 600.
[37] This is not entirely novel. Under the Criminal Procedure (Insanity) Act 1964, the court may appoint someone to put the defendant's case if the jury decides he is under a disability. Wilful refusal to have a lawyer in these cases amounts to placing oneself under a disability.
[38] HL Debates Official Report 1397 Feb 1.
[39] S 38(2).
[40] S 38 (4).
[41] S 40.
[42] S 38(5).
[43] *Doorson v Netherlands* [1996] 22 EHRR 330.
[44] Arts 3, 8.
[45] (1993) 16 EHRR 135.

Dubber has shown that the plea bargain is consistent with autonomy only where the distribution of power between negotiating parties is even.[46] Nevertheless, pragmatic interest in securing a greater proportion of uncontested trials has led to pressure being placed upon defendants to plead guilty.[47] Antony Duff argues that such pressure is inconsistent with the respect owed to defendants. A guilty plea should properly 'express the defendant's recognition, and voluntary admission, of her guilt.'[48] This is not the case if it is obtained by threats or inducements. The epitome of the pragmatic plea of guilty is the *Alford* plea in the United States.[49] This indicates that although the defendant wishes to plead guilty, he or she at the same time maintains innocence of the crime. The defendant thus can take advantage of a reduced sentence by pleading guilty to a lesser offence, while refusing to admit culpability. The United States Supreme Court upheld the validity of such a plea as long as the defendant acted voluntarily, and with full knowledge and understanding of the consequences. The trial judge, therefore, in deciding whether to accept an *Alford* plea, is concerned primarily with the issue of voluntariness, not with whether the defendant is in fact guilty. Truth is here subservient to defendant autonomy, or the appearance of it. On the other hand, in Sutcliffe's case the autonomous acceptance by the prosecution, in agreement with the defence, that the defendant was entitled to the defence of diminished responsibility was rejected and the prosecutor forced to the trouble and expense of pursuing a murder accusation in which he had no belief. Pragmatism apparently gave way to the need for catharsis. The result was a verdict which might have had powerful symbolic meaning, but little to do with the truth. Such an outcome is difficult to justify.

Control over one's case may not be the only factor affecting perceptions of fairness. Lind and Tyler also found that the more a trial format moved from inquisitorial to adversarial characteristics, the more satisfaction levels among their participants increased.[50] In their research, the key to approval was the extent to which each participant was given the opportunity to express his views. They tested 652 Chicago citizens in relation to their encounters with the police and the courts. Some of the evidence they gathered dealt with police encounters, although some concerned disputes that had been sent to arbitration. Subjects were asked questions such as, 'Do the authorities seem biased?' 'Do I trust them to be diligent and conscientious?' 'Do they treat me with respect?' Lind and Tyler found that ratings of procedural justice turned largely on values they described as 'group value' (emphasising the importance to individuals of their long-term relationship with legal authorities, in contrast to the short-term

---

[46] N 31 above.
[47] The Criminal Justice and Public Order Act 1994, s 48, requires judges to ensure that a defendant has been reminded of the sentencing discount that follows a guilty plea. In the context of the plea and directions (pre-trial) hearing, this could result in some clandestine and potentially unfair deals being struck by counsel and judges.
[48] Duff, n 25 above, at 141.
[49] *US v Alford* 400 US 25 (1970).
[50] E A Lind and T R Tyler, *The Social Psychology of Procedural Justice* (London, Plenum, 1988).

resolution of a particular dispute). Values such as 'trust' and 'group standing' were especially important to those in ethnic minorities. It appears from this research that perceptions of fairness depend not only on whether one is able to influence and control the conduct of the trial (with rather less emphasis upon the nature of the ultimate decision). The key feature seems to be the manner in which the encounter is handled—whether there are signs of bias, or of trust-worthiness and respect. Has either one of our two models of trial a greater claim to treat parties with dignity and respect? Defendants in continental trials are at the mercy of the presiding judge, lacking the protective shield of the Anglo-American exclusionary rules about bad character. On the other hand, witnesses in adversarial criminal trials are not allowed to express themselves freely, but have to give their evidence while contending with the rigid control and, some-times, downright cruelty, of the examining advocate.

Sanders records that a juror burst into tears when the hostile cross-examination of a witness with Down's syndrome lasted over two days and con-fused him completely.[51] It has been argued that the questioning style of the adversarial advocate is merely an enforcement of the social rules that govern coherence in ordinary conversation,[52] such as having to answer the question, not indulging in irrelevance, not giving more information than is asked for, and not interrupting. But the level of cross-examiner hostility tolerated by courts on a daily basis suggests otherwise.[53] Although it has been claimed that witnesses, most notably rape complainants, might undergo aggressive and humiliating questioning at the pre-trial hearing conducted in inquisitorial jurisdictions, con-frontation with the defendant is not always involved, and the hearing is not pub-lic.[54] Cross-examination is an extraordinarily oppressive way to challenge witness testimony, even when it is ostensibly polite and low-key. Frequently the questions are designed to confuse or humiliate witnesses by enmeshing them in minutiae of marginal or no relevance. A typical line of questioning in a road accident case would be: counsel (showing the witness a photograph of the road), 'Had you reached the second telegraph pole on the left in photograph number three when you saw the oncoming vehicle?'[55] This happens even in relation to child witnesses in cases of alleged sexual abuse, as, for example, 'What colour was the duvet?'[56] In its extreme form, in the United States, adversarial advocacy

---

[51] A Sanders, J Creaton, S Bird and L Weber, *Victims with Learning Disabilities: Home Office Research Findings* 44 (London, HMSO, 1996).

[52] R Penman, 'Regulation of Discourse in the Adversary Trial' (1987) 7 *Windsor Yearbook of Access to Justice* 3.

[53] Cairns, n 4 above, describes the admiration of legal historians for combative cross-examination.

[54] L Ellison, 'The Protection of Vulnerable Witnesses in Court: an Anglo-Dutch Comparison' (1999) 3 *International Journal of Evidence and Proof* 29.

[55] T Bingham, *The Business of Judging: Selected Essays and Speeches* (Oxford, Oxford University Press, 2000) 16.

[56] G Davies, C Wilson, R Mitchell and J Milsom, *Videotaping Children's Evidence: an Evaluation* (London, Home Office, 1995) 33.

can so disrupt the proceedings as to distort the outcome.[57] Luban sees adversarial proceedings as a licence to lawyers to trample over the truth and over moral principle. It survives because rival systems are not demonstrably better.[58]

Lawyers do not have the exclusive right to ride roughshod over the dignity of witnesses for the prosecution. Several notorious cases in Britain of sexual complainants being subjected to deliberate humiliation at the hands of unrepresented defendants[59] prompted the restrictions on cross-examination discussed above. In the United States, Colin Ferguson, a 'deranged gunman'[60] was tried for shooting and killing six people and wounding seventeen others on a commuter train. At his trial he conducted his own defence and, according to Pizzi, was allowed to 'milk' the dramatic aspects of the case. He cross-examined 'people whose lives and bodies had been permanently scarred by him', while walking arrogantly around the well of the court.[61] Pizzi asks 'Was Mr Ferguson *on trial* for these terrible crimes or should he more properly be thought of as the *host* of the trial?'[62] According to Lind and Tyler's research, those witnesses would not regard the trial as fair, whereas Ferguson certainly would. But it may be that the more a community identifies itself with 'liberty, egalitarianism, individualism, populism and laissez-faire'[63] the more aggressively adversarial it will expect its procedures to be—irrespective of their suitability for the pursuit of the truth. In other words, if a trial is perceived to be fair in the light of the prevailing culture of the society within which it takes place, less attention may be paid to the matter of whether questioning styles hinder witnesses from expressing themselves, or even whether the prospect of hostile treatment deters potential witnesses from testifying at all.

Pizzi argues that the 'adversary mentality' leads to the perception of trials as inevitably two-sided contests, with victims and others having no legitimate role. But in some jurisdictions the mounting influence of human rights jurisprudence has highlighted the need to recognise that all participants in trials, not only the parties, are entitled to respect for their rights to privacy and security,[64] and the right not to be subjected to degrading treatment.[65] Thus, a new interest has emerged, upsetting the traditional two-handed balancing of the defendant's

---

[57] W T Pizzi, *Trials Without Truth* (New York and London, NYU Press, 1999); P Danet and P Bogosch, 'Fixed Fight or Free-For-All: an Empirical Study of Combativeness in the Adversary System of Justice' (1980) 7 *British Journal of Law and Society* 36. But see, R Dunstan, 'Context for Coercion: Analyzing Properties of Courtroom Questions' (1980) 7 *British Journal of Law and Society* 61.

[58] Luban, n 11 above.

[59] J McEwan, 'In Defence of Vulnerable Witnesses: the Youth Justice and Criminal Evidence Act 1999' (2000) 3 *International Journal of Evidence and Proof* 1.

[60] Pizzi, n 57 above, at 84.

[61] Ibid, 85.

[62] Ibid 85–86. Author's italics.

[63] S M Lipsett, *American Exceptionality as a Double-Edged Sword* (New York, W W Norton, 1996) 33.

[64] Art 8 European Convention on Human Rights; *Doorson v Netherlands* [1996] EHRR 230.

[65] Art 3 European Convention on Human Rights.

right to a fair trial against society's interest in punishing and deterring crime. However, adversarial trials, with their bipolar configuration, are particularly unsuited to taking account of the interests of witnesses, including victims, and attempts to provide appropriate safeguards for them have been fraught with difficulty. Special measures for vulnerable witnesses have been introduced in common law jurisdictions all over the world. They tend to include closed circuit television, the use of screens, and in some jurisdictions, video-recorded interviews to replace the witness's evidence in chief.[66] Such measures have been held to be compatible with the fair trial requirement in Article 6.[67] Yet they inevitably carry the risk of creating the impression that the defendant is too terrifying to be faced directly. The risk of injustice is acute in the legislation of England and Wales. The Youth Justice and Criminal Evidence Act 1999 denies special measures to all defendants, irrespective of whether they could be regarded as vulnerable for reasons of youth, low intelligence, or communication difficulties. Juvenile defendants may find child witnesses for the prosecution, in some cases older than they are, benefiting from the use of videotaping and CCTV, while, as defendants, they are expected to testify in open court in the traditional manner. Indeed, failure to give evidence may give rise to an inference of guilt.[68] So far, courts seem untroubled by the potential unfairness in relation to the vulnerable defendant, whose right to be protected from degrading treatment is deemed to be satisfied by the operation of the presumption of innocence.[69] It is difficult to agree that the fact that a prosecutor is required to discharge the burden of proof can justify the unequal treatment of witnesses, whether they be the defendant or other individuals. The accused who testifies is not in the slightest assisted through that ordeal by the presumption of innocence, which affects only the weighing of evidence at close of trial. After all, there is a burden of proof also upon civil claimants;[70] should defendants in civil cases be treated differently from other witnesses if they decide to give evidence?

Lind and Tyler's findings suggest that there is a risk that the more that trials are adapted in line with human rights perceptions of appropriate treatment for victims and other witnesses, the less fair the trial will be perceived to be, unless we can preserve the dignity of the witness and afford the defendant equal respect at the same time. Any indication that defendants are losing the freedom to run their defence as they choose may also cause trials to be perceived as unfair. But

---

[66] J McEwan, 'Special Measures for Witnesses and Victims' in M McConville and G Wilson, n 12 above.

[67] *Baegen v Netherlands* A/327-B (1995); Application No 16696/90 (European Commission): *SN v Sweden* [2002] *Criminal Law Review* 831.

[68] Criminal Justice and Public Order Act 1994, s 35. Although in its original form, the provision prohibited the drawing of adverse inferences in relation to a defendant aged less than 14 who declined to testify, the age threshold was removed by the Crime and Disorder Act 1998, s 35.

[69] *R v Camberwell Green Youth Court* (*The Times* 13 February 2003) (closed circuit television). But in *T v UK* (4 December 1998, Application No 2488/94) the ECtHR expressed serious concerns about the treatment of juvenile defendants in Crown Court trials, and their ability to participate in them.

[70] Albeit to the lesser standard of the balance of probability.

how real was that supposed freedom? How much power over events has a defendant who cannot afford legal representation? When lawyers are involved, there is every indication that control is in their hands and that the trial is run for their benefit. Cairns argues that the adversarial model developed in the nineteenth century, partly as a consequence of the formation of a professional bar. This led to the increased participation of counsel in the conduct of the trial and gave them power over it. The judge retreated into the shadows of neutrality and the prisoner 'was rendered mute, and frequently helpless.'[71] The emotional commitment of the British Bar to traditional adversarial features such as cross-examination, non-disclosure of the defence case and the labyrinthine complexities of the rules on admissibility of the defendant's criminal record might thus be seen as reluctance in the legal profession to let go of its power.

Certainly, the decision whether or not the defendant should testify is frequently heavily influenced by counsel. According to Damaska, the adversarial tradition is hostile to one side of a dispute being able to use the other as a source of evidence. It would 'destroy the balance of advantages and the position of theoretical equality between the contestants.'[72] Duff argues that the process of trial 'aims to engage with the defendant in a communicative enterprise of argument and justification; but we recognise that we should, in practice if not ideally, allow her to refuse to take part in it.'[73] The 'right to silence' might be seen as a matter of autonomy insofar as the system respects the accused's exercise of the choice whether or not to testify. In England and Wales, that choice has been substantially reduced by the Criminal Justice and Public Order Act 1994.[74] The price for electing not to give evidence is that the court is entitled to interpret this as a sign of guilt. However, a right to autonomy, in the sense of being free to select the evidence to be presented,[75] cannot justify the exclusion of evidence that is probative. If silence in any particular case can legitimately be regarded as evidence of guilt, the defendant has no right to prevent the inference of guilt from being drawn.[76] The proceedings have recognised the defendant's right not to participate by not demanding that she gives evidence. Thus, the Act seriously threatens the fairness of the trial only if it is the case that refusal to testify is so infrequently an accurate indicator of guilt, and it is so difficult to identify those cases where it is indeed probative, that the drawing of adverse inferences seriously undermines the accuracy of verdicts.

The persistent legislative attempts[77] to demand disclosure of evidence and arguments by both sides to criminal proceedings can be seen further evidence of Parliament's indifference to the principle that parties cannot be used as a source

---

[71] L Farmer, 'Review of D Cairns' (n 4 above) (2000) 116 *Law Quarterly Review* 169.
[72] Damaska, n 8 above, at 563.
[73] Duff, n 25 above, at 133.
[74] Sections 34–37. See also Northern Ireland, Criminal Evidence (Northern Ireland) Order 1988.
[75] Dubber, n 31 above.
[76] I am grateful to Victor Tadros for this point.
[77] See now Criminal Justice Bill 2003; Auld, n 7 above—move to co-operation and transparency.

of evidence. It has been recognised that there is no equality of arms, so essential to adversarial theory, in a criminal prosecution. Thus prosecutors are obliged to hand over unused material, enabling the defence to take advantage of the State's superior resources. Enthusiasm for defence disclosure, however, springs from concerns about rationality and evidentiary quality. The drive to make trials more effective instruments to uncover the truth runs alongside pressure for efficiency in terms of time and money. Contemporary concern to protect the dignity of vulnerable witnesses derives as much from anxiety that failure to do so will deprive the court of valuable evidence as from recognition of the humanitarian obligation not to subject them to degrading treatment. The exclusion of the defendant from special measures suggests that anything he might have to say to the court is less valuable than evidence for the prosecution.

Relationship with Truth

The research of Thibaut and Walker and Lind and Tyler does not necessarily indicate that the experimental subjects considered values such as autonomy, dignity and respect to be more important than the need to discover the truth. Rather, their results may reflect a general acceptance that both inquisitorial and adversarial proceedings endeavour to get to the truth, and that in that respect there is little to choose between them. Given the lack of superiority of either system as an instrument of investigation, subjects were free to prefer adversarial procedures for the apparently greater emphasis placed upon those additional values. However, many advocates for the adversary system argue that partisan manipulation of evidentiary materials, under equality of arms, is the most effective way to place an independent tribunal of fact in a position to determine the truth—'an assumption at best unproven and at worst highly implausible.'[78] This philosophy has nevertheless most certainly had the incidental effect of expanding the role of the advocate. Over time, argues Cairns, the adversarial truth rationale was taken 'to sanction an aggressively adversarial mentality.'[79] Even Thibaut and Walker, whose research suggests that in evenly balanced cases adversarial process is better at establishing facts and combating internal and external bias, concede that in uneven cases the impact of evidence is distorted, making a weak case appear stronger than it is.[80] The inquisitorial system, on the other hand, places its faith in the integrity of the State and its capacity to pursue truth unprompted by partisan pressures of individual self-interest. Unconvinced, Wagenaar argues[81] that the requirement in The Netherlands that

---

[78] N Jörg, S Field and C Brants in C Harding, P Fennell, N Jörg and B Swart (eds), *Criminal Justice in Europe: a Comparative Study* (Oxford, Clarendon, 2002) at 43.

[79] N 4 above, at 165.

[80] *Procedural Justice*, n 32 above.

[81] W A Wagenaar, P J van Koppen, and H M Crombag, *Anchored Narratives: the Psychology of Criminal Evidence* (Hemel Hempstead, Harvester Wheatsheaf, 1993).

judges should read the evidence before the trial undermines the presumption of innocence. In one study, two groups of professional judges were compared. They heard identical cases, but one group read the file beforehand and the other did not. All of those who read the file beforehand convicted the defendant. Only twenty-seven per cent of the others did so. The prosecutor's opinion and the documents supporting it strongly influenced prior expectations.[82] In many inquisitorial systems the judge is required to read the file because a large part of the evidence will not be presented orally in court.

A system designed to pursue the truth does not easily accommodate the individual right to be protected from degrading treatment. This problem is arguably most acute in trials for sexual offences, where experience has shown that the adversarial trial has exposed complainants to humiliating, and frequently irrelevant, character assassination by the defence.[83] The struggle of common law jurisdictions to devise a workable 'rape shield' which allows relevant, but excludes gratuitous and prurient, questions about a complainant's former sexual relationships has been well documented.[84] In England and Wales, the House of Lords has failed to find a satisfactory solution to the conflict between the need to ensure that the defendant's right to a fair trial is not prejudiced by the exclusion of evidence relevant to his defence, and to ensure at the same time that complainants do not endure unnecessary embarrassment. In *R v A*,[85] the issue was whether the defendant, whose defence to a charge of rape was consent, could establish through cross-examination that he and the complainant had been enjoying a sexual relationship shortly before the alleged rape. It was clear that without this evidence, the defendant's version of events was implausible.[86] Recent legislation had provided that in cases of sexual complaint where the defence is consent, the relevance of the complainant's prior sexual behaviour, whether with the defendant or with others, depends upon whether that sexual behaviour falls within one of two exceptional categories. Questions about her relationship with the defendant may be relevant if the behaviour at issue is alleged to have taken place at or about the same time as the alleged offence,[87] or occurred longer ago but was so similar to her behaviour as described by the defence at the time of the alleged offence that the similarity cannot reasonably be explained as a coincidence.[88] Their Lordships considered that consensual intercourse between the complainant and the defendant a week before the

---

[82] B Schüneman, 'Experimentelle Untersuchungen zur Reform der Hauptverhandlung in Strafsachen' in H J Kerner, H Kurry and K Sessar (eds), *Deutsche Forschungen zur Kriminalitätsentstehen und Kriminalitätskontrolle* (Köln, Carl Heymanns, 1983).

[83] S Lees, *Carnal Knowledge: Rape on Trial* (London, Hamish Hamilton, 1996); Z Adler, *Rape on Trial*, (London, Routledge & Kegan Paul, 1987).

[84] N Kibble, 'The Sexual History Provisions' [2000] *Criminal Law Review* 274.

[85] [2001] 3 All ER 1.

[86] J McEwan, 'The Rape Shield Askew? *R v A*' (2002) 5 *International Journal of Evidence and Proof* 257.

[87] Youth Justice and Criminal Evidence Act 1999, s 41(3)(b).

[88] Ibid, s 41 (3)(c).

alleged rape was insufficiently close in time to fall within the first exception, although they recognised that,

> the man or woman in the street would find it strange that evidence that two young people had lived together or regularly as part of a happy relationship had had sexual acts together, must be wholly excluded on the issue of consent unless it is immediately contemporaneous.[89]

The 'similar facts' exception was not satisfied simply by dint of the coincidence of partner in each case, that is, that in each of the alleged sexual encounters the participants were the complainant and the defendant. For in some cases, the fact that the complainant once had a sexual relationship with the defendant has absolutely no bearing on the issue of consent, for example, if the relationship occurred a long time ago. So, although it was decided that 'rare or bizarre conduct'[90] was not required to establish sufficient similarity between the complainant's earlier behaviour and her conduct at the time of the alleged rape,[91] the best course would be to refer the case back to the trial judge so that he could investigate the case further to see whether there were sufficient coincidences of circumstance to justify the proposed cross-examination. This outcome prevented the House from having to make a declaration that the statute was incompatible with the ECHR in denying the defendant a fair trial under Article 6.[92] The tragic irony here is that complainants could face as much, if not more, degrading treatment than would be the case if they were merely asked, during cross-examination by the defence, whether they had not earlier enjoyed a consensual sexual relationship with the defendant. Instead, trial judges, mindful that in many cases, to conceal such information from the jury would be completely unfair to the defendant, apparently should quiz both parties about the exact details of the complainant's participation in her relationship with him in a search for some potentially superficial similarity of circumstance that would justify the proposed cross-examination. Parliament, from the best of motives, tried to devise a rape shield that acknowledged that for a woman to consent to sex with a particular man once does not mean that she consents forever. Unfortunately, the attempt has backfired badly, and courts are unable to reach a rational solution that accommodates the competing rights of the complainant, the defendant and the public who require offenders to be punished.

It is impossible to say whether either the adversarial or inquisitorial system is superior in terms of its quality of decision-making.[93] But I have argued that

---

[89] Lord Steyn, *R v A*, n 85 above, at 15.

[90] Lord Clyde, *ibid*, at 45.

[91] So that it was not at all clear how similar the complainant's behaviour would have to be in order for her earlier sexual encounters to become probative of consent.

[92] S 3 of the Human Rights Act 1998 directs that, so far as it is possible to do so, primary legislation must be read in a way which is compatible with Convention rights.

[93] P J van Koppen and S Penrod, 'Adversarial or Inquisitorial: Comparing Systems' in P J van Koppen and S Penrod (eds), *Adversarial versus Inquisitorial Justice: Psychological Perspectives* (New York and Dordrecht, Kluwer/Plenum, 2003).

many of the rules of evidence which owe their existence to the structural demands of the adversarial system are incompatible with the uncovering of the truth.[94] Increasingly, this is being recognised, and the law being reformed, in order to ensure that reliable evidence is brought before the court. This has the inevitable consequence of chipping away at the adversarial structure. Most significantly, perhaps, a series of notorious miscarriages of justice[95] have forced recognition that government cannot afford to regard trials as a matter of private interest between the parties. Jackson has shown that adversarial trials express 'a conception of the appropriate role of government in the resolution of disputes.'[96] Preferring to reduce governmental involvement to the most non-interventionist minimum, Anglo-American systems require only the provision of a forum for their impartial resolution. However, it is clearly no longer acceptable to restrict appeal hearings to issues of formal compliance with procedure rather than the reliability of verdicts. The insistence of the Court of Appeal that its role is not to retry cases already heard by the jury[97] led to the creation of the Criminal Cases Review Commission, which has the power to conduct investigations itself, to instruct police officers to investigate, and to demand production of documents from public bodies.[98]

Current proposals to allow the prosecution of an individual for an offence of which he was acquitted in the past clearly represent a derogation of the rule against double jeopardy;[99] it is a departure from the traditional adversarial principle that once the facility of the forum has been provided by the State and the parties had every chance to present their case, there is no rehearing.[100] But *ne bis in idem* is not exclusive to adversarial jurisdictions; it is a general principle of justice.[101] It may be explained by sympathy for the mental anguish of the defendant whose acquittal is not taken as final, and thus is 'not free thereafter to plan his or her own life, enter into engagements with other . . . if required constantly to have in mind the danger of being once more subject to a criminal prosecution for the same alleged crime.'[102] But, as Roberts has shown, distress

---

[94] J McEwan, *Evidence and the Adversarial Process* (2nd edn, Oxford, Hart Publishing, 1998).

[95] The 'Guildford Four' Richardson, Conlon, Armstrong and Hill (*The Times*, 20 October 1989); the 'Maguire Seven' (*Maguire and Others* (1991) 94 Cr App R 133); Judith Ward (*Ward* [1993] 2 All ER 577); the 'Tottenham Three' Silcott, Braithwaite and Raghip (*The Times*, 9 December 1991).

[96] J Jackson, 'Evidence: Legal Perspective' in R Bull and D Carson (eds), *Handbook of Psychology in Legal Contexts* (Chichester, Wiley, 1995).

[97] *McIlkenny* [1992] 2 All ER 417, at 424.

[98] 1995 Criminal Appeal Act, ss 15–25.

[99] Law Commission, *Double Jeopardy and Criminal Appeals* (Law Com No 267; London, HMSO, 2001). Criminal Justice Bill 2003; prosecutions will require new and compelling evidence, the consent of the DPP and should be in the interests of justice.

[100] As the famous actress told the exhausted Hamlet, 'You've had your chance—and you've missed it!'

[101] ECHR Article 4 of Protocol 7, subject to a proviso in (2) where there is evidence of 'new or newly discovered facts', or if there has been a 'fundamental defect' in the previous proceedings.

[102] *UK v Soering* 11 ECHR 439; cf *Green v US* 355 US 184 (1857), 187–88: 'It involves that person in expense, embarrassment and constant fear.'

in itself cannot be a bar to a second prosecution any more than it was a bar to the first.[103] A far more convincing rationale for *ne bis in idem* is, he argues, to remind the State of the limits of its power.[104] The Law Commission of England and Wales recognised that it is one of the principal terms of the bargain between the people and the State in relation to the exercise by the latter of coercive power. It respects the principle of limited government and the liberty of the subjects.[105] The knowledge that we have this kind of protection commands the respect and confidence of the public.[106] The commission, however, consider that the discovery of DNA, with its apparent infallibility, means that respect and confidence may be forfeit if people consider that the guilty are escaping justice for procedural and technical reasons.[107] Critics of the Criminal Justice Act note that a case may be retried on the strength of all kinds of evidence apart from DNA.[108] One of the most interesting aspects of the debate is the disagreement between those whose notions of fairness depend upon the finality of the verdict, and those who perceive fairness in terms of accuracy.

In the adversarial jurisdiction, the operation of the double jeopardy principle is complicated by the ban on evidence of bad character unless it is especially probative of guilt. Although the 'similar facts' rule would allow to be offered in evidence previous convictions which show that the defendant is guilty of the offence charged, English courts have struggled with the question of similar earlier alleged offences of which the defendant had been acquitted. In *R v Z*,[109] the defendant was charged with the rape of a young woman, C, in 1998. His defence was that C had consented to sexual intercourse. In the past, he had undergone four separate trials for rape, being accused in each by a different complainant. In each case, he had alleged that the complainant had consented. He had been acquitted three times, but was convicted on the fourth occasion. There were other similarities between the four earlier cases and the present allegation. The prosecution proposed to call evidence of these four previous alleged rapes to show that C had not consented. This procedure would not require any reference to the earlier trials, whose outcome was not material to the prosecution in relation to C, but would require the original complainants to come to court to give evidence again. All said that they were willing to do this. The defendant argued that their evidence would infringe the rule against double jeopardy, in that the prosecution argument would invite the current jury to decide that he had been

---

[103] P Roberts, 'Justice for All? Two Bad Arguments (and Several Good Suggestions) for Resisting Double Jeopardy Reform' (2002) 6 *International Journal of Evidence and Proof* 197; see also I Dennis, 'Rethinking Double Jeopardy: Justice and Finality in Criminal Process' [2000] *Criminal Law Review* 33.

[104] P Roberts, 'Acquittal Misconduct Evidence and Double Jeopardy Principles: from *Sambasivam* to *Z*' [2000] *Criminal Law Review* 982.

[105] Law Commission, *Double Jeopardy and Criminal Appeals* (Law Com No 267; London, HMSO, 2001), paras 4.12–4.19.

[106] *Connelly v DPP* [1964] AC 1254, 1353.

[107] See Law Commission, n 99 above; Criminal Justice Act 2003.

[108] *Briefing*, n 3 above.

[109] [2000] 3 All ER 385.

guilty on those earlier occasions and therefore was guilty in the present case. Lord Hutton replied:

> The principle of double jeopardy operates to cause a criminal court . . . to stop a prosecution where the defendant is being prosecuted on the same facts, or substantially the same facts as gave rise to an earlier prosecution which resulted in his acquittal (or conviction) . . . Provided that a defendant is not placed in double jeopardy . . . evidence which is relevant on a subsequent prosecution is not inadmissible because it shows or tends to show that the defendant was, in fact, guilty of an offence of which he had earlier been acquitted.[110]

In systems of justice which are used to dealing with issues of the defendant's personality, the problem would never have arisen.

The pursuit of truth seems currently to be preoccupying British and Commonwealth lawyers to a considerable degree. We see special measures for vulnerable witnesses introduced to help them give evidence more fluently (and therefore more convincingly). The rule against hearsay is under attack throughout the common law world. Its devotees have fought back hard;[111] many advocates from the adversarial tradition insist that the rule against hearsay is essential to allow cross-examination of opposing witnesses. But their faith in cross-examination is naïve.[112] Reformers, at any rate, are sufficiently disenchanted with it to propose a general power to admit hearsay where the maker of the statement is unavailable.[113] It cannot be denied that these reforms, like the double jeopardy proposals, have more to do with establishing guilt than the reverse.

3 CONCLUSION

All legal systems operate an evolutionary process of continuous reform, trying to adapt where concerns are expressed about the correctness of certain verdicts or the treatment of particular witnesses. But the adversarial system of England and Wales occasionally reacts to obvious unfairness by introducing a handicapping system more redolent of the Cheltenham Gold Cup than doing justice; because it is clear that prosecutors are more heavily resourced than the defence, they have a greater duty to disclose evidence; because the defendant has the advantage of being presumed innocent, he should not be entitled to special measures to allow more effective testimony. These responses may establish a rough and ready balance of disadvantages, but they have little to do with ascertaining the truth. Although we may not be able yet to ensure that criminal trials are fair, and may not even be very clear about what features a fair trial possesses, we can

---

[110] [2000] 3 All ER 403.
[111] See *Briefing*, n 3 above.
[112] McEwan, n 94 above, at 40–43, 106–8.
[113] Criminal Justice Act 2003; see *Briefing*, n 3 above.

be sure that handicapping does not represent even rough justice. For although we may have only hazy understanding of the symbolic function of a trial, it is clear that the public has a keen interest in the accuracy of the outcome, as was seen in the miscarriage of justice cases that led to the formation of the Criminal Cases Review Commission. Other features associated with fairness, including the ability of accused persons to present their case in the way they think fit, should be sacrificed only reluctantly. For, as Duff has pointed out, not only should society at large regard the criminal trial as fair, the defendant must perceive it as fair also.

4

'More Than Just Illogical': Truth and Jury Nullification

MATT MATRAVERS*

THE TITLE OF this chapter is taken from Sir Robin Auld's report on the criminal trial. He says of the phenomenon of jury nullification:

I regard the ability of jurors to acquit, and it also follows, convict, in defiance of the law and in disregard of their oaths as more than just illogicality. It is a blatant affront to the legal process and the main purpose of the criminal justice system—the control of crime—of which they are so important a part.[1]

The purpose of the chapter is not to provide a systematic, or even an unsystematic, defence of jury nullification, but is rather to pursue the thought that reflecting on the very peculiarity of jury nullification may teach us something about the trial. Jury nullification occurs when a jury acquits (or convicts) with deliberate disregard for the outcome that is dictated by the law and the facts as the jurors believe them to be. It can be distinguished from mistaken verdicts that result from juries' failure to understand the evidence or incompetent deliberations; from cases in which the jury doubts the credibility of a witness because of prejudice or anything else (so, for example, a jury that acquits because it believes that damning evidence provided by the police against a black defendant must have been planted because all policemen are racist, does not nullify); and from verdicts that result from corruption.

Jury nullification is a controversial aspect of criminal trials and one that divides the legal and political communities. Narratives of jury nullification thus emphasise the refusal of jurors to convict in some capital, or in 'three strikes', cases on the one hand, or, on the other, the refusal of white juries to convict white defendants for, for example, denying the right to vote to black citizens. In the USA, nullification has become controversial in politics because of calls—

* I am very grateful to Susan Mendus and to the members of the 'Trial on Trial' seminar for their comments on earlier versions of this chapter. I am particularly grateful to Robert Burns, Antony Duff, and Dudley Knowles for written comments.

[1] *A Review of the Criminal Courts of England and Wales by The Right Honourable Lord Justice Auld*, September 2001 <http://www.criminal-courts-review.org.uk/index.htm> 175.

most notoriously from a black law professor, Paul Butler—for black jurors to vote against conviction to stop other African Americans from ending up in prison. Butler does not believe murderers or other dangerous criminals should be spared from conviction, but in crimes like drug possession, he believes black jurors should protect their own. His arguments are many and complex, but in essence they appeal to the systematic racial bias in American law and society. Or, as he puts it, 'if African Americans simply followed the law because whites told them to, they'd still be slaves. The law doesn't come from God. It comes from people like Jesse Helms and Newt Gingrich.'[2] In what follows, I shall argue that jury nullification is best understood as occurring in the context of a conflict between the values embedded in the law and the values to which the jurors appeal, which may or may not be values of a more 'local' community to which the jurors belong.

1 TRIALS, JURIES, AND NULLIFICATION

In *A Theory of Justice*, John Rawls describes the criminal trial as an instance of 'imperfect procedural justice', which he contrasts with 'pure procedural justice'. In pure procedural justice, 'there is no independent criterion for the right result: instead there is a correct or fair procedure such that the outcome is likewise correct or fair, whatever it is, provided that the procedure has been properly followed' (think of a lottery: so long as it is fairly administered, the right outcome is simply that the person with the winning ticket wins). For Rawls, criminal trials are not like this because there is an independent criterion for the right outcomes: 'the offender should be declared guilty if and only if he has committed the offense with which he is charged.' Thus, the procedure of a criminal trial can be 'perfect' (not pure) or 'imperfect' and it is, of course, imperfect because it is not guaranteed to reach the right result.[3]

Rawls captures what is commonly believed: the purpose of the criminal trial is to get to the right answer, and it is an unfortunate fact that it does not always do so. Yet, many involved in the law dispute this. The English jurist, Frederick Pollock, for example, writes that 'perhaps the greatest of all the fallacies entertained by lay people about the law is . . . that it is the business of a court of justice to discover the truth.' Instead, he continues, 'its real business is to pronounce upon the justice of particular claims.'[4] Or, more flippantly, trials are designed to find not the substantive truth, but rather a definite winner.[5]

---

[2] http://www.erowid.org/freedom/jury_nullification/jury_nullification_media1.shtml. Perhaps the most notorious recent case of this sort involved the acquittal of Mayor Marion Barry of Washington DC who had been caught smoking cocaine on camera.

[3] All quotations from J Rawls, *A Theory of Justice* (Oxford, Oxford University Press, 1972) 85.

[4] F Pollock, *Essays in the Law* (Oxford, Oxford University Press, 1922) 275. Quoted in R Summers, 'Formal Legal Truth and Substantive Truth in Judicial Fact-Finding—Their Justified Divergence in Some Particular Cases' (1999) 18 *Law and Philosophy* 497, at 500.

[5] This phrase is adapted from Summers, ibid at 506.

This gap between the 'lay' and 'professional' understandings of the purpose of the trial can be closed simply by distinguishing different senses of 'the right answer'. Summers, for example, distinguishes between the actual truth, which he calls the 'substantive truth', and the 'formal legal truth', which is 'whatever is found as fact by the legal fact-finder.'[6] For Summers, the formal legal truth is created by the fact-finder. So, for example, in acquitting a defendant the jury creates the formal legal truth that the defendant is 'not guilty' even if the substantive truth is that he is. To borrow an example from the philosopher of language, J L Austin, just as the decision of an umpire in cricket to give the batsman not-out constitutes the formal truth (the batsman *is* then not-out even if the umpire is mistaken) so a jury's decision also constitutes the formal legal truth.[7] Of course, in normal cases we hope that a properly designed legal system will result in the formal legal truth coinciding with the substantive truth just as we hope that properly trained umpires will get their decisions right. However, unlike in the case of cricket, there are many instances in which a properly designed legal system will contain within it features that result in the formal legal truth and the substantive truth diverging. For example, there are burdens of proof, rules of evidence, rules of what the police may and may not do, and rules such as that which allows a spouse not to give evidence against his or her partner, which may (and presumably often do) mean that the formal legal truth and the substantive truth diverge. We uphold these rules for a number of reasons and presumably at least some of them are justified, all things considered.[8]

Rawls and Pollock, then, highlight different aspects of the criminal trial. The system is set up so as to arrive at the formal legal truth and, if it is set up properly, then it is hoped that where the formal legal truth and the substantive truth diverge that will be the result of other values that are embedded in the system. Thus, the system works when it rejects, say, a forced confession even if that confession is a good guide to the substantive truth. So, the jurors' roles are to come to a judgment about the facts of the matter up to some standard of proof and to apply the law as the judge gives it to them. The jurors aim at the formal legal truth and, unless there is good reason or a mistake is made, this will coincide with the substantive truth.

However, this is not the complete picture because the jury has the power to nullify. That is, *deliberately* to make formal legal truth and substantive truth diverge. In order to discuss this, we need a third category of truth. To see this, consider two cases in both of which the jury acquits although the substantive truth is that the offender is guilty of the charge. In the first, the jury acquits because it does not believe that the charge has been proven. That is, the jurors,

---

[6] Ibid, 498.

[7] J L Austin, *How to Do Things with Words* (Oxford, Oxford University Press, 1962) 153.

[8] The analogy with cricket is not entirely lost here. Technology could be used to give a more accurate decision in leg before wicket appeals than is achieved by leaving it in the hands of the umpires in the field (as it is in cases of appeals for a run out). However, opponents of this move cite values other than accuracy (such as not delaying the game and the importance of tradition).

applying the law as given to them by the judge to the facts as they believe them to be proven, decides against conviction. In the second, the jurors do believe the case proven, so they realise that applying the law as given to them by the judge to the facts as they believe them to be proven will result in a conviction, but they nevertheless acquit. In both cases, the fact that the jury acquits creates a formal legal truth that the offender is not guilty. However, it makes sense to distinguish the cases because surely we can say that there is a category—call it the 'actual legal truth'—which may be different from both the substantive truth and the formal legal truth. In the first case, the jury aspires to get the actual legal truth and it achieves this. It falls short of the substantive truth, but this ought not worry us as it is a result of the system having demanding standards of proof built into it. In the second case, the jury does not aim at the actual legal truth at all. Instead, it deliberately replaces the actual legal truth with its own judgment.

I want first to ask what is going on when the jury substitutes its judgment for the actual legal truth. The most straightforward account, which I shall call 'the naïve view' is to think of it as the jury lying about what it thinks. This seems to be the view of Sir Robin Auld, who notes that a nullifying jury is in breach of its 'oath or affirmation "faithfully [to] try the defendant and give a true verdict according to the evidence."' In support, he cites Glanville Williams asking 'if we really wish juries to give untrue verdicts, why do we require them to be sworn?'[9] Indeed, in many cases, a nullifying jury may deal a double blow to truth if the actual legal truth and the substantive truth coincide. On the naïve view, then, in putting the actual legal truth to one side, the jury establishes a formal legal truth by lying about what it believes to be both the actual legal, and the substantive, truth. Truth is sacrificed. Jurors pay this high cost in terms of truth in order to avoid a gross injustice (as they see it) being done; because, in the usual typology, '(1) they reject the law that criminalizes the wrong for which the defendant is being tried; (2) they reject not the criminalization of the act but the level of sanction attached to it; or (3) the jurors accept the law and concomitant sanction but simply have no wish to see them applied to the particular defendant on trial.'[10]

I call the view of jury nullification described above 'naïve' because it understands the deliberations of a jury in something like the following way. First, the jurors ask themselves, 'did the defendant do it?' Then, having established that he did, they ask themselves, 'ought the act to be criminal?', or (anticipating what will happen to the defendant) 'ought it to attract *that* level of sanction,' or 'ought this particular defendant to be punished in the way prescribed?' If the jurors feel strongly that one or other (or some combination) of these questions is correctly answered with a resounding 'no' then they report untruthfully that 'he did not do it.'

The trouble with this is that it is not at all clear what the 'it' is that the defendant did (or did not) do. A simple answer is 'the action', but that just invites

[9] Auld, n 1 above, at 175.

[10] D Allen, *The World of Prometheus: The Politics of Punishing in Democratic Athens* (Princeton, Princeton University Press, 2000) 5.

problems. Borrowing a phrase from Anscombe, of which great use is made by Donald Davidson, action is always action 'under a description'. The idea here is simple enough: one and the same action is always amenable to more than one correct description. My action of flipping the light switch can be redescribed as the act of turning on the light and also as the act of alerting the prowler who is lurking in the bushes outside. Generalising this point we can say that the same event can be referred to under quite disparate descriptions: the event of alerting the prowler is the same event as my flipping the light switch which is the same event as my moving my body (or a part of my body) in a certain way. Moreover, each of these descriptions is true.[11]

So, under what description do the jurors consider the action? Clearly there is one answer to this that supports the naïve view: under the description given to them by the law. So, in a murder trial, the 'it' in the 'did he do it?' question is not 'move his arm', or 'stab her', but 'stab her with the intent to kill or to cause grievous bodily harm' and so on. If the answer to whether he did *that* is yes, then the naïve view holds that there may be the further questions of whether killing someone in these circumstances ought to be criminal (presumably 'yes'), whether it ought to be punished with the particular sanction attached to it (possibly 'no'), and whether a given particular defendant ought to be so punished (again possibly 'no'). If the jurors answer 'no' to any of these questions then the possibility of nullifying—of being untruthful when asked whether he did it—emerges.

However, there is another possibility, which I will call 'the hermeneutic view'. Just because extremes are often more clear, take an extreme example: the jurors believe (as it happens rightly) that the defendant dishonestly took a piece of pizza from its owner with the intention permanently to deprive the owner of the pizza, that this is the defendant's third offence of the relevant kind (they are not meant to know that, but they have seen the defending attorney carrying a large folder labelled 'three strikes cases'), and so they believe that if found guilty he will go to prison for a minimum of twenty-five years. They find him not guilty. The naïve view says that the jurors believe him to be guilty (they believe that to be the actual legal, and the substantive, truth), but that when asked their verdict they report untruthfully that he did not do it (because they believe a gross injustice will be done if he is sentenced to a minimum of twenty-five years).

On the hermeneutic view, it seems to me that the relevant 'it' here (in the question 'did he do it?') is as follows: 'steal the pizza under conditions such that he deserves twenty-five years to life in prison.' That is, the hermeneutic view

---

[11] See G E M Anscombe, *Intention* (Oxford, Oxford University Press, 1957) 11. The example is taken from D Davidson, 'Actions, Reasons, and Causes', reprinted in his *Essays on Actions and Events* (2nd edn, Oxford, Clarendon Press, 2001) 3, at 4. The account of 'action under a description' owes much to J Malpas, 'Donald Davidson' in E Zalta (ed), *The Stanford Encyclopedia of Philosophy* (Winter 2003 edn); <http://plato.stanford.edu/archives/win2003/entries/davidson/>. I should add that nothing said here is meant to engage with complicated questions in the philosophy of action.

holds that the jurors ask whether 'he did it' where the 'it' is an action under the description relevant to the law *and* containing a claim about what is deserved by this defendant in response (it is an 'it' in which description and evaluation are mixed). Of course, this example is one which casts jury nullification in a good light. So, consider another: Luke is a white defendant charged with intentionally killing a black man in a jurisdiction where murder carries a mandatory life sentence without parole. Luke rightly believed that the victim was in a sexual relationship with his adult daughter. The jurors believe that Luke killed the victim and that under the description offered by the law, he is guilty of murder (that is, he meets all the conditions that make this murder rather than manslaughter or anything else); Luke shot the victim with the intention of killing him. The jury acquits and in doing so there is no question but that they nullify the law. The jurors deliberately put to one side the outcome of their deliberations that is dictated by the combination of the law as they understand it and the facts as they believe them to be.

There is no doubt that the jurors in both cases nullify the law; they do not give the verdict that they believe is required by the law as it is given to them and the facts as they believe them to be. However, it seems to me that it is nevertheless misleading to think of the jury as lying. There is one sense in which thinking of them as lying clearly is mistaken. This sense asks that we think of the jurors as reporting that it was not Luke or the 'three strikes' defendant after all who shot the victim or stole the pizza, but some unknown third party. This is implausible. What the jurors believe and express is something like 'Luke shot a nigger who had it coming to him' and that Luke is therefore undeserving of condemnation or punishment. Similarly, in the three strikes case the jury cannot seriously be thought to be indicating in its verdict that the defendant did not actually take the pizza. Rather, they report that what he did was not deserving of twenty-five years. If we are to think seriously about jury nullification then it seems to me important that we grant that in these cases the jury acquits, that we can infer under what description they acquit, and that that description is, for them, the truth of the matter.[12] If this is right then it raises (at least) two questions: 'How does this account fit into the analysis of the criminal trial?' And, 'What ought we to think about jury nullification?'

---

[12] In describing jury nullification in this way, I am restricting it to cases that are 'conscientious' (even if we may think the values of the racist jury repugnant). This is in part a consequence of distinguishing between jury nullification and mistaken or corrupt verdicts. However, it is possible to think of a case in which the jury is not corrupt or mistaken, but also not conscientious. In this case, the jury acquits a defendant they believe to be guilty simply because they like the defendant and do not wish to see the sanction applied to him. If this view is not 'desert based' then it is an instance of non-conscientious nullification. I think such cases are likely to be very rare, but if they exist then they are not covered by the analysis here.

2 THE TRIAL CONTEXT

The analysis of jury nullification given above should not be particularly controversial and might be thought obvious. It is, after all, implicit in the typology given of reasons for nullification—the jury rejects the law that criminalises the wrong for which the defendant is being tried; rejects not the criminalisation of the act but the level of sanction attached to it; accepts the law and concomitant sanction but has no wish to see them applied to the particular defendant—that the jury is not *really* saying when it acquits that the State has the wrong man, but is rather indicating that there is a problem with the law or with its application in this case. All I have said so far is that it is plausible to think of this finding as expressing a truth about what happened given that lots of things can be true of the same event under different descriptions. One objection to this might be to say that the jury is not, or ought not to be, in the business of evaluation at all. Rather, its business is in 'neutral' fact finding. However, as Robert Burns shows in his analysis of the trial in his contribution to this volume (and elsewhere),[13] this distinction between 'neutral facts' and 'evaluative judgments' has no part in an accurate description of the trial.

For Burns, the trial is in part a scene in which different narratives are woven by, for example, the prosecuting and defence lawyers. So, for example, one side tells of a malevolent woman who kills her husband for the insurance, while the other offers a tale of a sadistic and brutal husband killed by his terrorised wife. That the facts are used in the construction of these tales and that the verdict is a matter of which tale wins the day is, I think, compelling as an account of an adversarial trial. Moreover, what Burns's analysis makes clear is that the stories that are told are not just stories about the facts or about how the facts are to be understood, but are also about the desert of the defendant (and perhaps the desert of the victim).[14] In other words, what is often in question in a criminal trial is not 'what happened' or 'what are the facts of the matter?' in the normal way those phrases are understood, but rather how what happened is to be thought of; of what part of what story is what happened. This kind of analysis blurs the descriptive and evaluative aspects of judgment. It casts doubt on the common sense notion that we can entirely separate the relevant description of the act, which is in some sense neutral in merely reflecting facts about the world, from an evaluation of what the act is 'worth' (in some sense or other). And, it fits well with the idea that in nullifying the jury is reporting truthfully what it believes happened, where what happens in the world of criminal justice comes loaded with baggage about desert.

[13] R Burns, 'The Distinctiveness of Trial Narrative', this volume, and *A Theory of the Trial* (Princeton, Princeton University Press, 1999).
[14] D Graham Burnett, in his *A Trial By Jury* (London, Bloomsbury, 2002) has recently offered an account of his time as a jury foreman that is not only a good read, but gives ample support to Burns's analysis.

Allowing that my characterisation of jury nullification may capture what it is that the jury is doing when it nullifies, and that this account of what it is doing broadly fits with Burns's account of the trial, does nothing to resolve the question of whether jury nullification is a good or bad thing, or the question of how we ought to regard a jury that nullifies. Of course, our first reaction may depend on the case: we admire the jury that refuses to convict in the three strikes case and we feel outraged at the description under which Luke is acquitted in the race case. As already noted, this reflects the way discussion often goes when jury nullification is being considered. Yet, in both cases, the jury substitutes its judgment for that of the law and justifying *that* in something approaching a working democracy is a tall order.

One common argument appeals to the role of the jury as a buffer between the State and the citizen (in this case the defendant). As an example of this, Auld quotes from EP Thompson:

> The English common law rests upon a bargain between the Law and the People. The jury box is where people come into the court; the judge watches them and the jury watches back. A jury is the place where the bargain is struck. The jury attends in judgment, not only upon the accused, but also upon the justice and humanity of the law ...[15]

However, although this is, as Auld notes, a 'memorable passage', it does not provide a justification for ascribing this role to the jury. In a democracy, it is the legislature that is entrusted with making law. This, together with the rule of law, which is an essential element of liberal democracy, seems to require that jurors respect the law even where they disagree with it. Of course, many theorists of liberal democracy accept that there is a legitimate place for conscientious objection and their arguments may have a place here. But, arguments about conscientious objection do not apply straightforwardly to jury nullification (they may apply better to a refusal to accept jury service) and, in any case, what is of interest here is whether or not a justification can be found for the *systemic* feature of allowing juries to nullify. If that feature were to disappear—say, because the government accepted Auld's recommendation that the law should declare that juries have no right to acquit defendants in defiance of the law—it would still be possible for a jury to bring in a nullifying verdict or for a jury to refuse to bring in a verdict at all. It is just that such an action would not be a legitimate part of the system. What is at stake, then, is not something about the individual consciences of the jurors, but something about the system of the criminal trial.

3 EVALUATING NULLIFICATION

If nullification is to have a legitimate place as a feature of the system of criminal justice then an argument, or arguments, have to be found that support the idea

---

[15] Auld n 1 above, at 174.

of a buffer between the State and the citizen. One such argument appeals to the fallibility of the legislature and the vagaries of politics. Politicians, after all, are only human and, in a democracy, they are often under pressure to respond to public opinion even when that opinion is not well informed. Legislation that is ill thought through and the origin of which can be found in some public outcry or other can be found on the statute books of every country no matter how well governed. Given this, it might be argued, it is important that there remains a final hurdle (supporters of jury nullification might say 'a final hurdle of good common sense') for legislation to clear before its effects are felt by some unfortunate citizen.

This argument presupposes a good deal about the merits of juries, because, of course, it requires not just that the jury be *another* hurdle, but that it be a *valuable* one. The idea, after all, is that the jury stands between the mistake made by the legislature and the consequences of that mistake being visited on the defendant. One problem is that it is not at all clear what counts as a 'mistake' in a democracy. Thus, different accounts will emerge depending on whether making a mistake is thought of as a matter of misinterpreting the popular will or as a matter of allowing the popular will to violate certain fundamental standards of justice. In turn, different virtues will have to be claimed for the jury: in the first, the virtue of better reflecting what the people really want, and in the second, the virtue of being better able to discern the demands of justice. Nevertheless, the argument that juries play an important role in checking that the power of the State is not being misused (whatever we take that to mean) is not obviously wrong or inappropriate. Possibly, we might be able in time, and if such research were possible, to draw up a list of all the times nullification properly interfered with the application of a bad or unjust law and all the times it frustrated good or just laws. Then, making suitable adjustments for the significance of the cases, we might be able to decide as an empirical matter whether having juries with the power to nullify generally enhances or diminishes good and just government. Of course, in order to do this, we would need an agreed account of good and just government, including an account of the status of demands of justice in a democracy, but the difficulty of arriving at any such account need not affect the claims being made on behalf of jury nullification. In essence, this is a pragmatic argument that avoids having to consider too deeply the place of juries in a democracy by pointing out that democratic decision making is imperfect and fallible. Given that, there is then a simple test, either having the power to nullify built into the system enhances whatever value one cares for (justice, the 'real will' of the people, or whatever) or it does not. If so, there is something to be said for it.[16] If not, then there is not.

---

[16] Of course, that it brings about some value does not show that it is justified all things considered. We may, for example, think that fairness and the rule of law require that nullification be removed from the system even if we believe, say, that nullifying juries more often enhance justice than detract from it.

The above argument gives nullification instrumental value. It is a good thing only if it brings about something that we care about and we have reason to leave it in the system if it does this at not too great a price in terms of other values such as fairness. If we are to shape a more principled defence of nullification, we must appeal more directly to the role or purpose of the jury and show that having the power to nullify is partly constitutive of that role or purpose. Put provocatively, we need a defence of nullification that extends to the jury in the example of Luke, even if we abhor the particular use to which nullification is put in that example.

One argument that might provide such a defence is given, almost in passing, by Peter Bachrach in a paper in which the main discussion is of the Senate debate over how to respond to white juries in the American south refusing to convict white defendants of crimes connected with 'denying a Negro his right to vote.'[17] Providing background to the debate, Bachrach comments:

> In America, jury trial was regarded primarily as a means of insuring the local community against the possibility of a remote and tyrannical administration. Viewing it within its historical context, one can clearly see that the fundamental objective of the right to trial by jury was squarely in conflict with the right to vote provision of the civil rights bill. The purpose of the bill was to change, by the use of law, ingrained behavior patterns of the community, rather than to reflect—which is the objective of the criminal trial—attitudes and mores of the community.[18]

Although it is open to question whether '*the*' purpose of the criminal trial is to reflect the 'attitudes and mores of the community,' this is surely one of its purposes. And if so, then there is a role for the jury. Thus, if the jurors appeal to local understandings and values, and as a result bring in a nullifying verdict then, on this account, they are not perversely distorting the system, but are merely doing part of their job. That the local values might be repugnant is a separate matter. One can think that allowing juries the power to nullify in these circumstances is legitimate, even when one is dismayed at the use to which that power is put.

If we are to defend the power to nullify as intrinsically connected to the role and purpose of the jury then, I think, the argument must proceed along these lines. Nullification is part of the jury's armoury because part of the jury's function is to represent and reflect local norms in deciding what the defendant deserves. The jury is, after all, part of a process by which the community holds an offender to account for his wrongs. In a guilty verdict and in punishment the court expresses the community's moral condemnation of the offender.[19] If that condemnation is absent from the community then the trial cannot achieve this

---

[17] P Bachrach, 'The Senate Debate on the Right to Jury Trial Versus the Right to Vote Controversy: A Case Study in Liberal Thought' (1958) 68 *Ethics* 210 at 210.

[18] Ibid, 211.

[19] Not everyone would accept this account, but there is no space to defend it here. (See, among others, R A Duff, *Punishment, Communication, and Community* (New York, Oxford University Press, 2001), and my *Justice and Punishment* (Oxford, Oxford University Press, 2000.)

goal. That must be the shape of the argument, but it is of course too quick. A critic might simply reply that the trial and the jury ought to hold the defendant to account against standards that he, and the community, *ought* to accept, whatever it is that they do accept, or ask whether, in pluralistic societies, there are clear enough 'local' values to make this account at all plausible.

One advantage of taking the first route suggested by the critic is that it retains the idea of 'calling to account', but it distinguishes the three strikes and the racist juries. In the three strikes case, the jury substitutes standards that all ought to accept for the standards that are reflected in the law. In acquitting, then, it appeals directly to the demands of justice. The racist jury believes that it is doing the same, but its standards are not ones that anyone ought to accept. We may still wonder whether there is a legitimate place in a democracy for such direct appeals to values that everyone ought to accept, but all in all it seems to me that this approach is likely to result in the pragmatic view outlined above. The power of juries to nullify will be justified if the circumstances are such that allowing jury nullification is likely to promote rather than hinder justice. The second challenge offered by the critic is more fundamental. It is assumed above that there are substantive shared values of the community that may come into conflict with the values instantiated in the law. But most modern democracies are characterised by widespread pluralism. Thus, the racist jurors will come not from a homogenous community of racists, but from a society in which some people—say, whites in certain areas—believe that blacks are inferior and ought to keep to themselves except when working, and this view will not be shared by either the black community or other whites. In such conditions, the standard liberal view is that public rules must be formulated in terms acceptable to all reasonable people. In the formulation of precise legislation covering criminal justice what this means is that such legislation must be the outcome of democratic procedures constrained by a constitution that specifies basic rights. Moreover, the role of the liberal citizen is to put to one side his particular beliefs about what is good and bad, for example beliefs about interracial coupling, in favour of rules of rightness that can be justified by appeal to reasons acceptable to all in conditions of reasonable pluralism. If so, it would seem to follow that jurors ought to refer only to the description given by the law when deciding under what description to report on the act of the defendant. They may believe the law to be ungodly, but that category has no place in the deliberations of a liberal citizen when engaged in the public realm. If so, then in a democracy the jurors ought simply to match the facts as they believe them to be to the law as described by the judge because that law is generally representative of the liberal community of which they are part (even if they have comprehensive conceptions of the good that conflict with this liberal vision).

I think there are three interrelated reasons to resist this neat conclusion. They may not be decisive, but they are reasons that should, at least, make us pause. First is the pragmatic argument already discussed. Nullification may have a place in imperfect democracies and there may be no way of limiting the power to nullify so that it only occurs in cases where we approve of it. If so, we will cheer when juries acquit in three strikes cases and jeer when they release racists. In both cases the jury reports truthfully what it believes happened, where 'what happened' includes a desert claim, but in one case we agree and so think well of the jurors and in the other we disapprove and think badly of them. As long as jurors get it right more often than they get it wrong then there is at least something to be said for retaining the jury's power to nullify.

Secondly, we might wish to retain the power of juries to nullify as a valve that allows the release of the pressure of public discontent with the law and that, in so doing, informs the legislature of the existence of that pressure. This point can perhaps be best put negatively. A succession of cases that result in verdicts with which the public profoundly disagree, even if they ought not to disagree, might bring general discontent with the law and undermine the important relationship that ideally holds between the law and the citizens it regulates. Again, this argument is not decisive, but it applies even to the racist jury. Civil rights legislation, which outpaced changes in the values and mores of parts of the US, undoubtedly damaged the standing of federal law makers, and the federal law, in general in those parts. Persistent nullifying by juries informed the law makers of this gap. Of course, in this case, the price was worth paying, but in others it may be less obvious that that is so.

Thirdly, punishing an individual is an extraordinarily serious and messy business. In this sense, Foucault (and many others) have done a great deal to remind us that 'to punish is the most difficult thing there is.'[20] That is not to say that there cannot be general theories of punishment. (Indeed, I have offered such a theory elsewhere.)[21] Rather, the punishing of a particular offender for a particular crime and with a particular sanction is something that is not likely to be resolved by a plausible philosophical theory (philosophy, at most, contributes limits). Philosophers and legislators (and, for that matter, those who construct degree classification rules), even when they are good hearted and possessed of sound judgment, delude themselves if they think rules can be formulated that can be implemented without moral remainder. This holds in general and applies in spades to deliberations over desert.[22] That said, quite how this affects jury nullification is unclear (at least to me). At best, it seems to me to give rise to an inchoate commitment to the value of things that get in the way of the State and that allow the State's determinations of desert to be contested. And it is because the trial is an arena in which desert claims are made, contested, and (at least

---

[20] M Foucault, *Power: Essential Works of Michel Foucault 1954–1984* vol 3, ed J D Faubion (New York, The New Press, 2000) 464.

[21] Matravers n 19 above.

[22] Antony Duff has impressed on me that this speaks in favour not of jury nullification, but of sticking with the common law tradition of case-by-case reasoning that precisely does not rely on (would-be) clear and determinate rules, or of allowing courts to operate with a notion of equity. This may be right, although these are not mutually exclusive options, but then the common law tradition to which it appeals is increasingly under attack from an overbearing state and a series of hyperactive home secretaries.

provisionally, fixed) that jury nullification holds our attention. Against a background in which the trial is thought of as a procedure for arriving at the actual legal truth and the jury as a device for finding facts up to some standard of proof, nullification makes no sense. But trials are not like that. They are arenas in which desert is contested. This is true not just in the sense identified above in the brief discussion of Burns—that the defending and prosecuting lawyers offer competing narratives that speak to the desert of the offender—but also in the sense that the law itself might be the subject of contested narratives. Of course, in normal politics, the place for contesting the law is in the political arena—by voting, joining political parties or pressure groups, and so on—but this is a luxury not open to the jury if its worry is the way the law stands with respect to a particular offender whose fate is in its hands. Moreover, in contests over desert, inside or outside the court, the State has all the resources. Perhaps the inchoate thought to which I referred above is simply that jury nullification offers a means of resistance and that there are all too few of those.

4 CONCLUSION

What motivates this chapter is the apparent sense of Auld's view that jury nullification is a bizarre aberration in a system that is truth seeking above all else. In the first part, I have tried to show that the sense in which the trial is truth seeking is complex, and that one way of thinking of jury nullification is that it is a finding of truth, just a truth that contains both descriptive and evaluative elements. That account I find appealing given that nullifying juries cannot be thought of as simply reporting that the State has the wrong man. In this sense, it seems to me to fit the phenomenology of nullification. The argument depends on a blurring of the roles of evaluator and fact-finder and, borrowing from Burns, I claim that this blurring is characteristic of the trial.

In the second part of the chapter, I have attempted to show what kinds of things follow for how we should think of jury nullification in light of the characterisation offered in the first part. This section is more open ended and speculative. What underpins the section is the thought that once one thinks of the nullifying jury as reporting a truth, rather than as simply offering a 'blatant affront' to the legal system, then interesting avenues open up both for defending jury nullification and reflecting on the function of the criminal trial. That said, quite where these avenues lead is, as should be clear, a vexed question.

5

The Criminal Trial and the Legitimation of Punishment

MARKUS DIRK DUBBER*

WHATEVER ELSE·IT might be, a theory of the trial is also part of a theory of the practice of punishment as a whole. By the theory of a practice I mean (also) an attempt to legitimise it, ie, to develop—or at least to identify—relevant legitimising principles and to match the practice against these principles.

Now the practice of punishment can be divided for analytical purposes into three aspects, each of which requires legitimation if the practice as a whole is to be legitimised. The three aspects of punishment are the definition of criminal norms (the realm of substantive criminal law), followed by their application, which itself is divided into their imposition (the realm of criminal procedure, or the criminal process narrowly speaking) and their infliction (the realm of prison—or correction—law or, more correctly, the law of punishment execution).[1] The trial is one of the procedural means by which criminal norms are imposed. It is not the only imposition procedure, nor even the most common, though it may be the most significant. It certainly is the most visible, and the most studied, which is not to say that it is also the most theorised.

A theory of the trial thus would form part of a theory of the imposition of criminal norms, which in turn belongs to a theory of the practice of punishment, which in turn must find its place within a theory of law (given that punishment is a law practice), which in turn fits into a theory of state governance (of which law is but one mode; police is another).[2]

* Thanks to Lindsay Farmer and Paul Roberts for helpful comments and suggestions.

[1] These analytic distinctions carry no normative significance. In fact, the task of legitimation consists partly of overcoming the normative significance ascribed to them, as persons move closer to the inflictive end of the criminal process. For instance, one might attempt to render the *infliction* of punishment consistent with the principle of autonomy by breaking down the distinction between persons who are under a criminal sentence of some form, and those who are not (yet). Cf M Dubber, 'Reforming American Penal Law' (1999) 90 *Journal of Criminal Law and Criminology* 49, at 50.

[2] On this point, see M Dubber, 'Polizei-Recht-Strafrecht', in C Prittwitz, M Baurmann and K Günther (eds), *Festschrift für Klaus Lüderssen zum 70. Geburtstag* (Baden-Baden, Nomos, 2002) 179; M Dubber, *The Police Power: Patriarchy and the Foundations of American Government* (New York, Columbia University Press, forthcoming).

For purposes of this chapter, I will take for granted that the fundamental principle of legitimacy in a modern democratic state is autonomy, or self-determination (self-government, if you prefer). The goal of this chapter is to illuminate those features of the criminal process narrowly speaking that reflect the principle of autonomy.[3] Its goal is not to account for every feature of the criminal process, though I do think that its main, perhaps even its essential, features are comprehensible in terms of the principle of autonomy.

1 THEORIES OF THE CRIMINAL PROCESS AND CONSTITUTIONAL LAW

This chapter is written from an American perspective. Now one might think that this perspective would easily yield a comprehensive and well worked out theory of the criminal process. After all, American constitutional law, the traditional repository of theoretical sophistication in American legal doctrine, has lavished attention on the criminal process for decades. The study of American criminal procedure is synonymous with the study of *constitutional* criminal procedure.

This wasn't always so. Until the 1960s, criminal procedure had considerable difficulty finding a home in American legal education and scholarship. It was taught as an appendix to two other established subjects, criminal law and constitutional law. Criminal procedure attracted little attention until the US Supreme Court, under Chief Justice Earl Warren, took it upon itself to reform the American criminal process (particularly in the southern states) by means of the federal constitution. The federal bill of rights was applied to the states, and therefore to state criminal processes, and by the 1970s, criminal procedure had emerged as a respectable, self-standing subject.

Soon there was so much law on criminal procedure that it could no longer fit into the introductory criminal law class (which itself was struggling to keep up with developments triggered by the Model Penal Code of 1962) and there was so much *constitutional* law on criminal procedure that already bulging casebooks on constitutional law could not find room for it either. And so classes on criminal procedure, as constitutional criminal procedure, began to appear in American law schools. Eventually, the body of constitutional jurisprudence about the fourth, fifth, and sixth (and a little bit of the eighth) amendments grew so large, criminal procedure professors decided a single course would no longer do. Today, criminal procedure is often taught in three courses, one dealing with the early parts of the process (investigation), one addressing its latter parts

---

[3] For earlier suggestive remarks on this subject, see G Maher, 'Human Rights and the Criminal Process,' in T Campbell, D Goldberg, S McLean and T Mullen (eds), *Human Rights: From Rhetoric to Reality* (Oxford, Blackwell, 1986) 197; R A Duff, *Trials and Punishments* (Cambridge, Cambridge University Press, 1986); P Bal, 'Discourse Ethics and Human Rights in Criminal Procedure' (1994) 20 *Phil & Social Criticism* 71.

(prosecution and adjudication), plus a third one (survey) that covers the criminal process in its entirety.

Few people can remember when American criminal procedure was not a species of constitutional law. And yet, despite this overabundance of constitutional procedural jurisprudence, the American criminal process is oddly under-theorised.

Here the contrast to substantive criminal law is instructive. The substantive criminal law, everyone agrees, is grossly under-constitutionalised, particularly if compared with its sister discipline of criminal procedure. While the Supreme Court lavished attention on the criminal process, it remained strangely untouched by the constitutional constraints on the State's power to define the norms whose application it so vigilantly scrutinised. This is puzzling, to say the least for, as Henry Hart asked rhetorically long ago, just as the Warren Court was beginning its constitutional criminal procedure revolution: 'What sense does it make to insist upon procedural safeguards in criminal prosecutions if anything whatever can be made a crime in the first place?'[4]

Instead of adding up to a comprehensive view of the criminal process, driven by defined aims and structured by principles, norms, and rules, the avalanche of constitutional law has buried theorising about the American criminal process. Rather than highlighting the foundations of the criminal process, the Court's constitutional jurisprudence has kept them from view. Today the casuistry of constitutional criminal procedure is so Byzantine, it is difficult to teach—and think about—the subject as something other than a marvellously intricate, and gnarly, construct of precedent shaped by successive Supreme Courts and shifting majorities.

Substantive criminal law, by contrast, is largely untouched by constitutional jurisprudence, but thrives as a subject of theoretical inquiry. While the Supreme Court has shown virtually no constitutional[5] interest in such subjects as the basic requirements of criminal liability, including actus reus, mens rea, justifications, and excuses, commentators continue to debate them with great energy and at considerable length.

The point here is not, of course, to suggest that there is anything wrong with thinking about what constraints constitutional law might place on the criminal process. It's just that limiting thinking about procedural principles to constitutional jurisprudence runs the risk of obscuring as much as it illuminates. In Germany, for example, it may well be a good idea, as many commentators there suggest, to shift the emphasis from statutory interpretation of the comprehensive, but conceptually barren, Code of Criminal Procedure to constitutional jurisprudence. The US Supreme Court, however, has at the very least illustrated

---

[4] H M Hart, Jr, 'The Aims of the Criminal Law' (1958) 23 *Law and Contemporary Problems* 401, at 431. Cf M Dubber, 'Toward a Constitutional Law of Crime and Punishment' (2004) 55 *Hastings LJ* 509.

[5] As the highest federal court, the Court has not been able to avoid addressing some of these questions as a matter of statutory interpretation. See, eg, *Morissette v United States* 342 US 246 (1952) (mens rea).

how a constitutional jurisprudence of the criminal process originating in a commendable urge to remedy the worst abuses in practice can disintegrate into unprincipled patchwork.

2 PROCESS WITHOUT TRIAL

The bad news is, then, that the American literature has precious little to contribute to a British theory of the trial. The good news is, however, that the theoretical emptiness of American constitutional criminal procedure clears the way to a broader Anglo-American theory of the trial that rests not on constitutional law, but on another, older, common denominator, the common law.

For it turns out that one is more likely to find jurisprudential explorations of the nature of the criminal process in the preconstitutional era of American criminal procedure, when courts spoke in terms not of constitutional rights, but of common law rights. Not that the foundations of common law rights—other than their precedential pedigree—were plumbed with particular care, but at least judges had to render basic decisions without the crutch of constitutional provisions. For instance, the nature of the criminal process—and of legal processes in general—arose regularly when courts were forced to consider the results of various, and increasingly common, 'summary' proceedings that did away with certain rights associated with a proper criminal trial under the common law.

Consider, to take an early English example, summary proceedings under the 1823 Master and Servant Act.[6] The Act authorised local justices of the peace after an informal hearing to commit workers to the house of correction for breaches of their labour agreements, including quitting, temporary absence, or being neglectful or disobedient at work ('any other Misconduct or Misdemeanour').[7] The hearing had none of the hallmarks of common law protections associated with a criminal trial. Warrants of commitment were loosely drawn (failing to identify, for example, the occupation of the worker, a crucial condition of jurisdiction under the Act), the evidence supporting the adjudication need not be set out, nor need the evidence be given under oath or in the presence of the accused, who also had no right to cross-examine witnesses against him.[8]

When commitments under the Act were brought before common law courts under writs of habeas corpus, the judges often took the magistrates to task for failing to honour the common law rights of the accused, and Parliament for promulgating an act that 'is drawn as, I am sorry to say, most of them are,

---

[6] 4 Geo IV, c 34, s III (1823). In the following I rely heavily on Robert Steinfeld's excellent discussion of the Act in R J Steinfeld, *Coercion, Contract, and Free Labor in the Nineteenth Century* (Cambridge, Cambridge University Press, 2001).

[7] Steinfeld, ibid. 47–48.

[8] Ibid, 154–55.

imperfectly and loosely . . . ."[9] Ultimately the legitimacy of these summary proceedings turned on a number of formal distinctions. A criminal trial, after all, was not required if the proceeding was not criminal. The earliest distinction that separated criminal proceedings—and therefore trial—from other less formal ones, focused on the form of the adjudication resulting from them. As Robert Steinfeld reports, eighteenth century English cases held that:

> if a justice's adjudication result in an 'order' rather than a 'conviction,' even if the order result in 'severe penalties' as an order frequently did, it was not necessary for the justice to adhere to the formalities required for a conviction.[10]

So, if an adjudication under the Master and Servant Act was classified as an order, rather than a conviction, then the conviction would not have to identify the basis of jurisdictions, for instance. That is exactly what the common law courts decided—'commitments' were 'orders', and not 'convictions'. Thus, an adjudication could be informal as long as the magistrate did not make the mistake of mischaracterising it as a conviction, even if the commitment itself presumed a prior conviction.[11]

At bottom, the informal hearings under the Master and Servant Act did not require a trial because they were not criminal. And they were not criminal because they were not designed to punish, but to discipline. The 'commitment' after all was to the 'house of correction'. They were a means for enforcing obedience among workmen or, to use the language of labour law, to compel specific performance.[12]

The Master and Servant Act belongs to a class of disciplinary measures that has enjoyed a long tradition in English law and that continues to flourish in contemporary English, and American, law. The paradigm of these police measures is vagrancy. As Robert Shoemaker has pointed out, discussing seventeenth century English law:

> [m]ost authors of manuals believed that justices outside sessions had the power to commit a broad range of offenders to houses of correction . . . for custodial, but not punitive, purposes.[13]

---

[9] Ibid, 155 (quoting *Re John Gray and Hugh Blaney* (1844) 24 L.J. (n.s.) (mag. cases) 26, 29).

[10] Ibid, 155 n 206 (citing *Dominus Rex v Lloyd*, 2 Strange 996, 93 Eng Rep 992 (8 Geo II), 993, *Rex v Bissez*, Sayer, 303, 96 Eng Rep 888 (1756), 889).

[11] The struggle to differentiate criminal law from criminal police has continued. Cf L Farmer, 'The Obsession with Definition: The Nature of Crime and Critical Legal Theory' (1996) 5 *Social and Legal Studies* 57, at 64–65 (discussing attempts by English and Scottish courts, in the late nineteenth and early twentieth centuries, to distinguish between 'civil' and 'criminal' jurisdiction in response to 'the increasing significance of administrative or police offences'); A J Ashworth, 'Is the Criminal Law a Lost Cause?' (2000) 116 *Law Quarterly Review* 225, at 230–32 (discussing attempts by the European Court of Human Rights to distinguish between 'criminal' and 'other' proceedings).

[12] Steinfeld, n 6 above, at 49–53.

[13] R Shoemaker, *Prosecution and Punishment: Petty Crime and the Law in London and Rural Middlesex, c 1660–1725* (Cambridge, Cambridge University Press, 1991) 37–38.

It was, for instance, the case that:

> idle persons who lived above their station . . . could be committed by an individual justice to a house of correction to be put to hard labour, but they could not be punished [whipped] until the case was tried at sessions.[14]

American courts' struggles with police measures closely resembled those of their English colleagues, both in form and in outcome. One of the most articulate expressions of judicial attitudes toward non-criminal, administrative, sanctions imposed without a trial and its attendant protections appears in *United States v Hing Quong Chow,* a 1892 federal case addressing the then-nascent regime of policing immigration through sanctions that were on their face indistinguishable from criminal punishment. The statute in question provided that:

> Any Chinese person, or person of Chinese descent, arrested under the provisions of this act or the acts hereby extended, shall be adjudged to be unlawfully within the United States, unless such person shall establish by affirmative proof, to the satisfaction of such justice, judge, or commissioner, his lawful right to remain in the United States.

Furthermore,

> Any such Chinese person, or person of Chinese descent, convicted and adjudged to be not lawfully entitled to be or remain in the United States, shall be imprisoned at hard labour for a period not exceeding one year, and thereafter removed from the United States . . .

Quashing the indictment as not setting out a true crime, the judge explained that:

> The statute, as it seems to me, deals with the coming in of Chinese as a police matter, and is the re-enacting and continuing of what might be termed a 'quarantine against Chinese.' They are treated as would be infected merchandise, and the imprisonment is not a punishment for a crime, but a means of keeping a damaging individual safely till he can be sent away. In a summary manner, and as a political matter, this coming in is to be prevented. The matter is dealt with as political, and not criminal.[15]

The statute was political, not criminal, because it provided for what the English courts would have termed an order, and a commitment more specifically, rather than a conviction. Unlike the English statutes, however, this American immigration statute explicitly, and clumsily, invoked the term 'conviction', ordinarily a telltale sign of a criminal statute, and of a trial. So the judge was forced to look beneath outward appearances and excavate the true meaning of the statutory terms:

> The words used are those, which are ordinarily found in criminal statutes; but the intent of congress is, as it seems to me, unmistakable. What is termed 'being convicted and adjudged' means 'found', 'decided' by the commissioner, representing not the criminal law, but the political department of the government.[16]

---

[14] R Shoemaker, *Prosecution and Punishment: Petty Crime and the Law in London and Rural Middlesex, c 1660–1725* (Cambridge, Cambridge University Press, 1991) 37–38.
[15] *United States v Hing Quong Chow,* 53 F 233 at 234 (ED La 1892).
[16] Ibid, 234.

Although the statute was perhaps unartfully phrased, the informal process set out for its application made it clear that it could not, and therefore was not, a criminal statute defining crimes chargeable by indictment.

> By section 4 it is this finding [of being unlawfully in the US] which is to be followed by the consequence that, it is urged, authorizes a sentence under a criminal law. I cannot believe this was the intent of congress. A reversal of the presumption of conduct or presence being lawful might be introduced into procedures which were political in character, and assimilated to those relating to quarantine; but it seems to me well-nigh impossible that congress should have intended that in proceedings in their nature criminal there should be the presumption of guilt, and that the accused should be found guilty unless he proves himself to be innocent. The whole proceeding of keeping out of the country a class of persons deemed by the sovereign to be injurious to the state, to be effective of its object, must be summary in its methods, and political in its character. It could have no place in the criminal law, with its forms and rights and delays.[17]

Now, as I have argued elsewhere, the distinction between 'political' and 'criminal' matters spelled out in *Hing Quong Chow* and invoked, though generally less explicitly, in many other American cases dealing with summary proceedings reflects a more fundamental distinction between two modes of governance, police and law.[18] Police here is understood in the sense of the 'power to police', which itself derives from the patriarchal power of the householder and, later on, the quasi-patriarchal power of the king. As such, police is the heteronomous management of inferiors by quasi-householders (the ancient Greek art of 'economics'). Law, by contrast, is the autonomous government of citizens by citizens (the realm of 'politics').

The basic contrast in *Hing Quong Chow* between the political (police) and criminal (crime) thus itself reflects a more fundamental tension between two basic modes of governance that turn on different notions of the subject and object of government, and their relationship. It is, at bottom, the distinction between *Polizeistaat* (later renamed, focusing on its benign aspect, *Wohlfahrtsstaat* or *Sozialstaat*) and *Rechtsstaat*. Within this framework of police and law, crime and punishment appear as phenomena of criminal law, itself a species of law. The criminal process, in turn, is the procedural aspect of criminal law, governing the imposition of criminal legal norms. And the trial is one component of the criminal process thus conceived.[19]

One would expect that the principles of criminal law in general, and of the criminal trial in particular, would derive from, or at least fit with, the conception

---

[17] Ibid.

[18] Dubber, n 2 above, at 179.

[19] Here I think it is important not to confuse the trial with the criminal process. As even a casual observer of the American criminal process can attest, only a very small percentage–less than 10 per cent–of all criminal cases are resolved by trial. That is not to say that the trial isn't worth careful study as a social phenomenon with meaning beyond its actual occurrence, see, eg, R Burns, *A Theory of the Trial* (Princeton, Princeton University Press, 1999), just that a theory of the criminal process in general, and even of the trial in particular, needs to account of non-trial criminal processes as well.

of law as governance through equal self-government—as opposed to hierarchical other-government. The criminal process, and therefore the criminal trial, thus would be concerned with respecting, and affirming, the status of each of its participants as persons capable of self-government, rather than as objects to be processed. The police process, by contrast, would be governed by other considerations, if not principles. Given its origins in the notion of patriarchal household governance, or traditional economics, these aims might include efficiency or, more generally, the maximisation of 'economic' resources.[20] The process of criminal law, as law, is shaped by what process is due to the persons that populate it. The process of disposition, as police, has no similar concerns of 'due process' for the simple reason that it does not conceptualise its participants as persons, but rather as elements of cases to be processed.

3 AUTONOMY IN THE CRIMINAL PROCESS

In the law of the imposition of criminal norms in general, and of the criminal trial in particular, we find a host of manifestations of autonomy in current law that, however, are not always recognised as such.[21] At the outset, it might be useful to distinguish between two types of autonomy, active and passive.[22] Criminal procedure rights manifest both active and passive autonomy, where active autonomy is the freedom to participate in the process, and passive autonomy the freedom not to, or more generally, the freedom not to be interfered with, often referred to in American constitutional jurisprudence (somewhat misleadingly) as 'the right of privacy'.[23]

The first, and most basic, requirement of autonomy in the criminal process is that the defendant must be 'competent'. Without the ability to understand the nature of the criminal process and the charges against her, or the ability to co-operate with her representatives in that process, she cannot participate in it, and

[20] This distinction resembles Herbert Packer's distinction between the Due Process and Crime Control Models of the criminal process: H Packer, *The Limits of the Criminal Sanction* (Stanford, Stanford University Press, 1968).

[21] This is not to say that the criminal process, or for that matter the trial, is in fact solely, or even primarily, based on the concept of autonomy. The idea is instead to highlight some characteristics of the process that make sense if viewed in this light and that might feature in a theory of the criminal process, and of the criminal trial, built more consistently on the legitimating concept of autonomy.

[22] Nothing much turns on this distinction. Passive autonomy is not preferable to, or antecedent to, active autonomy, nor vice versa. What matters for my present purpose—to illuminate the place of autonomy in the criminal process—is that both active and passive autonomy are varieties of autonomy, not that they are active or passive. (The analytical distinction between passive and active autonomy thus should not be confused with Isaiah Berlin's distinction between negative and positive liberty. See Isaiah Berlin, 'Two Concepts of Liberty,' in his *Four Essays on Liberty* (London, Oxford University Press, 1969)).

[23] The freedom not to participate finds expression not only in particular procedural rights (like the right to remain silent), but in the right to *waive* those rights, or—as in the case of fourth amendment protections—to *consent* to state conduct that would otherwise would violate them.

thereby make it her own. This basic requirement of competence is traditionally labelled as 'competence to stand trial'. It is important to recognise, however, that it is a requirement that runs through the entire criminal process. Competence to stand trial is but one (impositional) manifestation of the general competence to participate in the criminal process, ie, to be not merely the object of the criminal process, but its subject as well. No incompetent defendant can enter a plea, can be convicted (assuming he was found competent to stand trial), sentenced, or 'punished'. The most dramatic instance of the requirement of (executional) competence, in fact, is not competence to stand trial, but competence to be punished by death, ie, literally to be 'executed'.[24] An incompetent defendant is a defendant whose capacity for self-determination is compromised to such a degree and in such a way that she could not be anything more than an object of inquiry that passively undergoes processing and eventual labelling, or in the case of capital punishment, slaughter.[25]

In sum, an incompetent defendant is incapable of exercising either active or passive autonomy. He would not only fail to participate in the criminal process, but would be incapable of doing so.

Prime examples of *passive* autonomy protections include the fourth amendment's protection against 'unreasonable searches and seizures,'[26] which the Supreme Court has read as protecting 'expectations of privacy,'[27] and the Fifth Amendment's privilege against compelled self-incrimination.[28] Note, however, that the passive self-incrimination privilege also has an active flipside, the right to incriminate oneself, whether outside the trial (most dramatically, in the form of a 'confession') or during it (in the form of testimony). It is often overlooked that *Miranda v Arizona*, for example, was a case not about confessions, but about *coerced* confessions.[29] The Court was careful to point out that it did not mean to preclude a suspect from 'talk[ing] to the police without the benefit of warnings and counsel.'[30] Otherwise, to protect the suspect's passive autonomy—by deterring police from obtaining coerced confessions—the Court would have interfered with her active autonomy—by preventing her from making a voluntary confession.

---

[24] See *Ford v Wainwright*, 477 US 399 (1986) (competence to be executed requires 'comprehending the reasons for the penalty [and] its implication').

[25] For clinical competence tests, see, eg, K Heilbrun and D Dematteo, *Forensic Mental Health Assessment: A Casebook* (New York, Oxford University Press, 2002).

[26] Cf C Slobogin and J E Schumacher, 'Reasonable Expectations of Privacy and Autonomy in Fourth Amendment Cases: An Empirical Look at "Understandings Recognized and Permitted by Society,"' (1993) 42 *Duke Law Journal* 727; W J Stuntz, 'Self-Incrimination and Excuse' (1988) 88 *Columbia Law Review* 1227; see also *R v Golden*, 2001 SCC 83 (constitutionality of strip search incident to arrest).

[27] *Katz v United States*, 389 US 347 (1967).

[28] US const amend V ('No person . . . shall be compelled in any criminal case to be a witness against himself').

[29] 384 US 436 (1966).

[30] Ibid, 478.

It is useful to remind ourselves at this point that until late in the nineteenth century, 'criminal defendants in this country, as at common law, were considered to be disqualified from giving sworn testimony at their own trial by reason of their interest as a party to the case.'[31] Continental criminal procedure to this day disqualifies defendants from testifying under oath. German criminal procedure law, for instance, categorically exempts the defendant from the oath requirement, along with children and the insane.[32]

That is not to say, of course, that continental criminal procedure precludes the accused from testifying, or confessing, altogether, anymore than American criminal procedure. After all the act of confession, most dramatically if it occurs in open court, can be regarded as the ultimate exercise of the accused's active autonomy, in that he literally applies the relevant provisions of the criminal law to himself, even as a procedural distinction between confession and conviction remains in all legal systems, along with a requirement that self-imposed punishment be *executed* by a third party.[33]

Contrast the right to testify with the *requirement* of a confession for conviction, which gave rise to torture as an evidence-gathering tool.[34] The right to enter a plea, unknown in continental criminal procedure, also should be seen in contrast to the requirement of a confession. The defendant in the American criminal process has the option of ending the proceedings against her by entering a plea, an option that is unavailable to continental defendants who, even after having struck a deal with the judge (the prosecutor tends not to play much of a role in negotiations), must go through the ordinary—though now shortened—criminal process, including the interrogation by the presiding judge and a public confession in open court.[35]

The availability of pleas—as opposed to confessions followed by conviction—is not of only passive significance, however, by allowing the defendant to opt out of the full-fledged process. It also empowers the defendant to participate in the resolution of the process through plea negotiations.[36] Whether plea negotiations are autonomy enhancing or limiting in fact depends crucially on the distribution of power among those doing the negotiating. As a matter of fact, the American prosecutor (often aided by the defence attorney and the judge) enjoys such enormous, and virtually unchecked, power that plea negotiations, again as a matter of fact, are autonomy limiting. To render plea bargaining consistent

---

[31] *Nix v Whiteside*, 475 US 157, 164 (1986) (citations omitted).

[32] StPO § 60. Discretionary exemptions—determined by the presiding judge—apply to youths (17–18 year-olds), the victim and her relatives, the defendant's relatives, and witnesses with a prior perjury conviction. StPO § 61.

[33] M Dubber, 'American Plea Bargains, German Lay Judges, and the Crisis of Criminal Procedure' (1997) 49 *Stanford Law Review* 547 at 604 (citing G W F Hegel, *Elements of the Philosophy of Right* 227 (addition) (A W Wood ed, H B Nisbet trans, Cambridge, Cambridge University Press, 1991) (1821)).

[34] See J H Langbein, *Torture and the Law of Proof: Europe and England in the Ancien Régime* (Chicago, University of Chicago Press, 1977).

[35] Dubber, n 33 above, at 597–98.

[36] Ibid, 603–5.

with the principle of autonomy would require a concerted effort to level the playing field, either by equipping the defendant with greater rights in the process (for example, by establishing meaningful voluntariness review) or limiting the prosecutor's power (for example, by constraining him charging discretion or reducing the level, and range, of penalties), or both.[37] Without these reforms, plea-bargaining remains a convenient mechanism for the mass processing of cases driven by the superior power of the State, rather than a legal procedure for the adjudication of persons.

The Sixth Amendment right to counsel likewise has an active and a passive, autonomy-enhancing, side. Passively, it works, indirectly, to put meat on the bones of the privilege against self-incrimination.[38] Actively, it enables the defendant to participate fully, though indirectly, in a lawyer-dominated process that disposes of 'her' case. At the same time, however, the defendant has the right to participate directly, pro se, and take her chances as a laywoman among trained jurisprudes.

Either directly, or indirectly, the accused also has the right to participate in the impositional process by assembling evidence, through investigation and 'discovery', and introducing it, in whatever form, as inanimate objects or records, or as 'live testimony' by himself or another 'witness', or an 'expert'. In fact, the accused has a constitutional right to state assistance in this regard, in particular 'to have compulsory process for obtaining witnesses in his favor.'[39] By contrast, the accused in the continental process has no such right of production. She instead has the right of petition. Only the court has the right, and the duty, to assemble and introduce evidence, either upon its own motion or upon motion by one of the parties.[40]

In this regard it should be noted, however, that German criminal procedure extends the right to question witnesses not only to defence counsel, but also to the defendant himself. In general, defendants in German criminal trials enjoy the same, parallel, procedural rights as their counsel, including the right to file motions, to question witnesses, to comment on the evidence, and to make a closing statement.[41] That is not to say that they exercise these rights. The ordinary German criminal trial continues to be dominated by the presiding judge, regardless of what procedural rights might be extended in theory to other process participants, including not only the defendant and her attorney, but also the prosecutor and other professional, or lay, judges on the panel, if any.[42]

In the American criminal process, the accused not only has the right to assemble and introduce his own evidence, but also to participate in the introduction of evidence by the *state*. In particular, the accused has the right 'to be confronted

---

[37] Ibid, 591–601.
[38] See *Miranda v Arizona*, 384 US 436 (1966).
[39] US const amend. VI.
[40] Dubber, n 33 above, at 570.
[41] Ibid, 570–73.
[42] Ibid, 580–91.

with the witnesses against him,' and to subject them to cross-examination.[43] Once again, the accused has the right to participate—or not to participate— in the assembly of evidence, through submitting to interrogation, cross-examination, and supplying other, non-testimonial, evidence to the state.

4 EMPATHY AND INDIRECT AUTONOMY

Several rights pertain to the selection of those who sit in judgment of the criminal defendant, i.e., those who are charged with applying criminal norms to him.[44] The defendant, after all, does not literally convict himself. Here the criminal process relies on what one might call *constructive* autonomy, or indirect self-government.

To see how indirect autonomy works, we need to introduce an enabling concept, empathy, or mutual roletaking.[45] In American political theory as in modern political theory more generally, the consent of the governed, including the punished (and the taxed), is crucial, but it need not be direct. The modern system of government is that of a representative, not a direct, democracy. The participation of the governed in their government is mediated through the transferral of the right of consent from the individual person to another, who acts as her substitute, agent, or representative. In the sphere of legislation, that representative is the legislator.

In the sphere of adjudication, that representative is the jury, first and foremost, but also the judge and, given the prevalence of plea bargaining in American criminal law, the prosecutor, at least in jurisdictions where these officials are elected.[46] (Here another factual legitimacy deficit of plea-bargaining becomes apparent. Not only is the prosecutor more powerful than the defendant. She also does not perceive herself as the defendant's representative, grand statutory proclamations about the duty of prosecutors to serve the public— including the defendant—notwithstanding. Instead, the modern prosecutor, if she thinks of herself as representing anyone in particular, regards herself as the representative of the *victim*, who is constructed in sharp contrast to the defendant, with radically incompatible interests, and (victims') rights).[47]

Punishment raises the problem of representation with particular urgency for two, related, reasons. The unique intensity of the state sanction of punishment places a particular strain on any attempt to legitimate its threatened, and actual, employment. At the same time, actual consent on the part of the object of the

---

[43] US const amend VI.

[44] For analogous rights in continental criminal procedure, see Dubber, n 33 above, at 571–72.

[45] For further discussion of the role of empathy in modern law, see M Dubber, *Law's Empathy: The Sense of Justice and the Life of the Law* (New York, New York University Press, forthcoming).

[46] Cf Dubber, n 33 above, at 591–93.

[47] See generally M Dubber, *Victims in the War on Crime: The Use and Abuse of Victims' Rights* (New York, New York University Press, 2002).

sanction is particularly unlikely. Nowhere is merely constructive consent less appropriate, and yet at the same time more necessary. Put another way, nowhere is the danger of hypocrisy greater than in the attempt to legitimate punishment as self-government, and yet nowhere is the need for that very legitimation more acute.

The precise nature of the relationship between representative and represented has been as contested as the best method for institutionalising it ever since the foundation of the American republic. In general, however, it is clear that—as a phenomenon—the representative relationship presumes a mutual identification between governor and governed. For representative self-government to work, the self of the representative and the represented must, if they cannot merge (through direct democracy), become so closely connected that one can easily take the position of the other. As none other than James Madison put it in the *Federalist Papers*, 'it is particularly essential that the [legislative] branch . . . should have an immediate dependence on, and an intimate *sympathy* with, the people.'[48]

Sympathy here should not be confused with affection. Instead, following Adam Smith, it should be understood as fellow feeling, enabled by the ability to put oneself in the other's shoes, to see things as she would see them.[49] That ability in turn presumes a mutual identification, ie, a basic sense of identity shared by the representative and the represented. Sympathy differs from affection because, as a cognitive process, it is emotionally neutral. To avoid the confusion between sympathy as a general cognitive mechanism and as a specific emotional effect (often contrasted with antipathy), the less ambiguous term 'empathy' is preferable. In contrast to sympathy—literally 'feeling-*with*' ('Mitgefühl' in German), empathy—'feeling-*in*' ('Einfühlung')—generally refers to the vicarious experience of another.[50]

Empathy is the mechanism that keeps the self in representative *self*-government. Without empathy, representative self-government turns into oppressive other-government, mediated self-judgment into immediate other-judgment, and indirect autonomy into direct heteronomy.

---

[48] *Federalist* No 52 (emphasis added).

[49] A Smith, *The Theory of Moral Sentiments* (1759); see also D Hume, *Enquiry Concerning the Principles of Morals* 10.1, 10.5 (1751); *Treatise of Human Nature* III.iii.1 (1739). To Smith, sympathy was a moral sentiment, a 'sense of justice.' Needless to say, it was not a sense of *police*. Recall that police, in Smith's view, had nothing to do with justice, and everything with 'expediency': 'Introduction' in RL Meek et al (eds), A Smith, *Lectures on Jurisprudence 1, 3* (Oxford University Press, Oxford 1978) (quoting D Stewart, *Account of the Life and Writings of Adam Smith, LL.D.*).

[50] See, eg, M L Hoffman, 'Toward a Theory of Empathic Arousal and Development' in M Lewis and L A Rosenblum (eds), *The Development of Affect* (1978) 227. For a useful overview, see L Wispé, 'History of the Concept of Empathy' in N Eisenberg and J Strayer (eds), *Empathy and Its Development* (1987) 17.

5 THE JURY

The principle of indirect, or representative, autonomy manifests itself in several features of the criminal process. The most obvious is the institution of the jury. The legitimate core of the idea that the jury manifests the 'sense of justice' of the community is that it represents not some community, but the community of the *defendant*. Composed of the defendant's peers, it speaks for the defendant and thereby makes possible a process of vicarious self-government, which respects the defendant's autonomy, or capacity for self-government, without forcing the defendant to literally judge himself.[51]

The challenge of the institution of the jury is to ensure that it functions as a forum of justice—a discourse among moral persons as such—without disregarding its role as a mechanism for indirect, or vicarious, self-judgment. That justice discourse and that vicarious self-judgment are possible only if jurors act on their sense of *justice*. But they can only act on their sense of justice if they identify with one another, and with the defendant, as members of the community of persons, ie the moral community.

This is not enough, however. While the *legitimacy* of their judgment is made possible through mutual identification among jurors, and between jurors and defendant, the enterprise of judgment itself only makes sense if the jurors also identify with the *victim* as another fellow moral person.[52] Without that identification, they will not experience the empathy that motivates them to pass judgment on the offender in the first place; they will not feel the vicarious resentment that turns an otherwise private conflict into a matter of public justice, and therefore of law.

As agents of self-government, jurors must be perceived, must perceive themselves, and—perhaps most important—must perceive the objects of their judgment, the defendant as well as the victim, not as members of this or that substantive community, but as members of a community of justice, ie a political community governed by principles of justice.

It is in this sense that the jury's representativeness and impartiality are crucial. Each juror must be representative in the sense that she must share, and be conscious of sharing, with the offender and the victim those characteristics that mark all three as subjects and objects of justice judgments. From this point of

---

[51] It is this capacity that makes the defendant a person. As a person in this sense, the defendant is entitled to respect, even if she is not *in fact* autonomous, just as a person is entitled to the protection of the criminal law even if she is not in fact autonomous—ie, incapable of exercising her capacity—for some reason or another (age, disability, imprisonment, extreme poverty, etc). The legitimacy of criminal law, and of law in general, turns on the extent to which it permits the defendant, as person, to exercise her capacity for autonomy. The challenge of justifying criminal punishment in particular arises from the fact that it interferes with actual autonomy (imprisonment is only the most obvious case), but must do so without negating the personhood—capacity for autonomy—of the punished. See Dubber, n 47 above, at 152–60, 253–65.

[52] Dubber, n 47 above, at 193–200.

view, representativeness and impartiality coincide; representativeness implies the juror's conscious possession of the relevant similarity (namely membership in the community of justice), while impartiality implies the juror's ability to disregard all other, irrelevant, similarities (such as membership in the same bowling team, or race, or whatever).

To ensure the representativeness of the jury, the defendant has the right to participate in the composition of the jury, through challenging potential jurors who would lack the capacity to empathise with him for one reason or another, notably various types of abstract or particular, such as prejudice or bias.[53] He also has the right to request the removal (recusal) of the judge, on similar grounds.[54] At the same time, the defendant does not have the right to adjudicators who are predisposed in his *favour*. Relatives of the victim and of the defendant alike are barred from adjudication—and so are the victim and the defendant himself. While relatives, or friends, might well be able to identify with the victim and the defendant, respectively, that identification would not be relevant in the legal process because it would be based on characteristics of the defendant other than his status as a person, ie as an object of justice.

The jury in this sense is the paradigmatic community of justice. Here individuals motivated by their sense of justice (*Rechtsgefühl*)[55] discuss what principles of justice apply to a particular case and how they might be applied. The jury's verdict is the outcome of that discourse. It is binding on the defendant—and the victim—because it represents the result they would have reached had they participated in the deliberation as moral persons, abstracting from accidental characteristics such personal preferences and membership in substantive communities. The defendant—and the victim—feel themselves represented by the jury, and its verdict, and accept the verdict as *just*, insofar as they recognise the jury as fellow persons who recognised them as persons in return.

[53] In continental criminal procedure, there is no directly analogous right. There *cannot* of course be an exactly analogous right if there is no jury, but that is not the point. The representativeness of the adjudicatory body, however composed, is thought to be sufficiently guaranteed by the adherence to a uniform, and nondiscriminatory, process for the selection and assignment of lay judges, who sit with professional judges on mixed panels and who are appointed for several years, rather than assembled for a particular trial. Challenges against the composition of the court thus are based on perceived deviations from this, rather cumbersome, selection process. Once the court has been properly assembled, the accused also has right to file recusal motion based on an allegation of bias, often said to have manifested itself in the court's denial of previous defence motions, including occasionally previous motions for recusal. See Dubber, n 33 above, at 588–89, 571–72.

[54] The right to request a change of venue belongs here as well. A defendant is entitled to venue change when the presumption of representativeness that ordinarily attaches to adjudicators drawn from the locus of the crime does not hold. That presumption of course is itself questionable given the mobility of modern society. Offenders are no longer as likely to live in the political community where the crime was committed as they once were. This also means, of course, that the notion of jurors as the defendant's peers, drawn from his vicinage, largely survives as a fiction, but an important fiction, because it properly shifts the inquiry from the level of judgment from intercommunal (neighbourly) sympathy to interpersonal empathy.

[55] See M Bihler, *Rechtsgefühl, System und Wertung: Ein Beitrag zur Psychologie der Rechtsgewinnung* (Munich, C H Beck, 1979).

6 A CONTEXTUAL THEORY OF THE CRIMINAL TRIAL

Perhaps we can do without a jury. (The Germans do.) Perhaps we can do without a trial. (We do, in the vast majority of cases.) Perhaps autonomy can manifest itself in proceedings before a mixed panel of professional and lay judges,[56] or even in bench trials without any lay participation whatsoever. Perhaps what we need to do is forget about the jury, and about the trial, altogether and focus instead on the legitimacy of the jury—and trialless criminal process as it operates in fact. Perhaps plea-bargaining can be reformed to render it consistent with autonomy, by legalising prosecutorial discretion, or by insisting on the representativeness of prosecutors vis-à-vis the defendant, and not merely 'the community', or more recently the victim. Elected prosecutors, or judges for that matter, clearly are not the answer, especially if the political community is confused with the community of actual and potential victims.

At any rate, a theory of the trial—and a theory of the jury—must arise from an analysis of the trial within the context of the practice of punishment as a whole. It is particularly easy to fall into an asystemic approach to the trial if one focuses on Anglo-American trials, which have been regarded—and celebrated—as the heart and soul of the common law criminal process for centuries, even as both the common law and the trial have given way to statutes, plea bargaining, bench trials, and summary proceedings. German criminal law provides a useful contrast. There the procedural analogue of the trial bears the prosaic, and functional, title of *Hauptverfahren* (or, more precisely, *Hauptverhandlung*) that has none of the trial's mysterious uniqueness, nor its medieval sword wielding connotations. (*Hauptverfahren* simply means 'main proceeding', as distinguished from *Vor-* and *Zwischenverfahren*, or preliminary and intermediate proceeding, which precede it.) Properly contextualised, a theory of the trial can make a crucial contribution to the still unfinished business of legitimising the practice of punishment as that state action most desperately in need of legitimation.

---

[56] I'm not so sure. The role of lay judges in German criminal trials is irrelevant at best, and hypocritical at worst. See Dubber, n 33 above.

6

Testimony

DUNCAN PRITCHARD

1 TESTIMONY IN EPISTEMOLOGICAL DEBATE

THE ISSUE OF the status of testimony is central to epistemological discussion, and it is easy to see why. Along with our senses, testimony is one of the two key ways in which we gain knowledge of the world.[1] Traditionally, when epistemologists talk of testimony they have in mind something quite broad which includes, for example, the written 'testimony' that one can gain from textbooks. Since our ultimate focus here is on the issue of legal testimony, however, we will understand testimony in a more strict fashion in terms of the intentional and verbal transmission of information.[2]

The debate surrounding the status of testimony in the epistemological literature has tended to cluster around two opposing models. On the one hand, there is the *inferentialist*—or, as it is sometimes known, often pejoratively, *intellectualist*—claim that one cannot gain a justified belief about a proposition solely on the basis of hearing someone assert that proposition (ie, one needs independent grounds to justify that belief). In contrast, others have argued for a *default* model—sometimes called, again often pejoratively, *credulism*—which allows

---

[1] A key difference between testimony and perception is that testimony, like memory, is not a *generative* source of knowledge and justification, but only a *sustaining* source. That is, while we gain new knowledge by using our perceptual faculties, we merely acquire knowledge that has already been gained by another source (such as by perception) from testimony, or transmit such old knowledge to others through our own testimonial acts. This, at any rate, is the standard view of testimony though, as J Lackey, 'Testimonial Knowledge and Transmission' (1999) 49 *Philosophical Quarterly* 471, points out, there are complications concerning exactly how we are to understand this claim.

[2] This also allows us to side-step the issue of whether an agent's *unintentional* transmission of information, whether verbally or otherwise, should qualify as testimony. For more on the issue of how we should define testimony, see C A J Coady, *Testimony: A Philosophical Study* (Oxford, Clarendon Press, 1992), ch 2—cf P J Graham, 'What is Testimony?' (1997) 47 *Philosophical Quarterly* 227—and E Fricker, 'Against Gullibility' in B K Matilal and A Chakrabarti (eds), *Knowing from Words: Western and Indian Philosophical Analysis of Understanding and Testimony* (Dordrecht, Kluwer, 1994) 125.

that provided there are no special grounds for doubt, then one can gain a justified belief in a proposition simply by hearing someone assert that proposition.[3]

There are certainly considerations that can be offered in favour of each position. As regards inferentialism, the natural motivation for the view is that without independent grounds there is, intuitively at least, no reason to accept testimonial evidence as being in any way indicative of the truth. Suppose that you have no independent grounds by which you can assess an instance of testimony—you do not know, for example, anything about the speaker's reliability as an informant or about the truth of what she asserts. In such a situation, why should hearing her make an assertion give you any reason for thinking that what is being asserted is true (let alone provide you with a reason which would suffice to *justify* your belief in that proposition)? After all, for all you know to the contrary, this person could be a compulsive liar, or completely delusional, or perhaps even someone who is having a joke at your expense.[4]

Historically, the inferentialist position is most often associated with the work of David Hume, who, it is claimed, argues that since there is no a priori reason for thinking that beliefs gained via testimony should be thought to be true, so we need independent grounds to justify our beliefs gained by testimony. Moreover, if we are to acquire a general justification for testimony, then this will have to be gained, ultimately, from non-testimonial sources since otherwise the justification would be circular. He writes:

> [T]here is no species of reasoning more common, more useful, and even necessary to human life, than that which is derived from the testimony of men and reports of eye-witnesses and spectators [. . .] [O]ur assurance in any argument of this kind is derived from no other principle than our observation of the veracity of human testimony, and of the usual conformity of facts to the reports of witnesses. It being a general maxim, that no objects have any discoverable connexion together, and that all the inferences, which we can draw from one to another, are founded merely on our experience of

---

[3] It is worth noting that this formulation of the contrast between inferentialism and the default model specifically focuses on epistemic *justification*. Accordingly, a quasi-credulist thesis which merely claimed that one can gain a reason—ie, as opposed to a *justification*—for a belief in a proposition simply on the basis of hearing someone assert that proposition would be counted as an instance of inferentialism by the lights of this formulation since it would still be demanding that testimony-based justified belief requires independent grounds. In what follows, when I talk of how default theorists allow that testimony-based beliefs have an innate epistemic status I will have in mind the specific claim that such beliefs have an innate justification. I take it that inferentialists will usually be inclined to reject even the weakened rendering of the default thesis, though it is not essential to the view as I understand it here that they do so.

[4] Of course, it is very difficult to imagine *any* situation in which one has no independent grounds by the lights of which one can assess an instance of testimony, and one might think that this fact counts against credulism. It is worth remembering, however, that it is not part of the credulist position to make an empirical claim to the effect that there are situations in which one forms justified testimony-based beliefs without having any independent grounds which one can bring to bear as regards assessing the truth of those beliefs. Rather, their claim is simply that where there are no special grounds for doubt, one can be justified in believing a proposition solely on the basis of hearing someone assert that proposition. Accordingly, credulists will claim that the fact that there usually are independent grounds available for belief in an instance of testimony merely indicates that we typically have *more* grounds available to us to justify our beliefs in such cases than is strictly necessary.

their constant and regular conjunction; it is evident that we ought not to make an exception to this maxim in favour of human testimony, whose connexion with any event seems, in itself, as little necessary as any other.[5]

It follows that as regards any particular testimony-based belief, that belief cannot be justified by that testimony alone. What will be required for justification will be further independent (ie, non-testimonial) grounds, such as our previous observations regarding the 'usual conformity of facts to the reports of witnesses.' Hume's position is often descried as *global reductionism*, in that he is interpreted as holding the view that testimonial justification must always be reducible to other forms of justification, such as perceptual justification.

Of course, we are very rarely in a situation in which, as we imagined above, we have *no* independent evidence by the lights of which we can assess an instance of testimony. Typically, for example, we can see the person making the assertion (or at least hear him), and this will reveal *something* to us about the pedigree of that assertion. Moreover, the content of the assertion is important in this respect. If it roughly conforms with our view of the world and what we deem to be likely to be true, then this will itself be independent grounds in support of belief in the proposition asserted, while if the assertion is of something which is, as far as we know, quite fantastic, then this will be prima facie grounds for thinking that what is asserted is false. What this reveals, according to the inferentialist, is that although the phenomenology of receiving someone's testimony seems to conform to the default model, in that we don't normally doubt such testimony unless there is special reason to do so, this is in fact because we are implicitly aware that we usually have good independent grounds for trusting testimony in this way—in particular, because we have independent reasons in favour of trusting the speaker or for thinking that what he says is true.

Nevertheless, if this is Hume's position,[6] then it will clearly lead to a form of scepticism about the epistemic status of a wide class of our beliefs. The reason for this is that the kind of independent evidence that we might wish to appeal to in justifying our testimony-based belief will often itself be gained via testimony. Think, for example, of the general world-picture that one has, including mundane facts about such things as how the postal service works, along with scientific facts concerning, for example, the way the gravitational pull of the moon affects the movements of the tides. Clearly, these are truths which very few of us are in a position to verify for ourselves, and it would be extremely difficult to gain sufficient inductive evidence about the reliability of an informant to ensure

---

[5] See D Hume, *Enquiries Concerning Human Understanding and Concerning the Language of Morals* (1777) ed L A Selby-Bigge (2nd edn, Oxford, Oxford University Press, 1972), 111. This passage from Hume incorporates some ambiguities that I have not the space to discuss here. For discussion, see Coady, n 2 above, ch 2.

[6] I actually have my doubts about whether Hume is best thought of as a global reductionist at all, since closer examination of the text reveals some important qualifications to what he says, and a contextual setting which undermines the apparent generality of the remarks just cited. In general, it strikes me that the 'Humean' position as regards testimony in the contemporary epistemological literature is not one that Hume would assent to.

that we were able to vouch for the testimony of that informant on matters like this without appealing to further testimonial evidence (eg, someone else telling us that this informant is reliable about these matters). As C A J Coady puts the point, 'it seems absurd to suggest that, individually, we have done anything like the amount of field-work that [global reductionism] requires.'[7] Thus, the range of empirical beliefs that we are able to possess justifications for on this picture is going to be much slimmer than we might have hoped. Nevertheless, this point is not in itself a decisive consideration against the view, since it could just be *true* that our beliefs are not as extensively justified as we often suppose, and thus that a limited form of scepticism about our testimony-based beliefs is entirely in order.

Still, the phenomenological pull of the default model of the epistemology of testimony is quite strong, in that the inferentialist account seems to unduly 'intellectualise' our understanding of how we acquire justified beliefs via testimony. The analogy with perceptual belief might be thought to be instructive in this regard, since this clearly seems to be a case in which insisting on an inferentialist model would be bizarre. We are quite happy to allow perceptual beliefs a default positive epistemic status. Intuitively, in normal circumstances where there is no special reason for doubt, one can gain justified beliefs about one's environment merely by observing that environment. Given that this is the case, the natural question to ask is why the same compliment should not be extended to our beliefs formed via testimony.

One might think that the obvious reason for this is that our perceptual faculties are *natural*—we are, as it were, *designed* to gain reliable information about our environment via these faculties. In contrast, it seems that our tendency to trust testimony is *acquired* rather than innate, and so is in need of some further justification. Closer inspection reveals, however, that this distinction is far from clear-cut. After all, it is well documented that our natural instinct is to tell the truth. The truth is something that 'slips out' when we are not being careful about what we say, and when telling a falsehood our bodies react in abnormal ways to indicate this (which is what ensures the general reliability of lie-detector tests). Moreover, it is a commonly observed feature of the intellectual development of children that they *learn* to be suspicious of what adults say in certain circumstances (eg, if they assert something in the middle of a 'make-believe' game)—their natural instinct is to trust the testimony of others, particularly adults. It could be argued, then, that just as we are naturally configured so as to gain information via our perceptual faculties, so we are naturally configured not just to tell the truth but also, in turn, to accept the word of others.

---

[7] See Coady, n 2 above, at 82. For two interesting—and recent—discussions of the manner in which a good deal of what we believe is ultimately based on testimony, see L Stevenson, 'Why Believe What People Say?' (1993) 94 *Synthese* 429, and E Sosa, 'Testimony and Coherence' in Matilal and Chakrabarti, n 2 above, at 59. This issue is also a recurrent motif in Wittgenstein, *On Certainty*, G E M Anscombe and G H von Wright (eds), D Paul and G E M Anscombe (tr) (Oxford, Blackwell, 1969).

Of course, this at best puts the epistemic status of testimony-based belief in the same boat as that of perception-based belief, and one might argue that such 'natural' justifications are not justifications at all, as regards *either* type of belief. For example, even if one grants the truth of an evolutionary story about how we came to have acquired the faculties that we did, this will only at best establish the practical *utility* of such faculties as regards our survival as a species,[8] and this alone will not ensure that they are reliable indicators of the truth. Indeed, there could be traits which are evolutionarily useful, because they help us to prosper as a species, and yet work precisely because they lead to false beliefs (perhaps because the true beliefs in question would be an impediment to our survival).

One way of understanding the default model in this respect is to construe the justification that accrues to one's testimony-based beliefs as a result of employing the principle of credulity along epistemologically *externalist* lines. Externalists about justification hold that an agent's belief can be justified, at least in certain cases, without that agent being in a position to offer *any* supporting grounds for her belief at all. All that matters on this view is that the belief is formed in the right kind of way, where this in turn is usually understood in terms of the agent forming her beliefs via a process that is reliable.[9] So just as long as the process of forming testimony-based beliefs by allowing testimony a default epistemic status is in fact a reliable way of forming such beliefs, then those beliefs can be justified, regardless of whether the agent is in a position to offer any grounds for, for example, thinking that such a principle is reliable.

While externalism might seem a plausible account of the justification of basic perceptual beliefs, however, it is far from obvious that it is applicable to the case of testimony. The reason for this is that the kinds of beliefs that are issue in basic cases of perception are very different from the potentially highly theoretical beliefs that one might acquire via testimony. For example, using one's perceptual faculties one might form the belief that there is a chair before one, and it seems plausible to suppose that provided there are no grounds to doubt this belief, and just so long as the perceptual faculties in question are in fact reliable in those circumstances, then one can be justified in forming such a belief. Contrast this case, however, with a situation in which one forms a belief that there are nine planets in our solar system solely on the basis of an isolated piece of testimony. Here it is not so plausible that just so long as a 'credulous' belief-forming process is a reliable way of forming beliefs then one would be justified in this case, and part of the reason for this concerns the 'theoretical' nature of the belief in question. Indeed, a related critical thought that one might have in this regard is that in the perceptual case there is a direct causal link between the

---

[8] And perhaps not even that. There is a great deal of debate about whether an evolutionary explanation of a creature's development ensures that there is an evolutionary 'merit' which accrues to all of that creature's cognitive faculties.

[9] For more on the epistemological externalism/ internalism distinction, see H Kornblith (ed), *Epistemology: Internalism and Externalism* (Oxford, Blackwell, 2001).

fact and the formation of the belief, whereas this is absent in the testimony case. Accordingly, this might be thought to constitute prima facie grounds for holding that the kind of epistemology appropriate to basic perceptual beliefs is not directly transferable to the case of testimony-based beliefs.

Moreover, the point made earlier about the phenomenological immediacy of our acquisition of testimony-based beliefs lends only ambiguous support to the default position for the simple reason that, despite the name, inferentialism is not normally understood as demanding that a certain inferential process needs to be involved in the acquisition of justified beliefs from testimony. Instead, the focus of the thesis is on the chains of epistemic support that need to be in place if a testimony-based belief is to be justified. It may be, for example, that an agent does not actually 'run-through' the relevant inference in his head in order to gain a justified belief from testimony, but merely that he would have been in a position to make such an inference if called upon to do so. The view is thus not obviously hostage to the psychological data, such as it is, about whether or not an inference does always take place when one acquires (apparently justified) testimony-based beliefs.[10]

Historically, this default position has tended to be most often associated with the work of a contemporary of Hume's, Thomas Reid. Indeed, we find in Reid an explicit statement of the view that we have a natural faculty that leads us to accord a default epistemic status to the word of others. He writes that we have a

> [. . .] disposition to confide in the veracity of others, and to believe what they tell us [. . .] [W]e shall call this the *principle of credulity*. It is unlimited in children, until they meet with instances of deceit and falsehood; and it retains a very considerable degree of strength though life [. . .].
>
> It is evident, that, in the matter of testimony, the balance of human judgment is by nature inclined to the side of belief; and turns to that side of itself, when there is nothing put to the opposite side. If it was not so, no proposition that is uttered in discourse would be believed, until it was examined and tried by reason; and most men would be unable to find reasons for believing the thousandth part of what is told them. Such distrust and incredulity would deprive us of the greatest benefits of society, and place us in a worse condition than that of savages [. . .].

He concludes:

> [I]f credulity were the effect of reasoning and experience, it must grow up and gather strength, in the same proportion as reason and experience do. But if it is the gift of nature, it will be strongest in childhood, and limited and restrained by experience; and the most superficial view of human life shows, that the last is really the case, and not the first.[11]

---

[10] In any case, it could well be that psychological inferences do take place but in such a way that the agent herself is not aware of making any such inference. At the very least, whether this hypothesis is true is an empirical issue that is not resolved simply by reflecting on the phenomenology of our acquisition of testimony-based beliefs.

[11] See T Reid, *An Inquiry into the Human Mind* (1764) T Duggan (ed) (Chicago, Chicago University Press, 1970) 240–41.

As we can see from this quotation, for Reid the fact that this trust of testimony encapsulated in the principle of credulity is thanks to nature is a reason for thinking that it can be relied upon, although it should be noted that this is largely because he regards our nature as God-given. Moreover, it is also worth noting that the further argument in defence of the principle of credulity that is implicit here—that it is only via the employment of this principle that we gain the 'greatest benefits of society'—offers at best only *pragmatic* rather than epistemic grounds in favour of that principle. It is quite consistent with the principle of credulity being practically beneficial in this way that testimony in no way correlates with the truth.

Nevertheless, there may be something more substantive underlying this issue about how we need some degree of credulity if we are to be more than savages, and this is the linguistic point that it is only by being generally accepting of testimony in the first place that one can acquire a language and thereby come to evaluate the truth of what is being conveyed in testimony. The inferentialist seems to be supposing that it ought to be possible, in principle at least, to *understand* what is being conveyed in testimony without going on to accept any instance of testimony on the grounds that we lack an independent justification for it. This is extremely dubious, however, in that in order to acquire a language and thereby gain an understanding of what is conveyed in testimony, one must clearly already be willing to accept some testimony in the first place. It seems, then, that there must be *something* right about the default model.[12]

We should tread carefully here, however, for one can grant that it may be necessary to assume the truth of a great deal of testimony if one is to be able to evaluate any particular instance of testimony without thereby granting that this constitutes grounds for thinking that there is any reason for maintaining that testimony tends towards truth, and it is this latter claim that is being proposed by defenders of the default model. Perhaps we need to make such an assumption

---

[12] As Wittgenstein (n 8 above, §160) writes at one point: 'The child learns by believing the adult. Doubt comes *after* belief.' This is a recurrent theme of Wittgenstein's later work and, as we noted earlier, does seem to possess some empirical support. As regards the recent literature on the epistemology of testimony, this view is most often associated with the work of Coady (see, esp, 'Testimony and Observation' (1973) 10 *American Philosophical Quarterly* 149, and *Testimony*, n 2 above) and T Burge, 'Content Preservation' (1993) 102 *Philosophical Review* 457, and 'Interlocution, Perception, and Memory' (1997) 86 *Philosophical Studies* 21, but see also Stevenson, n 8 above. The general point that one can only meaningfully engage in the activity of distinguishing truth from falsity by assuming from the outset that a large number of one's beliefs are true (this is, very roughly, the so-called 'principle of charity') tends to be most often associated these days with the particular brand of content externalism advanced by D Davidson: see, eg Davidson, 'A Coherence Theory of Truth and Knowledge', in E LePore (ed), *Truth and Interpretation: Perspectives on the Philosophy of Donald Davidson* (Oxford, Blackwell, 1986).

It is important to note that Hume himself (even on the standard interpretation) may well be willing to grant that we cannot help but take a great deal of testimony on trust. Insofar as this is the correct interpretation of Hume's position in this regard (and there are complex textual issues in play here), this doesn't necessarily mean that there is any inconsistency in Hume's stance for the simple reason that Hume is notoriously sceptical about the possibility of justifying testimony-based beliefs. More precisely, then, the issue for the inferentialist is how to deal with this problem while avoiding such scepticism.

in order to get the 'game' of evaluating testimony off the ground, but this does not mean that this assumption is *true*. Moreover, even if this argument were to establish a ground for maintaining that testimony-based beliefs should be accorded a default epistemic status, it is far from clear that the ground in question would be adequate for our purposes here. For all that has been shown is that we have reason to assume the general truth of testimony in order to enable the activity of evaluating testimony meaningfully to occur. Still, however, it could be that once one has mastered the language and is thereby able to understand what is being conveyed by testimonial assertions, one should then proceed as dictated by inferentialism and thus always seek independent grounds.

Given this *impasse* between these two opposing models of the epistemology of testimony, one might think that the way forward is to find a middle-ground between the two positions.[13] It is not at all obvious, however, that such a 'third-way' is possible. For example, some have proposed a *local reductionism* as a way of tempering the global reductionism of the Humean position while retaining its core anti-credulist tenor. The thought is that while we do not need to trace the justification for our testimony-based beliefs in general back to non-testimonial sources, as Hume apparently claimed, we do need to offer evidence in favour of each particular testimony-based belief which is independent of the testimony itself, where that evidence can include testimonial evidence. Such a view is most often associated with the work of Elizabeth Fricker.[14]

On the face of it, this might seem a common-sense amendment to the inferentialist position which enables it to evade some of the most pressing problems associated with the view. In particular, local reductionism appears to be able to account for our inferentialist intuitions without entailing a fairly radical form of scepticism about the justification of our beliefs. The problem, however, is that closer examination of the thesis reveals that it collapses into the global reductionism that it is meant to be an alternative to after all.

In order to see this, one need only note that unless some testimony-based beliefs are allowed to enjoy a default status, then the view will quickly become untenable. After all, as the thesis presently stands, my justification for one testimony-based belief may well depend on another testimony-based belief, the justification for which in turn rests on another testimony-based belief, leading to an indefinitely large regress of justification that leaves the issue of the epistemic status of the original belief moot. Indeed, what we have here is, at best, a very large *circle* of justification, in that we have a web of testimony-based beliefs

---

[13] For more on the main contours of the debate between inferentialist and credulists, see E Fricker, 'The Epistemology of Testimony' (1987) 61 *Proceedings of the Aristotelian Society (supplementary volume)* 57, and 'Telling and Trusting: Reductionism and Anti-Reductionism in the Epistemology of Testimony' (1995) 104 *Mind* 393; J McDowell, 'Knowledge by Hearsay' in Matilal and Chakrabarti, n 2 above, at 195.

[14] See, eg Fricker, 'Against Gullibility', n 2 above. For two other variations on the basic Humean reductionist account of the epistemology of testimony, see J Adler, 'Testimony, Trust, Knowing' (1994) 91 *Journal of Philosophy* 264, and J Lyons, 'Testimony, Induction and Folk Psychology' (1997) 75 *Australasian Journal of Philosophy* 163.

each supporting the epistemic status of each other. Now some have argued that circles of justification can be epistemically acceptable just so long as the circle is large enough,[15] but a moment's reflection reveals that, in the extremal case, the circle of justification could be extremely small. It could, for example, be that the justification for one testimony-based belief rests on another testimony-based belief, where the justification for this second testimony-based belief rests on the first testimony-based belief. Even proponents of epistemological theories which allow circular systems of justificatory support must concede that so small a circle of justification cannot be epistemically legitimate.[16]

Nevertheless, there may be ways out of this difficulty and, indeed, one can find the traces of one such response to this problem in the work of Fricker herself.[17] Recall that the key worry about inferentialism that proponents of the default model raised was that such a picture of the epistemology of testimony didn't seem to be able to account for our intellectual development—including, crucially, the learning of a language. One thought that one might thus have is to allow the testimony-based beliefs of agents in a developmental state a default justification and merely insist on inferentialism in the case of mature agents. Indeed, if one is worried about the rationale for such an amendment to the inferentialist view being of a purely pragmatic nature—in that it is only being proposed so that we can make sense of our intellectual development and not because we have any reason for thinking that such testimony is likely to tend towards the truth—then the view could be supplemented with the kind of epistemological externalism mentioned earlier. The thought would therefore be that there is a prima facie case in favour of the reliability of testimony in such 'basic' cases which is analogous to the putative reliability of our perceptual faculties when it comes to basic perceptual beliefs. Thus, the principle of credulity is permissible in this case only provided that, as a matter of fact, it is a reliable way of forming beliefs about this subject matter.[18]

---

[15] See, eg L Bonjour, *The Structure of Empirical Knowledge* (Cambridge, Mass, Harvard University Press, 1985).

[16] For a development of this line of argument against local reductionism, see Stevenson, n 8 above; M Weiner, 'Accepting Testimony' (2003) 53 *Philosophical Quarterly* 256. For a (rather limited) defence of global reductionism, see C Insole, 'Seeing Off the Local Threat to Irreducible Knowledge by Testimony' (2000) 50 *Philosophical Quarterly* 44.

[17] See, eg Fricker, 'Telling and Trusting', n 14 above, at 402.

[18] Accordingly, in possible worlds in which there is widespread deception taking place, agents would not be justified in accepting the testimony of others without seeking further independent support for that testimony, even where those agents are still in the 'developmental' stage. A slightly different suggestion in this regard might be to allow the principle of credulity, but weaken it so that an agent's assertion of a proposition merely gives one a *reason* to believe that proposition, not also a justification. As noted in n 3, this would still be a form of inferentialism in that it holds that no agent can be justified in believing a proposition solely on the basis of testimony alone. Nevertheless, such a proposal might be thought to be able to evade the regress problem facing inferentialism on the grounds that the additional reasons one needs in order to gain a justified testimony-based belief could be themselves 'default' testimonial grounds, thereby ensuring that one could gain a justified testimony-based belief while avoiding a regress of justification.

At a formal level, this has the potential to meet the problem just raised because if there is a wide enough class of testimony-based beliefs the justification for which does not depend on other testimony-based beliefs, then this could, in principle at least, ensure that the justification for most testimony-based beliefs does not depend on either an infinite regress of justification or else a small circle of justification. Moreover, with this class of default-justified beliefs in play one could then argue that the phenomenological attractions of credulism—principally, that we seem to be able to form justified testimony-based beliefs without needing to appeal to further independent grounds—could be explained away in terms of how it is part of an agent's intellectual development that she acquires certain traits—or, if you will, faculties—which enable her to form judgments about testimonial matters in a way that is sensitive to the truth.[19] In this fashion the quasi-local-inferentialist picture that we have in mind here could appropriate some of the theoretical machinery of the default position without acceding to its key claim concerning the need to accord all testimony-based beliefs an innate epistemic status.[20]

Still, the view would not be without its problems. For example, something would need to be said about whether the testimony-based beliefs that one gained in childhood should be subjected to further epistemic evaluation in adulthood if they are to retain their justified status. If this were the case, then the formal advantages of the view would start to diminish quite radically (and if it were not demanded that adults re-evaluate their childhood beliefs then that too would undermine some of the attraction of the view).[21] Moreover, the problem

[19] The key difference between this faculty-based approach to the epistemic status of mature agent's testimony-based beliefs and the faculty-based approach envisaged by some default theorists would be that on this view the mature agents involved ought to be, at the very least, in a position to offer grounds in favour of their beliefs that are being derived via their cognitive faculties in this way.

[20] Weiner has explicitly attacked the idea that a local reductionism could be combined with a limited acceptance of a default principle which is applied only to agents in the 'developmental' stage. He argues that such a model would not work because it would generate the result that an adult and a child could hear the same piece of testimony and form a belief solely on the basis of that testimony which was, respectively, justified in the latter case but not in the former. He claims that this is counterintuitive because if these two beliefs are to be accorded different epistemic evaluations at all, then it should be the *adult's* belief that is privileged and not the child's. His reason for this is that adults will typically have acquired a discriminative capacity to evaluate testimony that children will usually lack and he notes in this respect that the child in this case would be likely to believe in the existence of Santa Claus on the basis of an isolated instance of testimony ('Accepting Testimony', n 17 above, at 261). This remark about Santa Claus is revealing, however, since one might think that the reason why the adult would be more suspect than the child in this case is because she has gained a wider set of justified beliefs—many of them not derived from testimony—with which she can evaluate such testimony and find it questionable. In particular, the kind of discriminative capacity that we are to suppose adults acquiring is surely best understood in inferentialist terms as the product of a wide pool of general knowledge coupled with repeated exposure to cases of testimony which generates rough-and-ready rules by which such testimony can be (quickly, perhaps even instantaneously) evaluated. Thus, if anything, the kind of counterexample that Weiner has in mind to this proposal in fact lends support to it.

[21] My own feeling on this point is that we should opt for the second alternative, a view which I take to be implicit in Wittgenstein's remarks on 'hinge' propositions. The price you pay for such a move is that you have to either advance a scepticism-friendly theory of knowledge or else incorporate such a thesis into an externalist epistemology which limits the role that reasons play in the

that the class of justified testimony-based beliefs than we hold is more limited that we would wish might still remain, in that the epistemic status of a great many of our 'theoretical' testimony-based beliefs will not be traceable back to the default justification possessed by our 'developmental' testimony-based beliefs. Thus, the problems raised earlier about infinite regresses of justification and circular justifications would also remain even on this model. Finally, some of the difficulties that face the original credulist position would resurface here, such as concerns over allowing a default epistemic status to any instance of testimony and about the use of epistemological externalism where this further addition to the thesis is made.[22]

Nevertheless, I think that there are at least grounds for further exploration of this proposal. It is not my intention to mount a full defence of a particular model of the epistemology of testimony here, however, but merely to note the general contours of this debate between proponents of the inferentialist conception of the epistemology of testimony and proponents of the alternative default model. In what follows what I *will* be arguing, however, is that the inferentialist account *is* applicable to the specific case of legal testimony, and it is to this issue that I shall now turn.

2 LEGAL TESTIMONY

In order to simplify the discussion here, I would like to open my discussion of legal testimony by making a few stipulations. To begin with, we will understand 'legal testimony' as being the intentional and verbal transmission of information by witnesses (under oath) in a legal trial.[23] Moreover, in what follows we will confine our attentions to criminal trials where *all* the evidence that is presented for the consideration of the jurors in making their judgment about the defendant's guilt will be via the testimony of witnesses (we will set aside the issue of

acquisition of knowledge. Again, my preference in this regard is for the second alternative, though I have not the space to develop this line here. For more on this point, see D Pritchard, 'Radical Scepticism, Epistemological Externalism, and "Hinge" Propositions' in D Salehi (ed), *Wittgenstein-Jahrbuch 2001/2002* (Berlin, Peter Lang, 2001), 97.

[22] Another suggestion that has been made regarding the epistemology of testimony is that we can avoid the extremes of the inferentialist and default models by understanding the justification that we acquire from testimony along virtue-theoretic lines. On this view, rather than defining those traits which aid us in gaining knowledge and justification in terms of their knowledge/justification-conduciveness, we instead define knowledge and justification in terms of the epistemic virtues. The task in hand is thus to identify those epistemic virtues that are relevant to the acquisition of testimonial knowledge and justified belief and then define testimony-based knowledge and justified belief in terms of the appropriate application of such virtues. Further consideration of this proposal would take me too far away from the present discussion, but for more on such an account, see the exchange between M Fricker, 'Epistemic Injustice and a Role for Virtue in the Politics of Knowing', in M S Brady and D H Pritchard (eds), *Moral and Epistemic Virtues* (Oxford, Blackwell, 2003), ch 10, and S E Marshall, 'Epistemic Injustice: The Third Way?' in Brady and Pritchard, ch 11.

[23] Accordingly, we will be setting aside the epistemic issue of how, for example, juries can be influenced by the so-called 'demeanour' evidence of a witness.

whether or not there ever are any criminal trials that have this peculiar feature).[24]

One of the first points that we need to note is that in assessing the judgments formed by the jurors in response to the testimonial evidence that they are presented with, we cannot just focus on the justification for their belief about whether or not the defendant committed the crime in question. There are two reasons for this. The first is that it is at least possible that during a trial evidence that bears upon whether or not the defendant committed the crime in question may become available to the jurors which they are then explicitly instructed by the judge to disregard in their deliberations. One consequence of this is that a juror may well have adequate evidence to justify his belief that, say, the defendant committed the crime, even though, taking into account only the evidence that he is allowed to consider in making his judgment about the defendant's guilt, he simultaneously has insufficient evidence to form the belief that a 'guilty' verdict should be returned.[25]

The second reason why we cannot just focus upon the juror's beliefs, in the light of the testimonial evidence that is presented to them, about whether or not the defendant committed the crime in question concerns the presumption of innocence that is in operation in criminal trials, where the jury is instructed only to find the defendant guilty provided that her guilt has been established beyond all reasonable doubt. Since we do not normally make such an austere epistemic demand on justification, this means that a juror might have adequate evidence to justify her belief that the defendant committed the crime and yet at the same time lack adequate evidence to justify forming the belief that a 'guilty' verdict should be returned because whilst the evidence under consideration is sufficient to favour the belief that the defendant committed the crime over the possibility that she didn't, it isn't sufficient to favour the belief that the defendant committed the crime over the possibility that she didn't *beyond all reasonable doubt*.

In order to deal with these two issues, henceforth when we speak of the beliefs formed by jurors in the light of testimonial evidence we will specifically have in mind their belief that the defendant is (or is not) guilty beyond a reasonable doubt given only the testimonial evidence that the jury has been instructed to consider in this regard. It should be noted, however, that from the outset these two factors mark an important difference between the role of testimony in legal and non-legal contexts, since ordinarily we are interested in *all* the (testimonial)

---

[24] Of course, this doesn't mean that all the evidence that will be relevant to the jury's verdict will thereby be testimonial evidence. For example, the testimony of what the court agrees is an 'expert' witness implicitly brings with it further non-testimonial evidence that the witness is a reliable informant on the matters in question (though there is of course a further issue here, which I shall set to one side, as to whether even this additional information is not ultimately testimonial in nature).

[25] In practice, one would expect such a situation to be extremely rare in that if evidence were to be revealed to a jury in this way that could substantially alter the jury members' judgments about the defendant's guilt, then this would be a reason for, for example, changing the jury. This is especially the case if the illicitly revealed evidence were indicative of the defendant's guilt because of the presumption of innocence that operates in criminal trials.

evidence that is available (rather than just a sub-set of it), and typically (testi-monial) evidence need only favour belief in a proposition over belief in the nega-tion of that proposition for that belief to be justified (it doesn't need to favour belief in a proposition over belief in the negation of that proposition beyond all reasonable doubt). Indeed, I think that these two features of the legal context highlight one sense (we will consider others below) in which the epistemic standards in operation in legal contexts are more demanding than those in play in normal non-legal contexts.

The Pragmatics of Assertion

A further sense in which the legal context is more epistemologically demanding than non-legal contexts concerns the manner in which it requires a level of explicitness on the part of testifiers that we would not normally demand. One way in which this is manifested can be seen by considering the implicit rules which govern the pragmatics of assertion in normal non-legal contexts, and how they are, as it were, 'suspended' in a legal context.

It is often noted that in making an assertion one conveys—often quite inten-tionally—far more information than the literal content of what is asserted, and any account of the epistemology of testimony needs to be sensitive to this fact. In what follows I will primarily explore this distinction between the information explicitly stated and the information implicitly (and intentionally) conveyed in terms of the notion of *conversational implicature*.[26]

The standard account of conversational implicature is due to Paul Grice and concerns what one can reasonably take to be implied by an assertion (though which is not entailed by that assertion), given that one is able to make some plausible assumptions about the speaker (that he is, for example, honest, co-operative and otherwise rational).[27] If an assertion generates a conversational implicature that the agent making the assertion believes is false then, even if the assertion itself is of a proposition which is true, that assertion is conversation-ally inappropriate.

Grice uses the following example to illustrate this notion. Suppose that an agent, Ann, asks a by-stander, Bob, where she can get petrol from and Bob replies by asserting 'There's a petrol station around the corner.' Although Bob has not explicitly stated that this petrol station is open, and although this is not entailed by what he (literally) said, one would reasonably infer from such an assertion that the petrol station which Bob is speaking about *is* open (and that, for example, it is presently selling petrol). This is an example of a conversational implicature. If Bob did not mean to imply this by his assertion,

[26] For a sophisticated discussion of the role that conversational implicature plays in an account of testimony, see B Williams, *Truth and Truthfulness: An Essay in Genealogy* (Princeton, Princeton University Press, 2002), ch 5.

[27] See H P Grice, 'Logic and Conversation', in his *Studies in the Way of Words* (Cambridge, MA, Harvard University Press, 1989).

then we would expect him to have qualified his assertion in such a way as to cancel this implicature, perhaps by asserting, for example, 'There's a petrol station around the corner, but I'm afraid that it's not open.' Indeed, one can easily see that this implicature is generated by the original assertion by considering how odd it would be for Ann to reply to Bob's assertion by asking whether or not the petrol station in question is open (at least unless there was special reason to do so, such as that it was very late at night). In reply to such a question Bob might well respond by saying that of course it is, since why else would he have said what he did? In contrast, if Bob is aware that the conversational implicature in question here that the petrol station is open is false, then his assertion is conversationally inappropriate for this reason. Moreover, that this assertion is conversationally inappropriate is not changed by the (literal) truth of the assertion nor by the possibility that the implicature in question might, as it happens, be true (perhaps Bob thought that it was closed but was himself the victim of a trick played by the petrol station owner). An assertion can thus be true and generate a conversational implicature that is also true, but nevertheless be conversationally inappropriate because it is a conversational implicature that the agent making the assertion believes to be false.

The problem posed by these pragmatic features of assertion as far as legal testimony is concerned is that they can lead to important information being lost in a trial situation. Indeed, unscrupulous testifiers could use such pragmatic rules in order to suppress information that they do not wish to be heard by the jury. It is easy to see how such attempts to suppress information might work. Imagine, for example, that the accused is asked if she pushed the victim down the stairs and she replies by saying that she didn't. Ordinarily, a negative answer to a question of this sort by itself (ie, with no further qualifiers) would be taken to indicate that the agent had *nothing* to do with the event in question (or at least, nothing to do with it that wasn't already common knowledge), since if she did have something to do with it then she would have supplemented her reply with a further account of how she was involved in the event. In a trial situation, however, we cannot rely on the veracity of such implicatures and it is the responsibility of the lawyers involved to extract this further information from the accused (perhaps by asking a second question about whether the agent had *anything* to do with the victim falling down the stairs). Indeed, if the threat of the witness being tried for perjury is to get a grip, then it will be necessary for the lawyers concerned to extract fully what the agent's testimony is so that there will no subsequent ambiguity over whether the agent has, in fact, perjured herself (as opposed to merely asserted propositions which, while literally true, generated conversational implicatures that she believed to be false).[28] So while it

---

[28] For a subtle discussion of the demand that a necessary condition of perjury is that the testimonial assertions in question be literally false, and which also includes a useful overview of the literature in legal theory on this topic, see S Green, 'Lying, Misleading, and Falsely Denying: How Moral Concepts Inform the Law of Perjury, Fraud, and False Statements' (2001) 53 *Hastings Law Journal* 157.

may well be plausible to suppose that we ordinarily tend to assume that agents are being co-operative in their assertions unless we have specific reason for thinking otherwise, it seems to be in the nature of a trial situation to offer just such a standing reason to doubt the full co-operation of at least some of the agents who are presenting their testimony.[29]

The witness need not be intending to suppress information, of course, since it could just be that he fails to present a fully explicit answer because what is commonly taken for granted in normal non-legal contexts cannot be legitimately taken for granted in the context of a criminal trial. We can bring this issue into sharp relief by considering the role of the so-called *evidence maxim* as regards the pragmatics of assertion. This is the maxim that in making an assertion an agent represents himself as being in the possession of adequate contextually relevant evidence that will back-up that assertion. Accordingly, one's assertion, if not qualified appropriately, will carry the conversational implicature that one is in a position to offer adequate contextually relevant evidence to backup that assertion.[30] As a result, if one makes such an assertion while aware that one lacks such grounds, then that assertion will be conversationally inappropriate, even if true.

Consider our example of Bob and Ann that we looked at above. A conversational implicature that would clearly be generated by Bob's assertion in that conversational context is that he has appropriate evidence to backup his

---

[29] As Bernard Williams points out, the legal case is not the only scenario in which this is true. He mentions in this respect the subtle rules that govern declarations by political representatives: 'In the British Parliament, there is a convention that ministers may not lie when answering questions or making statements, but they can certainly omit, select, give answers that reveal less than the whole relevant truth, and generally give a misleading impression. [. . .] It is clear what the point of this convention is. No-one can expect a government to make full disclosure about everything, and often it is unclear anyway what full disclosure would be. It is equally undesirable that they should be able to get away with anything they like in order to deceive the public. The rule makes it harder to get away with deceit, since answers will be suspiciously inspected and questions pressed and ministers who are debarred from lying can be forced to a position in which they either produce the truth (if they know it) or are left seriously embarrassed and with nothing to say.' He goes on to note the parallel between this case and legal testimony: 'These are quite special circumstances: the situation is at once adversarial and rule-governed. The rule works, a good deal of the time, because it has a point and there are strong sanctions against breaking it. There are other situations with a similar structure, such as courts of law [. . .]. But, apart from such cases, not much of life has just this structure of expectations. Most of it is either better or worse. It is better when we can more or less rely on what people imply as well as on what they assert; it is worse when we cannot even rely on what they assert' (*Truth and Truthfulness*, n 27 above, at 108–9). An example from the political sphere that might be useful for illustrative purposes in this regard is Bill Clinton's famous assertion (in a press conference) that 'I did not have sexual relations with that woman.' Depending on how one interprets 'sexual relations' here, and to whom one takes 'that woman' to be referring to in this conversational context, his assertion could well be literally true even though it clearly carries the conversational implicature (which he knows to be false) that he did not engage in *any* kind of sexual activity with Monica Lewinski. Significantly, perhaps, Clinton's original training was in law. Green (n 29 above) offers an interesting discussion of the legal ramifications of the Clinton/Monica Lewinski affair.

[30] Indeed, typically at least, in asserting a proposition one represents oneself as *knowing* that proposition. For a robust defence of this claim in one of its strongest guises, see T Williamson, 'Knowing and Asserting' (1996) 105 *Philosophical Review* 489.

assertion. For example, we would expect him to have some knowledge about this petrol station, such as when it is open, its location, and whether or not it currently sells petrol. If Bob were to make such an assertion while aware that he lacked such evidence (perhaps because he was new to the area himself), then his assertion would generate a false conversational implicature and thus be conversationally inappropriate, even if (as it happens) it were in fact true.

One way of drawing out the importance of paying due attention to the conversational implicatures generated by the evidence maxim in the case of legal testimony is by considering the role of contrast classes in this respect. In making an assertion I usually have an implicit contrast in mind, where this contrast is dictated by the shared presuppositions of that conversational context. One consequence of this is that, depending upon what contrast I have in mind, the evidence that I represent myself as having in making that assertion will be different.

Consider the following example, due to Fred Dretske.[31] In asserting the proposition 'Mary stole the bicycle,' I could have one or more of the following contrasts in mind. I could be intending to emphasise that it was *Mary* (as opposed, say, to John) who stole the bicycle, or I could be intending to emphasise that it was Mary who *stole* (as opposed, say, to borrowed) the bicycle, or I could be intending to emphasise that it was the *bicycle* (as opposed, say, to the car) that Mary stole. The contrast in question will usually depend upon the shared presuppositions of that conversational context. For example, in a conversational context in which everyone takes it as given that it was the bicycle that was stolen, and stolen by either Mary or John, then the goal of the assertion will clearly be to draw the contrast in John's favour. The kind of contextually relevant evidence that will be needed to support this assertion will thus relate to this particular contrast. In this case, for instance, in making an assertion of this sort one only needs adequate grounds for thinking that John did not steal the bicycle (perhaps he was around one's house at the time); one does not need adequate grounds specifically for thinking that Mary is the culprit (such as seeing Mary taking the bicycle), much less does one need grounds for thinking that, for example, the bicycle was stolen (as opposed to merely innocently borrowed).

The importance of this to a trial situation is that one needs to draw out exactly what grounds are being implied as supporting the assertion in question. If one's grounds for making the assertion about Mary already assume that either she or John stole the bicycle, then while the assertion may well be true, the evidence offered by this testimony is somewhat limited in this context. Accordingly, it is going to be crucial to elicit from the witness just what evidence is being implicitly presented in support of the assertion in question. In general, the interest here is in stripping away the presuppositions that may be informing that assertion in order fully to identify the exact informational content of the testimony being offered.

---

[31] See F Dretske, 'The Pragmatic Dimension of Knowledge' (1981) 40 *Philosophical Studies* 363.

We have thus seen two further senses in which the epistemic standards employed in a legal context are more demanding than in normal non-legal contexts. The first concerns the general issue of how in a legal context it is necessary to explicate the relevant conversational implicatures that are generated by a witness's assertion so as to unearth all the information germane to the trial (especially in cases where there is reason to suppose that the witness might have a motive for suppressing such information). The second more specifically concerns the manner in which in a legal context it is important to make explicit just what evidential claims are being conversationally implied by the witness's testimony.

The Case for Inferentialism

As it stands, neither of these consequences of the pragmatics of assertion directly speak to the issue of how the original debate that we introduced regarding the inferentialist and default models of the epistemology of testimony bear on the specific issue of legal testimony. The reason for this is that our focus has not been on the truth of the assertions in question, but rather on the truth of what is conversationally implied by those assertions (indeed, more specifically still, the focus has been on the truth of the agent's *beliefs* about the conversational implications of her assertions). Nevertheless, what we have seen is that in the legal context there is at least a standing reason not to trust the reliability of these conversational implicatures, especially where those implicatures concern the evidential basis of the agent's assertion and where there is reason for thinking that the witness has a motive for suppressing relevant information. Accordingly, these considerations, while not impacting directly on the application of the principle of credulity (taken literally) to the legal context, do have an impact on the application of a sister credulity principle—what we shall call *super-credulity*—to the legal context.

Recall that the principle of credulity endorsed by proponents of the default model of the epistemology of testimony held that unless there were specific grounds for doubt, one should take testimony at face-value as true. Given the previous discussion on the pragmatics of assertion, however, we need to clarify just what is meant by this principle. As it stands, all it seems to commit one to is the *literal* truth of the testimony in question, but as we have seen there is a more to a testimonial assertion than the conveyance of the information contained in the literal assertion itself. Accordingly, we can distinguish a stronger credulity principle, the super-credulity principle, which demands that we should not only regard testimony as literally true (pending specific reasons to the contrary at any rate), but regard that testimony as *fully informative* in the sense that the agent does not intend it to generate false conversational implicatures. The principle of super-credulity is clearly stronger than the principle of credulity because it could be true that there is a default assumption in favour of the literal truthfulness of testimonial assertions without there being a default assumption in favour of the literal and, as it were, *conversational*, truth of testimonial asser-tions (ie, what is conversationally implied by that assertion, particularly about what the agent believes is conversationally implied by the assertion). Whatever one might say about the application of the principle of credulity to legal contexts (where this is explicitly understood in terms of the literal truth of the testimo-nial assertions in question), it is certainly true that the principle of super-credulity is inapplicable to legal contexts because, as we have seen, there *are* good standing reasons for thinking that we should press the conversational implicatures of a testimonial assertion in a legal context, even if we do not also think that we should query the literal truth of the assertion itself. That is, even if one is willing to grant the application of the principle of credulity in legal contexts, this does not ensure the legitimate application of the principle of super-credulity to this context.

Although the principle of super-credulity is stronger than the principle of credulity, they are in the same spirit, in that what motivates the former also motivates the latter. If one thinks that one should regard people as generally truthful in their assertions because it is part of our nature to be truthful, then it would be odd to insist that one should be suspicious of the conversational impli-catures of one's assertions. After all, part of what constitutes being truthful is being fully informative in the sense just specified. It might be psychologically easier to deceive in such a way that preserves the literal truth of what is said, but such evasiveness would still be contrary to the veracious nature that authors like Reid take to be a natural feature of our cognitive character. Accordingly, it would be strange to maintain the principle of credulity while rejecting the prin-ciple of super-credulity. Whatever one might say about the application of these principles in general, then, there are good reasons for thinking that the principle of super-credulity is inapplicable to the legal context and thus, given their com-mon motivation, there are also good grounds for thinking that the application of the principle of credulity in this regard is suspect also.

Nevertheless, even despite these indirect reasons for rejecting the application of the principle of credulity in legal contexts, there remains an overwhelming consideration that speaks in favour of this principle (but not the principle of super-credulity) having application in a legal context, and this is the conse-quences of bearing false witness. Unlike testimony in normal non-legal contexts, making literally false assertions in a legal context carries with it a very definite legal sanction—*viz*, the possibility of criminal prosecution and, thereafter, legal punishment. Accordingly, while there is no presumption in favour of witnesses being as informative and explicit in their testimony as is appropriate to the legal context, there is a presumption that they will not literally bear false witness and thereby perjure themselves.[32]

---

[32] Of course, this is not to deny that there are sanctions against both lying and (where this is thought to be different) deceiving in non-legal contexts as well, such as the moral opprobrium from one's peers that can result. The point is only that the sanction in this regard is both very specific and very austere. Furthermore, it is worth noting that it is not part of the claim here that all witnesses

Even so, this conclusion does not lend support to the default model as regards the epistemology of legal testimony for the simple reason that what is motivating the application of this principle in this context is precisely the fact that we have independent non-testimonial grounds in favour of the application of the principle—namely, our knowledge that agents will want to avoid the undesirable consequences of perjuring themselves on the witness stand. Indeed, that the overwhelming consideration in favour of applying the principle of credulity in this context rests upon an independent ground lends support to the opposing inferentialist model of legal testimony. That is, whatever one might want to say about the default epistemic status of testimony in general, there does seem to be a standing reason for seeking independent grounds in favour of an agent's legal testimony.[33]

Subconscious Prejudice

I want to close by briefly considering one further motivation that one might have for preferring the inferentialist model of the epistemology of testimony, at least when it comes to legal testimony, and this concerns the issue of unconscious prejudice. Clearly, jurors might be consciously prejudiced in the beliefs that they form, and if they are then this will undermine the justification that they have for their beliefs since gaining one's beliefs via prejudice is, by its nature, an unreliable way of gaining true beliefs. Naturally, since the goal of a criminal trial is to get to the truth about the specific matter of which verdict should be returned in this case, we do not want consciously prejudiced individuals on the jury (at least where the prejudices are relevant to the case in hand). The epistemic advice that one should give the consciously prejudiced is thus obvious, and I will not dwell further on this issue.

---

who tell the (literal) truth on the witness stand will be motivated merely by their desire to avoid this sanction, since one would expect a large majority of witnesses to regard themselves as being under an obligation to tell the truth in this situation which is independent of any concerns they might have about the legal consequences of bearing false witness. The point is simply that given this very specific and austere sanction imposed on asserting literal falsehoods in the witness stand, this consideration alone will give us reason for thinking that there is a presumption in favour of the truth of a witness' testimony, regardless of any further evidence one might possess regarding the moral character of the witness in question.

[33] That is, the correctness of inferentialism as regards the epistemology of the specific class of beliefs at issue in the case of legal testimony does not prejudice the issue of which epistemological model is applicable as regards testimony-based beliefs in general. More precisely, the (local) inferentialist claim that there is no possible situation in which one's testimony-based belief in a legal context could be justified in the absence of independent grounds is perfectly consistent with the general default theorist's claim that there *are* possible situations in which one's testimony-based belief could be justified in the absence of independent grounds. (In a similar way, the general sceptical worries about inferentialism raised in §1 have no direct application to an inferentialist account of legal testimony for the simple reason that it is not being denied by such a thesis that there are *no* testimony-based beliefs that are justified in the absence of independent supporting grounds.)

Where the prejudice is unconscious, however, then matters start to become a little more complicated since the agents concerned may consciously desire to form their beliefs in an unprejudiced manner and yet habits of thought lead them inexorably towards forming prejudiced beliefs (albeit, perhaps, true ones). Here the advantages of advising the jurors to proceed, epistemically, along the lines dictated by inferentialism are clear, since it is by seeking further independent grounds that one can bring to light any prejudice that may be informing the formation of one's beliefs. If one's natural and subconscious instinct is groundlessly to count, say, the accent of the defendant as evidence for thinking that his testimony is false (and thus for finding him guilty of the crime in question), then further consideration of the supporting grounds in favour of one's beliefs in this respect will be the best way to bring this to light. A juror might find, for example, that his 'grounds', when exposed to the clear light of day, are, if genuine grounds at all, inadequate to justify the belief that he instinctively formed and thus, given that he consciously wishes to avoid prejudice of this sort, his belief (unlike that of the consciously prejudiced juror) will change in response to this revelation. This then is a further reason to recommend inferentialism as the correct model of the epistemology of testimony in the legal context.[34, 35]

[34] For a further discussion of the problem of unconscious prejudice and how it bears on the issue of the epistemology of testimony in the legal context, albeit a discussion that takes a very different approach to that taken here, see M Fricker, n 23 above (cf Marshall, n 23 above).

[35] I am grateful to the organisers and participants at the two 'Trial on Trial' workshops—held at the Universities of Edinburgh and Stirling—at which an earlier version of this chapter was discussed. Special thanks go to my commentator at the second of these events, Victor Tadros, and to Michael Brady, Rowan Cruft, Antony Duff, Stuart Green and Tony Pitson. Finally, I am indebted to The Leverhulme Trust for the award of a Special Research Fellowship which afforded me the time to conduct work in this area.

7

Managing Uncertainty and Finality: The Function of the Criminal Trial in Legal Inquiry

JOHN D JACKSON*

1 INTRODUCTION

T HROUGHOUT THE TWENTIETH century an expanding literature emerged which was critical of the way legal procedures are used to
represent truth. It is important to distinguish here between claims that
were specifically sceptical of the ability of legal procedures to represent the truth
and more sceptical claims about the possibility of justifying belief even outside
the legal context. Although influential currents of post-modern or post-
structuralist thought have embraced extreme forms of scepticism, few of the
critics of legal methods of proof have been sceptical of the possibility of knowledge or justified belief.[1] Thus Jerome Frank, the American realist who coined
the term 'fact-skepticism', contrasted the 'fight' theory of justice as practised in
the United States with a 'truth theory' which would put a higher priority on the
discovery of truth in criminal justice.[2] Many of the critics have been scientists
who have been shocked by what they see as the lack of commitment to truth
on the part of lawyers and legal procedures.[3] Others have been historians and

---

* I would like to thank all the participants at the 'Trial on Trial' workshop at the University of
Stirling on 21–22 June 2003 for their comments on an earlier draft of this chapter. Special thanks
are owed to Sarah Summers, Lindsay Farmer and Mike Redmayne for their detailed written comments.

[1] See W Twining, 'Some Scepticism about Some Scepticism' in *Rethinking Evidence* (Oxford,
Blackwell, 1990) 92.

[2] See J Frank, *Courts on Trial* (Princeton, Princeton University Press, 1949).

[3] Huber has commented that most scientists view the legal system much as humans view reptiles
with about equal parts horrified fascination and profound disgust: P Huber, *Galileo's Revenge:
Junk Science in the Courtroom* (New York, Basic Books, 1993).

journalists shocked again at the way in which legal inquiry is conducted in particular *causes célèbres* which they have reported or written about.[4]

The targets of this scepticism have ranged from the specific to the general. Jerome Frank was a particular critic of the jury system which, in his view, encouraged excessive partisanship.[5] Some have targeted judges and lawyers who play 'games' with the truth in cases rather than engage in a serious search for it.[6] Others have been critical of the entire adversarial enterprise. Sociologists such as Doreen McBarnet have claimed that particular miscarriages of justice such as the Confait case in England in the mid 1970s, in which a number of youths were found to have confessed falsely to murder and arson, are systemic in a system based on adversary investigation and advocacy where convictions are constructed by zealous and partial investigators and lawyers.[7] Fire has also been directed at more inquisitorial procedures. Critics have pointed to miscarriages of justice in France and the Netherlands where supposedly more neutral professionals are put in charge of investigating and adjudicating cases but where there has often been a similar dependence on the police file as in adversarial systems.[8] This raises questions about the incentives on official investigators to unearth enough evidence, and about the degree of trust we can have in officials to act with independence and impartiality.[9] When inquisitorial processes have been adopted closer to home, these have also come in for criticism. The first official inquiry under Lord Widgery into the events of Bloody Sunday in Londonderry when British soldiers killed thirteen unarmed civilians was widely regarded as flawed, particularly when allegations were made about the biased way in which inquiry lawyers took statements for the tribunal.[10] The most recent attempt by the Saville Inquiry to unearth what happened has also come under criticism for its methods of inquiry. The journalists whose original

---

[4] For a journalist's insight into the miscarriages of justice in Britain in the 1980s, see B Woffinden, *Miscarriages of Justice* (London, Hodder & Stoughton, 1989). For a critique by an Italian historian of a striking miscarriage of justice arising out of the killing of a senior police officer during civil unrest in Italy in 1969, see C Ginzburg, *The Judge and the Historian* (London, Verso Books, 1999).

[5] 'More than anything else in the judicial system the jury blocks the road to ways of finding the facts': Frank, *above* n 2, at 138.

[6] See the latest outburst of the Metropolitan Police Commissioner, Sir John Stevens, against lawyers who play an uneven game of tactics against the prosecution in front of 'an uninformed jury with the disillusioned victims and a bemused defendant looking on': 'Police chief renews attack on criminal justice "game"', *The Guardian*, 7 March, 2002. This is a well worn theme of police chiefs: see D Pollard, *The Guardian* 23 July 1993 for an earlier version of the same complaint.

[7] See, eg D McBarnet, 'The Fisher Report on the Confait Case' (1978) 41 *Modern Law Review* 455.

[8] See, eg W A Wagenaar, P J van Koppen and H F M Crombag, *Anchored Narrative: The Psychology of Criminal Evidence* (New York, Harvester Wheatsheaf, 1993).

[9] On incentives, see R Posner, 'An Economic Approach to the Law of Evidence' (1999) 51 *Stanford Law Review* 1477, 1488–93 .

[10] *Report of the Tribunal appointed to inquire into the events on Sunday, 30 January 1972, which led to the loss of life in connection with the procession in Londonderry on that day, by the Rt Hon Lord Widgery* (1972). For a critique, see P Taylor, *The War Against the IRA* (London, Bloomsbury Publishing, 2001) ch 8.

account for the *Sunday Times* was hailed as edging closer to the truth than any public report have been critical of the way in which the inquiry has privileged the gladiatorial approach of lawyers which exposes every inconsistency in witnesses' accounts, over a more historical approach which would have put more credence on the primary sources unaffected by fading memories.[11]

If there is one particular feature of legal inquiry that has come in for sustained criticism, however, it has been the common law criminal trial. Jerome Frank focused much of his criticism on the criminal trial process, and many of his views on the unreliability of trial testimony have been supported by the work of experimental psychologists. Psychologists such as James Marshall have represented the trial as a world of 'make-believe' where relevant evidence may not be presented, counter evidence may not be made known and contradictions are left unresolved.[12] They have also been critical of the manner in which testimony before the court is elicited by means of examination and cross-examination and of the over-reliance on demeanour evidence.[13] The exclusionary rules of evidence associated with the adversary trial have also come in for criticism, even from lawyers themselves. This criticism can be traced as far back as Jeremy Bentham who devoted much energy to a critique of the rules of evidence and a growing number of critics have advocated a freer process of proof at trial whereby all relevant evidence is admitted.[14] In more recent years the trial process has come under the direct scrutiny of actual participants in the legal process—victims of crime, witnesses and police officers—who have been horrified at the way in which their stories have been misrepresented at trial.[15]

It is not perhaps surprising that critics have focused so particularly on the criminal trial, even though today only a minority of cases actually end up in trial. Common lawyers have for long identified the guilt determining stage of the trial with the criminal process as a whole. Damaska has pointed out how to this

[11] P Pringle, 'We return to Derry under Fire', *The Observer*, 24 February 2002. For their account of the events, see P Pringle and P Jacobson, *Those are Real Bullets: Bloody Sunday, Derry, 1972* (Berkeley, Grove/Atlantic Inc, 2002).

[12] J Marshall, *Law and Psychology in Conflict* (New York, Anchor/Doubleday, 1969).

[13] See, eg J Marshall, K H Marquis and S Oskamp, 'Effect of Kind of Question and Atmosphere of Interrogation on Accuracy and Completeness of Testimony' (1971) 84 *Harvard Law Review* 1620; O G Wellborn III, 'Demeanor' (1991) 76 *Cornell Law Review* 1075. It has been suggested, however, that systematic empirical research has contributed little to examining the value of cross-examination: see R Park, 'Adversarial Influences in the Interrogation of Trial Witnesses' in P J van Koppen and S Penrod (eds), *Adversarial versus Inquisitorial Justice: Psychological Perspectives* (New York and Dordrecht, Kluwer/Plenum, 2003), 131.

[14] On Bentham, see W Twining, *Theories of Evidence: Bentham and Wigmore* (London, Weidenfeld & Nicolson, 1985). According to one classic statement, there never was a more slap-dash, disjointed and inconsequent body of rules than the law of evidence, founded 'apparently on the principle that all jurymen are deaf to reason, that all witnesses are presumptively liars and that all documents are presumptively forgeries': C P Harvey, *The Advocate's Devil* (London, Steven & Sons, 1958) 79. Sir Rupert Cross is reputed to have said that he was working for the day when his subject would be abolished: Twining, *above* n 1, at 1.

[15] See the experiences of victims and witnesses recounted in J Jackson, *Called to Court: A Public View of Criminal Justice in Northern Ireland* (Belfast, SLS Publications, 1991); P Rock, *The Social World of an English Crown Court* (Oxford, Clarendon Press, 1993).

day Kafka's '*Der Prozess*' is translated as 'Trial' in English.[16] As the trial is the centrepiece of the criminal process, critics have naturally focused on its weaknesses. This chapter examines the responses that can be made to these criticisms. One response is to claim that legal procedures and the trial in particular are not concerned centrally with truth. Another is to claim that while truth is important these criticisms fail to take account of the constraints on truth which are inevitably placed on legal inquiries and on the particular function which the criminal trial plays in bringing finality to criminal disputes. A third response that will be developed in this chapter is that, when seen in the context of this function, trial procedures have provided much more rational mechanisms for finding the truth than is sometimes supposed. But it will be argued that recent challenges from the media and science questioning the truthfulness of trial verdicts are calling into question the trial's ability to bring finality to criminal disputes and at the same time providing alternative means of settling such disputes. Accordingly, the criminal trial is undergoing perhaps one of the greatest crises of confidence that it has faced since trials by ordeal came to be challenged and replaced in the thirteenth century.

2 THE IMPORTANCE OF TRUTH AND EVIDENCE

It is not intended to dwell long on the first response. Few have denied that truth and evidence play an important role in legal procedure, as one of its central purposes is to apply the substantive law.[17] Substantive law is of little use unless it is enforced and to this end there is a need to devise procedures like the trial to determine whether there has been a breach of the law. Although this may involve questions of legal interpretation, more often it involves questions about what happened—questions about evidence and truth. Hence the centrality of truth and evidence in legal inquiry.

To establish the centrality of evidence in legal procedure does not mean that truth finding is given the same weight in each type of case.[18] A distinction is sometimes made between legal processes which are concerned with resolving conflict and those concerned with the implementation of state policy.[19] In so far as criminal procedure is about enforcing the criminal law, however, it may be said that it is vital that those who have breached the law are pursued and this

[16] M Damaska, 'Models of Criminal Procedure' (2001) 51 *Zbornik* (collected papers of Zagreb Law School) 477.

[17] For a compelling defence of the view that one of the central aims of legal procedures is to produce true or accurate judgements, see A Goldman, *Knowledge in a Social World* (Oxford, Clarendon Press, 1999) ch 9.

[18] M Damaska, 'Truth in Adjudication' (1997) 49 *Hastings Law Journal* 289.

[19] For discussion, see M Damaska, *The Faces of Justice and State Authority* (New Haven, Yale University Press, 1986). For a critique of this dichotomy, however, see I Markovits, 'Playing the Opposites Game: On Mirjan Damaska's *The Faces of Justice and State Authority*' (1989) 41 *Stanford Law Review* 1313.

policy would be defeated if the wrong persons were punished. Of course, criminal justice processes do not have to enforce the law in every case. Langbein has argued that one reason why in fact there was so much tolerance for the truth defeating aspects of adversary procedure in the second half of the eighteenth century, when these processes were developed, was because a central function of the criminal trial at that time was to mitigate the harshness of the criminal law which arose out of the over-prescriptive nature of capital punishment.[20] As he puts it, 'too much truth meant too much death.'[21] But even in this environment, truth and evidence played an important role. It was important first of all, to establish whether defendants had broken the law, and then in deciding which offenders were worthy of capital punishment and which were not, to take account of which crimes had been committed and in what circumstances.

3 TRUTH AND FINALITY

The second response is to accept the importance of truth and evidence in legal inquiry but to argue that there are certain constraints on the legal truth finding enterprise which are not so evident in other fact finding inquiries. One of these is the limited time and resources available for conducting the legal inquiry. Of course, limited time and resources may affect other truth finding inquiries as well, but a crucial difference is that there is not the same pressure on many of them to reach a definitive conclusion on a particular question. Article 6 of the European Convention on Human Rights requires that in the determination of his civil rights and obligations or of any criminal charge against him, everyone is entitled to a fair and public hearing within a reasonable time. This can be particularly important in criminal proceedings where the European Court of Human Rights has recognised that there is a particular need to ensure that defendants do not remain too long in a state of uncertainty about their fate.[22] It is important, however, to see that the need for legal proceedings to be brought to a conclusion is not just a desirable state of affairs, as delay in reaching a conclusion can be harmful to the parties and lead to a loss of memory about the original events in dispute. It is a necessary constraint on the proceedings. In the end a decision must be reached because the very point of the proceedings is to bring closure to the issues in contest.

The need for finality need not always constrain truth finding. One of the arguments that has been made for the double jeopardy rule, whereby acquittals cannot be re-opened after trial, is that it has the effect of galvanising the police and prosecution to put their best case together at one concentrated trial. Although

---

[20] J H Langbein, *The Origins of Adversary Criminal Trial* (Oxford, Clarendon Press, 2003).
[21] Ibid, 6.
[22] *Stögmuller v Austria* (1979–80), 1 EHRR 155, para 5. For commentary on how this requirement is affecting UK domestic law, see J Jackson, J Johnstone and J Shapland, 'Delay, Human Rights and the Need for Statutory Time Limits' [2003] *Criminal Law Review* 510.

there are doubts as to whether the prospect of finality actually motivates the behaviour of criminal investigators in this way,[23] examples can be found where the prospect of finality has helped to crystallise matters and bring about a satisfactory verdict. A recent civil example is to be found in the libel case concerning David Irving's writings on the holocaust where a leading expert witness in the trial has commented that the trial provided a good opportunity to settle the historical and methodological points at issue in the case.[24] In historical debates he claimed it was often possible to evade your opponent's questions or get away with irrelevant answers. In a court of law answers had to be given to questions and this proved very helpful in moving the court towards a definite conclusion on the issues.

This was an exceptional case where there was an opportunity for full disclosure of the relevant evidence before the trial. In other cases where there is more limited time and resources, the danger is that not all relevant evidence is unearthed and disclosed in time. Of course, legal inquiries are not unique in requiring final and speedy decision making. In medical emergencies, for example, it can be crucial for practitioners to ascertain all the relevant facts or symptoms as quickly as possible in order to reach a definite diagnosis. The limits on resources can also demand that diagnoses are made speedily as there are obvious resource implications for any health system if a thorough diagnosis involving a large number of tests were carried out in the case of every patient who complained of certain symptoms. But here another contrast between the legal inquiry and other inquiries looms large, which is that the matters under investigation can be shrouded in considerable factual uncertainty. One reason for this is that the matters under investigation can become the subject of a bitter contest where claims and counter-claims are vigorously disputed. Of course, it may be that there is no dispute to the claims made, but where the parties are contesting issues which can have profound consequences for them, there can be considerable incentives for concealing material evidence. Steps can be taken to force parties to disclose evidence but in this event parties may deliberately deceive each other, with the result that it may be just as difficult to reach accurate conclusions.[25] The subject matter of the dispute, often events that occurred in the past, may also constrain truth finding. The passage of time may make it very difficult to reach conclusions about the events that occurred and about the motivations and intentions of the parties at the time, although much will depend here on the substantive legal norms that form the subject of the dispute.[26] A

---

[23] See P Roberts, 'Justice for All? Two Bad Arguments (and Several Good Suggestions) for Resisting Double Jeopardy Reform' (2002) 6 *International Journal of Evidence & Proof* 197, 211–14.

[24] R Evans, *Telling Lies About Hitler* (London, Heinemann, 2002) 196.

[25] On the effective role deception can play as a means of suppressing the truth, see D J Seidmann and A Stein, 'The Right of Silence Helps the Innocent: A Game-Theoretic Analysis of the Fifth Amendment' (2000) 114 *Harvard Law Review* 430.

[26] These may limit the number of perspectives that may be taken and hence make the task of fact finding actually *easier* than might be the case in other disciplines where there may be more scope for numerous interpretations: a point made by Damaska, above n 18.

further cause of uncertainty is that unlike certain other inquiries such as medical diagnoses, there are few established procedures for determining questions of fact that arise frequently in legal inquiry, such as whether someone is telling the truth or not. It is true that medical diagnosis is not as rule-bound as is sometimes thought. Some conditions, such as whether someone is HIV positive, may be tested on the basis of a simple blood test but many illnesses are less straight-forward. Even in the case of psychiatric diagnoses, however, where there is no simple test for mental disorders, doctors attempt to adopt rule-based procedures such as the application of several criteria from a list to meet 'diagnostic crite-ria'.[27] By way of contrast, the contested nature of legal procedures demands that considerable formality needs to be attached to the process of eliciting evidence at trial, even if there is very little formality attached to how to derive conclusions from the evidence assembled at the trial.

The need for final decisions to be reached in conditions of uncertainty about disputed claims imposes a number of constraints on the procedures for legal truth finding. First of all, finality requires decision rules spelling out what should happen in the event of the claim not being proven. The issues in dispute are sometimes called the 'material facts' or 'facts in issue'. If in a criminal trial the facts are proved, the defendant is guilty. But if they are not proved, it does not follow logically that the defendant is not guilty.[28] Without a decision rule to enable a decision to be reached that D is not guilty, the court could avoid mak-ing a decision, leaving the parties in a state of uncertainty. Secondly, the need for a conclusion means, as we have seen, that a decision may have to be reached under fairly extreme conditions of uncertainty and this requires that legal pro-cedures establish standards of proof setting out when facts will be considered proved. This requires the courts to operate an error preference on the basis of which some mistakes such as wrongful convictions are worse than others such as wrongful acquittals.[29] Thirdly, the need for a conclusion puts pressure on the legal system to develop procedures and rules to justify the outcome reached. The criminal courts have been notoriously reluctant to interfere with verdicts at a later stage even when they appear to be wrong. This is what Nobles and Schiff have described as a 'tragic choice' in the very nature of appeal proceedings.[30] On the one hand, if the system is too ready to admit error this may undermine confidence in the ability of the courts to reach binding final decisions and create great uncertainty for the parties. On the other hand, if it disregards the error and reinforces the original judgment it risks being undermined by revelations that the conclusion was wrong.

---

[27] For a discussion of the use of diagnostic classification in psychiatry, see F Margison, 'Practice-based Evidence in Psychotherapy' in C Mace, S Moorey and B Roberts (eds), *Evidence in the Psychological Therapies* (Hove, Brunner-Routledge, 2001) 174.

[28] N MacCormick, *Legal Reasoning and Legal Theory* (Oxford, Clarendon Press, 1978) 44.

[29] A Zuckerman, *Principles of Criminal Evidence* (Oxford, Clarendon Press, 1989).

[30] R Nobles and D Schiff, *Understanding Miscarriages of Justice* (Oxford, Clarendon Press, 2000).

But this tension between the need for finality and the need for truth does not only operate at the appeal level. In the criminal context accusations are made against individuals which can have profound consequences for them. If a conclusion is reached that the defendant is guilty, this is more than a descriptive statement of fact; it is also a normative judgment endorsing the justification for some blame to be attached to D.[31] In view of the consequences that attach to such a judgment and for the full normative force of such a judgment to be brought to bear on the defendant and the public, the legal system needs to find expressive means of communicating the accuracy of the verdict. This is particularly necessary where defendants are contesting the claims made against them. As it is difficult to establish formal rules and procedures for justifying the *substance* of the decisions reached, various means have been adopted for justifying the *manner* in which they are reached in order to 'copper-fasten' their accuracy. Examples of such measures include holding a public trial, ensuring that decision makers in it carry particular authority, according due process to the proceedings, and reinforcing the verdict with various rules of evidence or with some form of reasoned judgment. These might be viewed as means by which the system seeks to legitimise its verdicts over and above the need for factual accuracy.[32] But another way of viewing these is as devices for *reinforcing* accuracy which is in itself the primary goal of the trial process. Given the pressures for finality, there is often an inevitable evidential gap between what the evidence points to and the conclusion reached in the form of a verdict. The system therefore needs to find means of justifying that conclusion as best as it can to the parties and the public. Ironically, however, the need to justify the accuracy of verdicts can lead to devices which serve as obstacles to truth finding. One of the conditions of a fair trial in Article 6 of the European Convention, for example, is that hearings take place in public. Open justice is a means of demonstrating the accuracy of the conclusions reached from the evidence, but it may inhibit persons from disclosing information relevant to the dispute.

It is against this background that our present trial procedures are to be judged. A distinction is sometimes made between rules of evidence that are internal to the legal fact finding process, designed to further the accuracy of verdicts, and rules of evidence that impose external constraints on the system as a result of values which have nothing to do with truth finding at all, for example rules which exclude reliable evidence obtained unlawfully or in breach of other

---

[31] Although attaching blame is most commonly associated with criminal procedures, it can play a part in civil proceedings as well where there can be just as much concern about compliance with the law. A much overlooked purpose of tort law, for example, has been said to be to keep wrongdoing under control and in that way to supplement the criminal law: see Lord Stein, 'Perspectives of Corrective and Distributive Justice in Tort Law', John Maurice Kelly Memorial Lecture, University College Dublin, 1 November 2001.

[32] For a recent attempt to ground verdicts in a theory of legitimacy, see I H Dennis, *The Law of Evidence* (2nd edn, London, Sweet & Maxwell, 2002) ch 2. According to Dennis, 'the factual accuracy of the decision ceases to be the primary goal of the adjudicative process', 40. See also C Allen, *Practical Guide to Evidence* (2nd edn, London, Cavendish, 2002) 48–49.

values.[33] In reality, however, there is seldom such a clear cut distinction between these types of rules. Rules preventing coerced confessions, for example, may be seen as an internal constraint on the trial system as they may be factually inaccurate as well as an external constraint in that this is a gross violation of human rights. Even exclusionary rules which do not appear to enhance truth finding at all, such as rules governing the admission of evidence obtained in breach of the laws on search and seizure, are seldom applied without regard to a principle of proportionality whereby due weight is given to the interests of truth finding and law enforcement, on the one hand, against the need to convey a public message that the trial cannot condone breaches of fundamental rights by law enforcement officials.[34] This can easily lead to an incommensurable conflict between the need to justify verdicts as founded on truth and the need to protect the defendant's rights.[35] If the trial is viewed as a public forum for justifying the verdicts of the legal system, however, it may be possible to resolve the conflict by appeal to the principle that whatever the truth of the defendant's guilt and the nature of the violation to the defendant's rights, verdicts cannot be publicly sanctioned by the legal system unless they have been constituted in a lawful manner. It may be considered a failing when apparently reliable evidence is excluded from the courts as this can skew the truth of the final verdict which the system is seeking to justify. But the system cannot condone gross violations of its own rules of process as it is only through compliance with them that it is able to pronounce that a verdict is both lawful and enforceable.[36]

It is next proposed to turn to the third response—that within the constraints of having to justify verdicts publicly within the law in order to bring finality to proceedings, legal procedures and more particularly the criminal trial that emerged to settle contested claims have in fact provided rational mechanisms for finding the truth. We shall do this by way of a brief historical look at the

---

[33] The distinction is derived from Wigmore's distinction between 'rules of extrinsic policy' and 'rules of auxiliary probative policy': see J H Wigmore, *Evidence in Trials at Common Law* (rev Tillers; Boston, Little Brown, 1983) vol 1:11 at 689.

[34] See C Bradley, 'The Exclusionary Rule in Germany' (1983) 96 *Harvard Law Review* 1032. There are, of course, examples where breach of a constitutional right leads to automatic exclusion, for example breach of the Fourth Amendment to the US Constitution on search and seizure: see *Mapp v Ohio* 367 US 643 (1961).

[35] See A J Ashworth, 'Exploring the Integrity Principle in Evidence and Procedure', in P Mirfield and R Smith (eds), *Essays for Colin Tapper* (London, Butterworths, 2003) 107, 118–19.

[36] This would seem to resemble what has been called the principle of judicial integrity, whereby it is wrong for a court to act on the results of a gross violation of fundamental rights or law as it is then condoning the violation. For discussion of this principle, see P Mirfield, *Silence, Confessions and Improperly Obtained Evidence* (Oxford, Clarendon Press, 1997). There is not space here to develop the argument but this principle is often argued on the basis that a failure to exclude evidence obtained in breach of fundamental rights would lessen the moral authority of the law. But on a somewhat narrower view, it may be argued that the courts' primary responsibility is to protect the integrity of the processes that have been laid down by law for the acquisition of evidence. Where evidence has been acquired in gross violation of these processes, the courts would be failing in their responsibility to protect these processes if they were to allow the evidence to be acted upon. For further discussion of the importance of upholding process values, see J H Ely, *Democracy and Distrust* (Cambridge, Mass, Harvard University Press, 1980).

development of methods of proof. It will be argued that the various devices used to copper-fasten the verdict may be viewed as rational when seen in the light of justifying verdicts according to the intellectual and social climate of their time.

4 THE DEVELOPMENT OF LEGAL METHODS OF PROOF

Much of the literature has contrasted early irrational methods of proof with the later supposedly rational ones. Although legal procedures today are largely designed to give effect to substantive law, this was not always so. For long periods of European history lawsuits were designed to resolve disputes on the basis of the party which had right or God on its side.[37] The old modes of proof—ranging from a simple oath through to oaths sworn by oath-helpers or compurgators who swore that the party's oath was unperjured, through to more arduous forms of proof of trial by ordeal or battle—appear magical and irrational to us today, but it has been argued that if they are seen in the wider context of dispute resolution they made sense.[38] Damaska argues that most disputes were not actually resolved by these magical means but by what might be called 'alternative dispute resolution', where more natural truth revealing methods were used by people who knew something about the dispute coming forward to give their version of events. The judicial apparatus only came into play when the local community was unable to resolve the dispute or the dispute was too important to be left in its hands. Even when these methods were employed, however, much more weight was put on evidence and accurate outcomes than might appear. Oath helpers would be unlikely to come forward and invite divine wrath if they were not satisfied about the justice of their party's cause. Trial by ordeal then only came into play when the required number of oath-helpers was missing or when the party's own oath could not be relied upon because of past crimes or when the dispute could not be settled in any other way. In other words, these magical trials were used as a last resort in hard cases and even then were not as irrational as they might seem. The ordeals put psychological pressure on litigants to drop their claims or confess and it seems that the severity of the tests could vary according to the demeanour and body language of the litigant. In many cases the appeal to divinity merely put the final seal on a result that had been determined beforehand by other more rational means. This ties in with our theory that legal methods of proof require some means of justifying or demonstrating the accuracy or justice of a decision, especially in hard cases, to the parties and the public over and above the simple adjudication of the court that X should succeed in his claim. In a society that believed emphatically in divine revelation, appeals to divinity were entirely rational.

---

[37] H Berman, *Law and Revolution: The Formation of the Western Legal Tradition* (Cambridge, Mass, Harvard University Press, 1983) 57–60.

[38] M Damaska, 'Rational and Irrational Proof Revisited' (1997) 5 *Cardozo Journal of International and Comparative Law* 25.

When, however, it became clear that trials by ordeal were often manipulated by the clergy, this mode of proof was no longer so useful as a means of demonstrating the rightness or justice of the judgment, and in 1215 the Lateran Council condemned clerical involvement in unilateral ordeals. Continental systems under pressure to create a more systematic application of rules adopted Roman law as a means of bringing a corpus of rules to bear upon society. Enforcement was to be provided by judges who were organised within a strict hierarchy of control and also by a series of rules of evidence which prescribed what was to constitute proof for giving effect to the law. Judges could only base a decision on a written record, and in criminal trials could only convict for serious crimes on the testimony of two eye-witnesses or on the accused's own confession.[39]

In England too another mode of proof had to be found when trial by ordeal was abolished by royal ordinance in 1219. Henry II created a bench of royal judges whose task was to develop a law 'common' to the whole land, but instead of working on their own they were to work in partnership with local juries who were given power to decide disputes. Originally these juries were self-informing in the sense that they were presumed to know the facts of the case because they lived in the local neighbourhood. Gradually over time, however, the jury's role changed to one where they listened to witnesses who were called to court to testify before them and evaluated evidence on the basis of information and testimony introduced in court by private accusers and government appointed justices of the peace.

It can be argued that the new modes of proof developed after 1215 in both England and the Continent represented a move towards a much more rational mode of adjudication. The move towards a system where parties and juries would swear to particular facts rather than to the rightness of their claim, and where the final disposition of the case was in the hands of men rather than God, more closely resembles what we would recognise as an attempt to base judgments upon evidence and reason rather than upon superstition and emotion. But in a number of respects the new modes of proof fell short of modern methods of legal proof. It has been suggested that trial by jury and by torture became the new trials by ordeal.[40] If the jury swore to the truth of facts, that was the end of the matter. Similarly, if torture produced a confession, that determined the case and no further inquiry was made by the court. The weight of a piece of evidence, in other words, depended upon the authority of the person who swore to it or to the document which provided it rather than upon the probability that it was true.

At the same time, just as there was scope for the evaluation of evidence under the old systems of trial by ordeal, so there was also much more scope for this

---

[39] See J H Langbein, *Prosecuting Crime in the Renaissance: England, Germany, France* (Cambridge, Mass, Harvard University Press, 1974) 157; *Torture and the Law of Proof: Europe and England in the Ancien Régime* (Chicago, University of Chicago Press, 1977) 5–8.

[40] R Bartlett, *Trial by Fire and Water: The Medieval Judicial Ordeal* (Oxford, Clarendon Press, 1986) 139.

under the later numerical proof and jury systems. It has been suggested that a reading of the primary sources of the time reveals that the architects of Roman-canon proof never contemplated that judges should merely count evidence and that their scheme encouraged the application of an empirical method of inquiry.[41] What this suggests is that before it was recognised that the evaluation of evidence on the basis of inductive probability could play a role in justifying beliefs, other forms of justification were found on the basis of authority, whether this was by divine revelation, by numerical rules of proof or by other oaths of witnesses or jurors. It may be that *in practice* these modes of proof played a much less decisive role than has traditionally been recognised, but they nevertheless seemed to play a significant symbolic and 'copper-fastening' role in the acceptance of verdicts. When the evaluation of evidence on the basis of inferences came to be more accepted, however, it was possible to move more towards what has been called a rationalist theory of evidence and a system of free or natural proof where weight is not assigned a priori to certain items of information and credence is no longer placed on the authority of sources.

5 TOWARDS FREE PROOF?

There was nevertheless some reluctance on the part of writers and judges to acknowledge the central role that evaluation of evidence played in legal proof. It was easier in many ways to latch on to the fiction that juries were self-informing about the facts, for so long as juries acted purely on their own knowledge their verdicts could continue to be accorded a kind of oracular authority. When they became evaluators of evidence their personal evaluation could not command the same authority as personal knowledge of the evidence. As the intellectual current of the time moved more in the direction of accepting that triers of fact were able to estimate for themselves the probative value of the evidence, however, the reality that juries had to engage in the evaluation of evidence came to be accepted and judges began directing juries to weigh the credibility of witnesses and to base their verdicts on belief and 'satisfied conscience'.[42]

Continental procedures took even longer to adapt to the principle that triers of fact had to base their judgments on their actual belief rather than on legal proofs. The requirement of two witnesses or a confession before there could be a conviction continued throughout the sixteenth and seventeenth centuries. Many continental jurisdictions also resorted, however, to a discretionary power to impose penalties known as 'poena extraordinaria' when there was persuasive circumstantial evidence against the accused.[43] In these cases the accused was not

---

[41] Damaska, *above* n 38, at 35.

[42] B Shapiro, *Beyond Reasonable Doubt and Probable Cause* (Berkeley, University of California Press, 1991) 13–14.

[43] *Langbein, above* n 39, 45–60.

technically convicted but was punished for the suspicion that had accumulated against her. This meant that full proof in the form of two sworn witnesses or a confession was no longer essential for punishment, and seemed to open the door for the abolition of judicial torture long thought necessary in order to obtain full proof. But judicial torture was not actually abolished until the late eighteenth century when a more full blown assault on the system of legal proofs came to be mounted by a number of Enlightenment figures influenced by the ideas of Locke and Newton.[44]

The shift in Anglo-Saxon procedure towards a reliance on the beliefs of triers of fact did not lead, however, to a system of free proof. Indeed it had the opposite effect, heralding various rules of evidence, first in civil trials and later in criminal trials. Although the legal treatise writers of eighteenth century England were heavily influenced by the works of John Locke which emphasised the need for a satisfied conscience, this did not mean that they gave up the quest to guide and at times mandate how this conscience should be satisfied. Throughout the sixteenth and seventeenth centuries certain categories of witness were considered incompetent and unable to testify. On top of this certain types of evidence came to be privileged over others. In one of the first English legal treatises devoted exclusively to evidence, published in 1754, Geoffrey Gilbert, the Lord Chief Baron of Exchequer, organised various types of evidence in a hierarchical fashion around a best evidence principle under which pieces of evidence were categorised with various degrees of weight in advance of the trial.[45]

Gilbert's work was devoted mostly to evidence in civil cases and such a rigid categorisation of evidence did not find total favour in the practice of the criminal courts where there was much greater reliance on oral evidence at a public trial. Unlike continental Europe where professional magistrates and prosecutors were allocated a central fact finding role, the investigation conducted by lay justices in England was much less thorough and this meant that the oral public trial became a central feature of English criminal procedure.[46] At this trial accusations were put to the accused 'in altercation'. This proved, however, to be a very one-sided exercise capable, as the treason trials of the 1670s and 1680s showed, of producing miscarriages of justice. As the political classes voiced their discontent, a process of 'evening up' took place in which the accused came to be represented by counsel and rules of evidence such as rules on corroboration and confessions were developed to give the accused additional protection. In time a system of adversarial justice developed which laid the foundations for the modern adversarial trial where lawyers dominated the proceedings, the accused was largely silent, and exclusionary rules of evidence such as the hearsay rule came to be used by lawyers to full effect.

---

[44] The influence of English empirical thought on French Enlightenment thinkers is traced in B Russell, *A History of Western Philosophy* (London, Allen & Unwin, 1946), 641; F Copleston, *A History of Philosophy* (New York, Doubleday, 1960) vol 6, 15.

[45] G Gilbert, *The Law of Evidence* (Dublin, S Cotter 1754).

[46] Langbein, *above* n 20, at 46.

6 THE MODERN ADVERSARIAL CRIMINAL TRIAL

Critics of the modern adversarial trial and the exclusionary rules associated with it have viewed it as an aberration from a rationalist theory of proof whereby triers of fact are given free rein to make inquiries as to the facts and draw their own conclusions as to guilt. On this view the most natural thing to do when it was accepted that the truth was best realised by an evaluation of evidence would have been to establish a professional corps of magistrates or prosecutors for this purpose, as was done in continental Europe. Instead the modern adversarial trial has retained a number of key irrational vestiges from its past. The old fiction that juries could swear to the truth of the facts has long since disappeared, but the oral tradition whereby witnesses swear to the truth of the facts at a public hearing has been retained. The oath continues to play an important ritualistic role in the modern trial. The idea that the oath itself is a guarantee of truthfulness disappeared as cross-examination became the primary means for testing the validity of claims in the modern adversarial trial. But the oath continued to be used as a means of encouraging witnesses to tell the truth as its underlying effect was to convey the message that those who lied on oath would be punished by divine vengeance.[47] The lay jury has also been retained as the body responsible for handing down the verdict and a number of rituals associated with the jury have been retained in many jurisdictions, such as the public summation by the judge to the jury of the law and the facts, the secrecy of the deliberation process that follows upon this summation, and the sphinx-like verdict that emerges from this deliberation without any indication of the reasons behind it.[48] The adversary trial itself has also assumed a number of ritualistic formalities as battle lines are drawn up between the two sides, each with their respective teams of witnesses who give evidence in a courtroom which is laid out in a highly formalised manner, the witness box representing the central stage but with other equally significant props such as the elevated bench from which the judge presides from on high and the much more lowly 'dock' where the prisoner sits. The symbols communicated by the bible placed beside the witness box, the raised dais for the judge and the lowly position of the dock are further reinforced by the red ermine traditionally worn by the judge and the wigs and gowns of the learned counsel.

Although it is easy to characterise these ritualistic features of the adversarial trial as irrational vestiges of a trial system which is badly in need of modernisation, they have proved remarkably resilient to change. This would seem to be

---

[47] Indeed well into the late twentieth century it was not uncommon for judges to question child witnesses about their religious understanding on the ground that they could not be sworn to give evidence unless they had some comprehension of the divine sanction of the oath. See *R v Hayes* [1977] 2 All ER 288.

[48] For discussion of the lack of accountability of the jury, see J Jackson, 'Making Juries Accountable' (2002) 50 *American Journal of Comparative Law* 477.

because, just as with the ordeals of the old trial, they have a played an important part in conveying the impression of the trial as a solemn search for the truth and invest the verdict with the authority that is needed for imposing the sanctions that follow a determination of guilt.[49] It is true that a number of these rituals have been represented as displaying the majesty of the law itself and upholding its moral view—the public charge to the jury by the judge, for example, communicating and legitimising the moral values of the law before the verdict is handed down. Hay, for example, has shown how the public charge delivered by the judge to the jury in the Hanoverian period was directed beyond the jury to a wider audience in the court room and took the form of a secular sermon on the virtues of authority and obedience.[50] But scenes leading up to the public charge, such as putting witnesses on oath and exhorting juries to weigh the evidence carefully, also help to convey the impression that there can be faith in the truth of the verdict.

On this view the rules of evidence and procedure play an important role in reinforcing the truthfulness of the verdict. At one level they can be a useful tool for judges to employ in addressing some of the inequities and frailties inevitably associated with this mode of trial. The competency rules forbidding certain classes of witness from testifying were a means of excluding the testimony of witnesses who were deemed to be unreliable. This perpetuated the idea that the testimony of witnesses who were sworn was entitled to a certain value.[51] In a similar manner the hearsay rule was originally devised as a means also of validating the significance of the oath, as it forbade the testimony of witnesses who were not sworn on oath.[52] Gradually, as trials became more adversarial and testimony came to be tested by cross-examination, the hearsay rule came to be adapted to encourage parties to tender their witnesses for cross-examination.[53]

Two schools of thought have emerged to explain the modern rules of evidence—the so-called 'adversary control theory' and the so-called 'jury control theory'. The adversary control theory holds that the contested nature of the adversary trial requires special quality controls to be put upon the admission of evidence.[54] When the proof process is dominated by the evidence which the parties have gathered and collected, there is a particular need to be sceptical

---

[49] For discussion of the importance of the visual in representing the truth in law, see P Goodrich, *Languages of Law: From Logics of Memory to Nomadic Masks* (London, Weidenfeld & Nicolson, 1991) 191; P Haldar, 'The Evidencer's Eye: Representations of Truth in the Laws of Evidence' (1991) 2 *Law and Critique* 171; J Jackson, 'Law's Truth, Lay Truth and Lawyer's Truth: the Representation of Evidence in Adversary Trials' (1992) 3 *Law and Critique* 29.

[50] D Hay, 'Property, Authority and the Criminal Law', in D Hay, P Linebaugh, J G Rule, E P Thompson and C Winslow, *Albion's Fatal Tree: Crime and Society in Eighteenth Century England* (London, Allen Lane, 1975).

[51] The fact that only prosecution witnesses could be sworn in criminal trials gave them considerable advantage over defence witnesses in the seventeenth century trial: see Langbein, *above* n 20, 51–52.

[52] Ibid, 237–38.

[53] See J Hunter and K Cronin, *Evidence, Advocacy and Trial Practice: A Criminal Trial Commentary* (Sydney, Butterworths, 1995) 17.

[54] See D Nance, 'The Best Evidence Principle' (1988) 73 *Iowa Law Review* 227.

about the nature of this information and a need to impose rigorous testing devices and foundational requirements.[55] According to this theory the institutional environment of the adversary system is the best explanation for the rules of evidence.

The jury control theory was most famously articulated by James B Thayer, the Harvard law professor and first great American evidence scholar, when he said that the law of evidence is the 'child of the jury system'.[56] This theory was to dominate much twentieth century evidence scholarship.[57] The argument was that judges developed exclusionary rules to prevent juries placing more weight on certain kinds of evidence than they really merited. A jury may give undue weight, for example, to hearsay evidence or character evidence. According to this theory, it is not enough to trust lay triers of fact to evaluate evidence on their own. When the legal system accepted that juries could only reach verdicts by evaluating evidence, means had to be found to control this process of evaluation. Exclusion of unduly prejudicial evidence and formal directions on how certain kinds of admissible evidence should be used became the tools used to control the natural reasoning processes of the jury.

Although these theories have been portrayed as rivals, they are in fact interdependent. Without an adversary system, judges would inevitably take on a more active truth finding stance and would be able to control juries, as indeed they did before the lawyerisation of the criminal trial in the eighteenth century, without the need to exclude evidence. Conversely, however, without the jury system, exclusionary rules could not be enforced as judicial fact finders would obtain knowledge of the very evidence they had to exclude and it is difficult to expect triers of fact to 'unbite the apple of knowledge.'[58]

In addition, a number of formal directions have also come to be given to juries as to how to approach matters of evidence. As some of the more exclusionary rules have declined in significance over the past century, these formal directions have assumed greater importance, extending beyond matters concerning the burden and standard of proof to issues such as handling particular kinds of potentially unreliable evidence such as identification evidence, the evidence of particular witnesses, and the effect of the accused's silence or of lies told by the accused. Much debate has been generated on the practical effectiveness of these directions,[59] but they may also be seen as serving the function of conveying the standards that should be applied in evaluating the evidence to an audience wider

---

[55] M Damaska, *Evidence Law Adrift* (New Haven, Yale University Press, 1997) ch 4.

[56] J B Thayer, *A Preliminary Treatise on Evidence at the Common Law* (Boston, Little Brown, 1898) 266, 509. For a modern version of the theory, see E J Imwinkelried, 'The Worst Evidence Principle: The Best Hypothesis as to the Logical Structure of Evidence Law', (1992) 46 *University of Miami Law Review* 1069.

[57] Nance, *above* n 54, at 279. Cogent criticism of the theory is to be found, however, in E Morgan, 'The Jury and the Exclusionary Rules of Evidence' (1937) 4 *University of Chicago Law Review* 247.

[58] M Damaska, 'Free Proof and its Detractors' (1995) 43 *American Journal of Comparative Law* 343, 352.

[59] For discussion see Damaska, *above* n 55, 33–34.

than the jury and also a sense of closure that the system has done its best to ensure that these standards will be applied.[60]

All this is not to argue that the ritualistic trappings associated with the modern adversarial criminal trial are the most rational means of organising truth finding arrangements. But it does suggest that there is more to the trial than simply devising the best fact finding arrangements. Within the context of contested allegations of criminal conduct, the trial serves the function of communicating to a wider audience a message that the system has done its best to determine the truth. At this point it is worth comparing the experience of what has happened across the European continent where a more rational system of proof is said by critics to have developed. From an early stage a professional corps of magistrates and prosecutors was established to conduct a thorough investigation of the facts before the trial and the oral public trial never assumed the importance that it did in England. At the same time a public trial did develop, albeit within a very different mode of procedure, and mechanisms had to be found to communicate the message that an accurate judgment had been reached.

7 THE CONTINENTAL ALTERNATIVE

Langbein has argued that during the eighteenth century when the English criminal trial was being transformed from altercation to adversary trial, hardly any attention was given to a highly visible alternative to adversary criminal procedure on display across the English Channel.[61] One reason for this was that, as Langbein himself has shown,[62] up until the late eighteenth century the European alternative continued to exhibit serious weaknesses such as the use of rigid legal proofs and torture. In the course of the nineteenth century however, these shackles were swept aside and professional triers of fact were given the free rein necessary to seek out the truth.

It is important to see, however, that in developing their modern system of proof continental systems adopted some aspects of English criminal procedure which in the English context have been criticised as truth-defeating, such as the oral public trial, the use of defence counsel and the use of juries, or more commonly lay judges sitting with professional juries. A purely rationalist model of proof might suggest that it is enough to appoint trusted professionals to seek out the truth. But the history of continental procedure has shown that even professionals entrusted with seeking out the truth can become one-sided and that, as Langbein has put it, seeking the truth does not guarantee finding it.[63] As a result

---

[60] See, for example, S Doran, 'The Symbolic Function of the Summing-Up in the Criminal Trial: Can the Diplock Judgment Compensate?' (1991) 42 *Northern Ireland Legal Quarterly* 365; M Seigel, 'A Pragmatic Critique of Modern Evidence Scholarship' (1994) 88 *Northwestern University Law Review* 995.

[61] *Above* n 20, at 338.

[62] *Torture and the Law of Proof, above* n 39.

[63] *Above* n 20, at 342.

further guarantees of trustworthiness had to be found and a public trial dominated, unlike the wholly adversarial trial, by triers of fact, but allowing scope for
defence counsel as well, has become the norm in many systems.[64] Although the
trial is not therefore the determinative phase in the criminal process, it nevertheless serves the important function of providing public judicial confirmation
of the conclusions of guilt drawn from the investigation phase.[65] Other quality
controls have also emerged such as the requirement that judges justify their
factual findings in a written opinion in a manner which makes appellate review
easier than when there is a simple guilty or not guilty verdict. Exclusionary rules
of evidence, on the other hand, have never featured as prominently as in the
common law trial. The institutional constraints which operate to create scepticism of the evidentiary sources presented in the adversarial trial do not operate
so intrusively in continental processes, where the evidence is built up and tested
incrementally before trial and recorded in the case file or dossier as it goes along.
Similarly, although reformed continental processes have given greater
opportunity to the parties to influence the shaping of the evidence, evidence is
still largely controlled by investigating or trial judges. It can therefore be argued
that there is less need for rules of evidence in the continental institutional environment, and in the absence of a tribunal of fact like the jury from which evidence can be hidden there is also not the means for enforcing them as effectively
as in the common law tradition.

Yet a number of standards regulating the approach that should be taken
towards evidence have emerged in continental jurisdictions. Many continental
jurisdictions operate rules whereby evidence obtained unlawfully or in violation
of human rights should not be used and there are robust rules of privilege and
rules regarding the qualification of experts.[66] These restraints may be said to be
externally imposed in order to enforce certain values and have nothing directly
to do with enhancing truth finding. It is much less common to find rules man-
dating the exclusion of certain categories of evidence or requiring corroboration
of them for reasons to do with the enhancement of truth-finding.[67] Yet a number of standards designed to guide the decision making of fact finders can be
found and appellate courts have not hesitated to reverse judgments which have
relied too heavily on hearsay evidence or on inferences about a person's character.[68] In addition the European Court of Human Rights has recently laid down
standards which prevent convictions being based upon evidence that has not

---

[64] For classic, if somewhat out-dated, illustrations of the workings of a range of continental
trials, see S Bedford, *The Faces of Justice: A Traveller's Report* (London, Collins, 1961).

[65] See B McKillop, 'Readings and Hearings in French Criminal Justice: Five Cases in the *Tribunal
Correctionnel*' (1998) 46 *American Journal of Comparative Law* 757.

[66] See, eg C Bradley, above n 34, at 1032; Damaska, *above* note 55, at 13–14.

[67] Damaska, *above* n 55, at 16–22. An exception is to be found in The Netherlands where a conviction can still not be based on the statement of a single witness and some jurisdictions demand that
convictions are not based purely on confession evidence: ibid, 21.

[68] See M Damaska, 'Of Hearsay and its Analogies' (1992) 76 *Minnesota Law Review* 425;
'Propensity Evidence in Continental Legal Systems' (1994) 70 *Chi-Kent Law Review* 55.

been subject to cross-examination.[69] These standards are hardly exclusionary rules in the classic common law sense, but they are constraints imposed on trial decision makers as decisions may not be justified on the basis of such evidence. What then is the explanation for this? The common law jury and the adversary system are commonly said to justify the rules of evidence in the adversarial trial. In continental jurisdictions principles and standards of evidence would seem to have emerged instead as part of the process of appellate review whereby appellate courts have made authoritative statements on what is to constitute adequate evidentiary support for the factual findings of the court below.[70]

It would seem that there is a need for legal systems to develop standards or principles of evidence to justify the factual basis for their decisions. We have seen that the constraints of litigation inevitably mean that decisions must be made in a state of evidential uncertainty. Decision rules allocate a system of error preference but beyond this it has been difficult in the legal arena to prescribe particular modes of inference for coming to decisions. Instead rules of evidence and procedure have been devised to give maximum credibility to the decisions that are reached. In recent times the need to give credibility to decisions would seem to require that, so far as possible, the fact-finding processes are conducted in the public arena, with evidence being elicited orally from those who can give the most direct evidence of the facts in issue and with an opportunity for cross-examination of these witnesses so that decisions are not based purely upon unsubstantiated hearsay. These rules are clearly addressed to the litigants and the triers of fact but also, most importantly, they are addressed to the wider public as a means of securing acceptance for the accuracy of verdicts. According to this theory, the principles of evidence are best explained therefore not on account of the frailty of lay fact finders nor on account of the deficient quality of evidence adduced in adversary litigation, but on account of the need for *any* system of litigation predicated on the application of law to justify its verdicts, *whoever* the triers of fact and *whatever* the particular procedural environment. To be sure, there will continue to be arguments about the most suitable tribunal for determining questions of fact and about the best procedural environment for reaching decisions of fact. In some climates there may be greater deference and authority given to triers of fact than in others and this may affect the degree to which evidence is regulated. However, this theory suggests that there will still be a need for public justification of the basis for these decisions and rules of evidence play an important public role in this justification.

---

[69] As breaching Art 6(3)(d) of the European Convention on Human Rights: see, eg *Kostovski v Netherlands* (1990) 12 EHRR 434.

[70] Damaska, *above* n 55, 22.

8 THE MODERN CRIMINAL TRIAL UNDER CHALLENGE

It has been argued that the rules of evidence and procedure developed for the criminal trial may be seen as a rational response to the constraints imposed on legal fact finding. Legal systems need to find conclusive means of settling disputes, especially in the criminal arena where it is unacceptable to leave people in a state of uncertainty about accusations and where the judgments reached can have coercive consequences for them. Given the uncertainty that attaches to making findings of fact about the past, it has been impossible to establish definitive methods for reaching certainty about the events in dispute. Instead there has been a need for a process like the criminal trial to attempt to bring finality to the various contested claims by having them tested and justified. Within this process the rules of evidence serve the purposes of guiding the various participants on how to present and justify the claims made and of justifying to a wider public that the best is being done to reach an accurate conclusion.

In order for the verdicts that arise from criminal trials to be accepted, however, it is arguably not enough for there to be a public adjudication where public standards and principles are applied to justify the decision. In the eighteenth century trial where the public regularly attended the trial spectacle, the public trial was available for all to see.[71] But for the trial process to win acceptance among a larger populace, the legal system has to have ambassadors and other conduits to represent its procedures in the best light. Farmer has shown how throughout the nineteenth century historical trial narratives played a central role in constructing a broader cultural understanding and legitimation of the adversarial criminal trial in England and Scotland.[72] It would seem that during this period the legal system was largely successful in promoting a positive image of the criminal trial. This was to change in the twentieth century, however, when a variety of forces came to undermine the legitimacy of the trial as a process that can produce accurate verdicts.

One of these has been a greater willingness to subject established institutions to greater public scrutiny and accountability.[73] This demand for greater accountability has not escaped the justice system.[74] Campaigns on behalf of victims and defendants, focusing often on particular *causes célèbres*, have drawn attention to deficiencies in the system. Investigative journalists have cast doubt

---

[71] Hay, *supra* n 50, at 27–28.

[72] L Farmer, 'Notable Trials and the Criminal Law in Scotland and England 1750–1900', in P Chassaigne and J-P Genet (eds), *Droit et société en France et en Grande-Bretagne (XII–XX siècles). Fonctions, usages et représentations* (Paris, Publications de la Sorbonne, 2003).

[73] This began with calls for government to be more accountable but has extended to all public services: see D Oliver and G Drewry, *Public Service Reforms: Issues of Accountability and Public Law* (London, Pinter, 1996).

[74] This scrutiny has even extended to demanding that jury decision making which has traditionally been shrouded in secrecy be made more accountable: see Jackson, *above* n 48.

on the accuracy of verdicts in specific cases by pointing to gaps in the evidence presented at trial or to mistakes that were made in the assessment of evidence.[75] Although many of these revelations have exposed deficiencies in the pre-trial investigation rather than at the trial itself, the trial process has inevitably been compromised by reaching verdicts that have not been accurate. The deficiencies have been remedied by imposing more rigorous standards of investigation and prosecution in the pre-trial process. A less coercive regime for interviewing suspects has been introduced, requiring interviews to be tape recorded and giving suspects the right to a solicitor.[76] Prosecution standards have been tightened up with the creation for the first time in 1985 of a fully professional prosecution service to review every case that the police have charged.[77] A statutory disclosure regime requiring the defence to be given notice of material which the prosecution do not intend to use at trial has also been established.[78] As greater pre-trial regulation has been established, so some of the excesses of the adversarial trial system have been mitigated and there has been growing pressure for some of the more rigid exclusionary rules such as the hearsay rule to be relaxed at trial.[79] More recently, reform proposals aimed at bettering the lot of victims in the criminal justice system have included relaxing other rules such as the character evidence rules so that triers of fact gain more knowledge of offences committed by the accused in the past which are similar to those charged.[80]

Just as the criminal trial has had to be accommodated to public criticism, however, another arguably more fundamental challenge has come to the fore from the domain of science. In the early twentieth century, experimental psychologists challenged methods of eliciting testimony at trial and although this did not prompt a re-examination of the traditional adversarial methods of examination and cross-examination,[81] the legal system has had to refine its approach towards certain kinds of witness testimony such as children's evidence.[82] More critical has been the growth in forensic science which has enabled challenges to be made to particular trial outcomes. The growth of particular

---

[75] See Woffinden, *above* n 4.

[76] See the Police and Criminal Evidence Act 1984.

[77] See the Prosecution of Offences Act 1985.

[78] See the Criminal Procedure and Investigations Act 1996.

[79] Much of the impetus for relaxation of the rules came from the Eleventh Report of the Criminal Law Revision Committee in 1972. Although some its proposals including those calling for a relaxation of the right of silence were heavily criticised at the time, many of its proposals have seen the light of day in the intervening 30 years.

[80] See Home Office, *Justice for All* (2002), Cm 5563 and the proposals in the Criminal Justice Bill 2003.

[81] For an account of the fierce debate engendered by the work of experimental psychologists, see D S Greer, 'Anything but the Truth? The Reliability of Testimony in Criminal Trials' (1971) 11 *British Journal of Criminology* 131.

[82] For an account of the special provisions permitting the video-recording of children's evidence before trial, see J Spencer and R Flin, *Children's Evidence* (London, Blackstone, 1992). Recent legislation has proposed extending these provisions to other vulnerable witnesses: see Youth Justice and Criminal Evidence Act 1999. See L Ellison, *The Adversarial Process and the Vulnerable Witness* (Oxford, Clarendon, 2001).

techniques such as DNA profiling, has led in the last ten years in the United States to the uncovering of numerous miscarriages of justice and has caused legislatures and courts to reconsider their approach towards the death penalty.[83]

All this has inevitably challenged the criminal trial's ability to bring finality to legal proceedings. It has led to large numbers of cases being challenged on appeal and has caused legislatures to relax a number of finality rules. In the United States, for example, a number of jurisdictions have enacted statutes allowing convicted prisoners access to DNA testing.[84] Statutes of limitations have been increased in respect of crimes for which DNA evidence may be available and prosecutors have executed 'John Doe' warrants identifying suspects by their DNA so that arrests may be made when their DNA turns up in databanks. In the United Kingdom the ability of DNA evidence to show that certain defendants have been wrongly acquitted in the past has sparked a debate about whether the long standing double jeopardy rule should be abandoned in certain kinds of cases.[85]

Beyond undermining the trial's ability to bring finality to proceedings, these developments also present a direct challenge to the methods of the trial by suggesting that scientific methods can produce more accurate results. It has been argued that in the absence of a definitive manner of establishing the truth about a defendant's guilt, the strength of the trial has been that in the face of the uncertainty that attaches to making judgments about past events, it establishes a basis for resolving disputes about evidence and justifying the outcome to the community. Safeguards such as a fair and public hearing together with rules of evidence have helped to justify the outcome by providing defendants with a mechanism for disputing the claims made against them. But if science can show that it has superior methods of fact finding which can claim to take away the uncertainty surrounding past events, this may be said to eradicate the need for evidence to be presented in a trial process at all. There would still be a need for a formal legal procedure to proclaim the accused's guilt and determine sentence. But the need for formal rules and procedures to govern contested claims about the evidence might no longer be necessary.[86]

We are a long way from this yet. For one thing it is a mistake to assume that the methods that scientists use are necessarily more reliable than the methods of non-scientists. It is true that the natural sciences have been so successful that we tend to give precedence to scientific explanations over other forms of knowledge.[87] This has led to a naïve belief, which the courts themselves have sometimes perpetuated, whereby all scientific knowledge is assumed to be

[83] See B Scheck, P Neufeld and J Dwyer, *Actual Innocence* (New York, Doubleday, 1999). See also http://www.innocenceproject.org.

[84] K Swedlow, 'Don't Believe Everything You Read: A Review of Modern "Post-Conviction" DNA Testing Statutes' (2002) 38 *California West Law Review* 355.

[85] See P Roberts, 'Double Jeopardy Law Reform: A Criminal Justice Commentary' (2002) 65 *Modern Law Review* 393.

[86] See, however, the arguments of R A Duff, *Trials and Punishments* (Cambridge, Cambridge University Press, 1986).

[87] S Richards, *Philosophy and Sociology of Science* (Oxford, Blackwell, 1987).

reliable knowledge. In the famous ruling in *Daubert v Merrell Dow Pharmaceuticals, Inc.* where the United States Supreme Court was faced with the difficult question of determining what the courts should count as 'expert' evidence, the majority of the Court took the view that the courts should look here not only for relevance, but for reliability and in doing this the courts should consider whether the evidence is really 'scientific . . . knowledge'.[88] Self-evidently, however, the equation of scientific knowledge with reliable knowledge does not help a court determine in a particular case whether certain evidence which professes to be scientific is reliable, for there have been many examples where scientists have been shown to be incompetent, mistaken or partisan. While the development of new techniques in forensic science has challenged the correctness of trial verdicts, there are plenty of examples in the miscarriages of justice in England and Wales in the 1970s and 1980s where forensic scientists made mistakes in the conclusions they reached from the tests they had performed.[89]

Nor is it correct to think that there is one scientific method which can help differentiate reliable science from unreliable science. The Supreme Court attempted to lay down tests to determine whether the proffered evidence had been subjected to a scientific methodology such as Popper's falsifiability thesis. But those philosophers of science whom the Court invoked in order to demarcate genuine and reliable science from other forms of knowledge did not claim that their theories could distinguish between reliable and unreliable evidence.[90] It is a mistake to think that there is one particular 'scientific method' used by all scientists and only scientists. While we do associate certain qualities with science such as rationality, consistency, objectivity and accuracy, these are qualities that are associated with non-scientific empirical inquiries as well. It has been suggested that every kind of empirical inquiry, from everyday questions as to why a bus was delayed to more complex inquiries of historians, detectives and scientists, involves making guesses about the explanation of some event, figuring out the consequences of its being true, and checking how well those stand up to evidence.[91] While this approach is adopted within all inquiry, scientists have, of course, developed complex instruments and techniques to advance their particular fields of knowledge, but these techniques are not used by all scientists and do not guarantee reliable results. Techniques vary according to what is acceptable within scientific communities where what counts as knowledge is not

[88] 509 US 579, 113 S Ct 2786 (1993).
[89] See Royal Commission on Criminal Justice, *Report* (1993) Cm 2263. The locus classicus on the subject is to be found in Glidewell LJ's judgment in *R v Ward* [1993] 1 WLR 619, 674: 'For lawyers, jurors and judges a forensic scientist conjures up the image of a man in a white coat working in a laboratory, approaching his task with cold neutrality, and dedicated only to the pursuit of scientific truth. It is a sombre thought that the reality is sometimes different.'
[90] For a penetrating critique of the Supreme Court's decision in *Daubert*, see S Haack, 'Disentangling Daubert: An Epistemological Study in Theory and Practice' (2003) *Science in the Law*. Newsletter of the American Philosophical Association.
[91] Ibid.

simply the result of following one particular scientific method but of what practices have become conventionally accepted within a particular scientific community.[92]

It is therefore mistaken to think that there is some unique scientific mode of inquiry to which the factual claims in legal disputes should be subjected.[93] This is not to deny that the growth of scientific knowledge poses considerable challenges to the traditional manner in which these claims have been resolved. It is noteworthy how many issues of fact are increasingly coming within the domain of expert or scientific evidence.[94] This 'creeping scientisation of factual inquiry,' as it has been called,[95] has arisen as a result of science's ability to generate knowledge by means of sophisticated technical instruments well beyond the ken of laypersons. Just as significant has been the growth in the sciences of the mind which has had led to the recognition of new forms of psychological evidence such as post-traumatic stress disorder, battered women's syndrome, rape trauma syndrome, recovered memory syndrome and the like. Even the task of assessing the credibility of witnesses which has been considered best left to the common sense of the lay jury has now been challenged by the growth of experts willing to testify on witness credibility and by such 'scientific' techniques as polygraph evidence. All this has posed difficult questions of admissibility for the courts of the kind that the Supreme Court tried to solve in *Daubert*. But it also challenges the traditional means of eliciting evidence by examination and cross-examination. Are those who testify to such advances to be treated simply as ordinary witnesses by the courts? And does it make sense for juries, or even judges, to retain supremacy over the fact finding domain if they are being asked to assess evidence well beyond their competence?

All this challenges the traditional mode of proof in adversary trial procedures which have set so much store on oral evidence elicited by witnesses in a concentrated hearing and assessed by lay fact finders. Although it is unlikely to subvert the adversarial trial completely, it may be that scientific evidence will have to be integrated more effectively into existing procedures, with accredited experts given a greater role in the assessment of evidence than hitherto, and trial fact finders a more active role in interacting with experts so that they can understand what they say. This may have repercussions for the concentrated trial as lay jurors may require more time to be educated about the evidence. Already there is a greater willingness for certain witnesses to give evidence at pre-trial hearings which are video recorded.[96] In this manner the trial may come to resemble more a continental-style review of scientific evidence and witness evidence already

[92] For further discussion see Nobles and Schiff, *above* n 30, at 186–87.

[93] For further limitations on the use of scientific evidence in legal settings, see P Roberts, 'Science, Experts and Criminal Justice', in M McConville and G Wilson (eds), *The Handbook of the Criminal Justice Process* (Oxford, Oxford University Press, 2002) 253.

[94] See M Redmayne, *Expert Evidence and Criminal Justice* (Oxford, Clarendon Press, 2001).

[95] Damaska, *above* n 55, at 143.

[96] *Above* n 82.

elicited rather than the climactic event to which all attention is drawn in the criminal process.[97]

But it may be doubted whether scientists themselves will ever be able provide a complete alternative to the trial format. Efforts are being made to use artificial intelligence to simulate models of common sense reasoning and it is tempting to think that advances such as these hold the key for future factual inquiries within law.[98] We have seen how, in the past, seemingly magical or irrational elements accepted by the community were allowed to permeate the trial to give verdicts the seal of certainty and finality. For some, science may seem like the new saviour as there is an attraction in the verdict being based on hard evidence and models of formal reasoning rather than on the frailties of common sense reasoning. But the difficulty, as sociologists of science have been saying for some time, is that scientists can disagree as much as other witnesses can disagree and reach different interpretations of reality.[99] It is, indeed, in the nature of scientific endeavour constantly to seek better evidence, to be prepared to revise even the most entrenched claim in the face of unfavourable evidence.[100] This chapter has argued that this spirit of inquiry is incompatible with the constraints of legal inquiry where decisions have to be reached in the interest of finality. It is suggested therefore that although legal inquiries may have much to learn from science, the criminal trial will be with us for some time while continuing to evolve, borrowing models of proof from elsewhere, in the face of the continuing need to bring finality to contested claims.

---

[97] On the growing convergence between inquisitorial and adversarial systems, see P Fennell, C Harding, N Jorg and B Swart (eds), *Criminal Justice in Europe: A Comparative Study* (Oxford, Clarendon Press, 1995).

[98] See the forthcoming special issue on papers delivered at a conference on Inference, Culture and Ordinary Thinking in Dispute Resolution to be published in the *Journal of Law, Probability and Risk.*

[99] See, eg B Barnes, D Bloor and J Henry, *Scientific Knowledge: A Sociological Analysis* (Chicago, Chicago University Press, 1996).

[100] See S Haack, 'Inquiry and Advocacy, Fallibilism and Finality: Culture and Inference in Science and the law' (2004)(forthcoming).

8

Nothing But the Truth? Some Facts, Impressions and Confessions about Truth in Criminal Procedure

HEIKE JUNG

1 INTRODUCTION

TRUTH IS MORE than just a first principle in law and procedure, in science, in politics, in social life. Truth is an essential, and for many the essential, moral value of humanity. It relates to honesty and reliability, but also to progress. In many social settings the question 'true or false' is the ultimate test, almost synonymous with right or wrong. Only recently, the activities of the South African Commission for Truth and Reconciliation have shown the extent to which social peace depends on truth.[1] A forensic setting such as a criminal trial is, of course, somewhat unique and follows its own rules, though even then the search for truth in the criminal process cannot be disassociated from the general prospect of discovery and sincerity in communication.

The ranking of truth among the highest of moral values is not uncontested. Hobbes' famous statement '*auctoritas, non veritas facit legem*' (authority, not truth makes law) indicates that there are rival contenders for this position, which at least requires that we are sensitive to historical changes in the balance between values. Not telling the truth may be motivated and justified for different reasons. In some cases disclosure will amount to self-destruction or entail serious personal harm to others. As a lawyer, I am of course convinced of the formula that truth should not be sought at any price,[2] a formula which stands

---

[1] Interestingly enough the commission distinguishes between 'factual and forensic', 'social', 'personal and narrative' and 'healing and restorative' truth: Truth and Reconciliation Commission of South Africa, *Report* (Cape Town SA, Juta 1998), vol I, 111–14.

[2] This formula has been coined by *Entscheidungen des Bundesgerichtshofes in Strafsachen* (BGHSt) vol 14, 358 (365).

in marked contrast to that other well known formula, 'I do solemnly swear to tell the truth, the whole truth, and nothing but the truth.'

Historians have become disillusioned as to the reliability of memory which introduces subjectivism and margins of interpretation into the fact-finding process. The French social historian Noiriel reminds us that: '*Le regard que les historiens portent sur le passé est fortement tributaire de leur expérience vécue.*'[3] We know already that truth cannot be 'found', and that it can only be reconstructed should be of help in preventing constant frustration, since absolute correspondence is an illusion, perhaps not even an ideal perspective. Beginning with the concept of reconstruction entails a somewhat reduced programme which may allow us to cope better with the inherent limitations of the project and to pay tribute to rival interests.

Thus, rival general concepts of truth and discovery impose themselves commandingly on 'truth in adjudication',[4] commonly embodied in the juxtaposition of correspondence and consensus theories. Moreover, our fact-finding takes place in procedural contexts with potentially diverse objectives and structures. Therefore, we will have to look more closely at the particulars of legal proceedings, their theoretical background, their cross-cultural differences and their ritual character.[5]

2 TRUTH AND THE AIMS OF PROCEDURE

Neumann has eloquently defended the concept of objective truth against functionalisation.[6] He opposes Luhmann's '*Legitimation durch Verfahren*' (legitimation through procedure),[7] which disconnects the process from the material programme of substantive law. This controversy recalls the traditional German preference for substantive law, with procedure being limited to the function of serving substantive rules.[8] In essence this boils down to the question of whether the moral backdrop of law is derived from the confirmation of the objective truth, that is from reaching a result in accordance with the law as it stands, or from the respect for a certain procedure or from both. Rosen carries this insti-

---

[3] 'The gaze which historians bring to bear on the past is strongly derived from their own lived experience' (my translation): G Noiriel, *Penser avec, penser contre. Itinéraire d'un historien*, (Paris, Belin, 2003) 4.

[4] Adopting the title of an article by M Damaška, (1998) 49 *Hastings Law Journal* 289.

[5] For the ritual aspect see A Legnaro and A Aengenheister, *Die Aufführung von Strafrecht. Kleine Ethnographie gerichtlichen Verhandelns* (Baden-Baden, Nomos, 1999).

[6] U Neumann, 'Funktionale Wahrheit im Strafverfahren', in L Philipps & H Scholler (eds), *Jenseits des Funktionalismus* (Heidelberg, Decker & Müller, 1989) 72.

[7] First published in 1969. Cf the critical comments by D Krauß, 'Das Prinzip der materiellen Wahrheit im Strafprozeß', in *Festschrift für Schaffstein* (Göttingen, Schwartz, 1975) 411, 420.

[8] For a more general outlook on the German position see H Jung, 'Making Sense of the German "Straftatlehre"' in *Festskrift till Nils Jareborg* (Uppsala, Iustus Förlag, 2002) 369. See also J F Nijboer, 'Common Law Traditions in Evidence Scholarship Observed from a Continental Perspective' (1993) 41 *American Journal of Comparative Law* 299, at 319ff.

tutional aspect further when he speaks of the power of the courts to create things and the power of the law 'to make things by declaring them so.'[9] Yet, as if he wanted to reconcile Neumann's and Luhmann's position, he continues:

> There always remains this curious relationship between the ability of the law to make things so by saying they are so and the evident need to perform this task in a way that remains broadly consonant with the sources of the judiciary's own legitimacy.[10]

Dwelling on Rosen's own ethnological research on qadi justice we realise that the idea of 'legitimation through procedure' is only a sophisticated version of a more general paradigm: the relevance of truth in procedure may depend on the aims and the relevance of procedure in the settlement of conflicts. Let me be more specific: if the procedure is aimed at the re-establishing of broken personal ties between the litigants this relational aspect may outweigh any striving for truth, or at least call for a specific approach to it.[11] Equally, if criminal procedure pursues the aim of rehabilitation, the process of discovery will be, at least partly, oriented towards a different goal.[12]

Procedures do not only address a legal issue; they also settle a social conflict. I suppose that Neumann, in his attempt to distance himself from Luhmann's position, did not really want to opt for or against the social embedding of procedures, but rather to relate the social effects of procedure and their regulatory potential to the search for material truth. The term 'striving' allows for restrictions, but also for competing considerations. The main contender here is the protection of privacy, which has been implemented in law in a variety of forms, from the right to silence, exclusionary rules of evidence and professional privileges to the prohibition of torture. In this area the personal values which are at stake require a balancing process.[13] Such normative aspirations are often viewed as inherent restrictions on the process of discovery, yet they should rather be conceived as the normative presuppositions of this process.[14] It would not be compatible with the peace-keeping function of the criminal process for the procedure to end with the destruction of those who are involved in the evidentiary process.

This relates to the classical antagonism between 'Funktionstüchtigkeit der Strafrechtspflege' and 'schützende Formen', or to Packer's more or less analogous antagonism between crime control and due process. A crime control model will be tempted to 'establish' a case—to find the truth by whatever means. A due process model will provide in-built detours.[15] These detours are not simply

---

[9] L Rosen, *The Anthropology of Justice* (Cambridge, Cambridge University Press, 1989) 20.
[10] Ibid.
[11] For the classical example of qadi justice see Rosen, ibid, at 20ff.
[12] For further reading see H Müller-Dietz, 'Der Wahrheitsbegriff im Strafverfahren', (1971) 15 *Zeitschrift für Evangelische Ethik* 257.
[13] T Weigend, 'Is the Criminal Process about Truth?: A German Perspective' (2003) 26 *Harvard Journal of Law and Public Policy* 157, at 168.
[14] For a classic statement, see W Hassemer, 'Konstanten kriminalpolitischer Theorie' in *Festschrift für Lange* (Berlin and New York, de Gruyter, 1976) 501.
[15] D Salas, 'Etat et droit pénal' (1992) 15 *Droits* 77, at 78.

complications on the way to the same end. They may well lead to a different end, since one has to adapt to the routes that are available. It is worth recalling that the European Court of Human Rights has in *Klass* stated that 'the Contracting States may not, in the name of the struggle against espionage and terrorism adopt whatever measures they deem appropriate.'[16] Equally, the concept of a right to be tried on evidence not obtained by the violation of fundamental rights alludes to a particular method for the fabrication of truth which does not allow for a free-floating discovery process.[17] This is not only a question of method but also of content.

3 CORRESPONDENCE V CONSENSUS

Our approach to truth is somehow intertwined with the aims and role of procedure. This sheds some light on the theories of truth, but it does not give a complete answer to the question of which theory we should follow. The rival contenders are well known: the debate has traditionally been focused on correspondence and consensus theories of truth.[18] Damaška has recently made a strong case for the reconciliation of correspondence theories of truth with social constructionism, and at the same time rejected consensus theories of truth as a foundation for fact-finding arrangements in legal proceedings. He worries about conflating truth with the successful justification of knowledge claims and wonders about how far the consensus idea should be carried in criminal procedure:

> Should it encompass the criminal defendant? Should witnesses be permitted to confer with one another to establish whether they can reach an agreement on what they witnessed?[19]

Still, in opting for 'correspondence' he underestimates the dynamics of a reconstruction process which degrades correspondence to the rank of a pious wish.[20]

The attraction of consensus models flows not only from the apparent deficiencies of the correspondence model, but from a certain mixture of conceptual and methodological aspects. However, the emphasis on process differs from Luhmann's concept of 'legitimation through procedure', as consensus models

---

[16] *Klass v Germany*, Series A No 28, §49.

[17] Discussed by A J Ashworth, *Serious Crime, Human Rights and Criminal Procedure* (London, Sweet & Maxwell, 2002) 35ff.

[18] The 'linguistic turn' in philosophical theories of truth, embodied in the various deflationary theories, does not—for our procedural purposes—help us to avoid the predicament of having to choose between suboptimal approaches, ie consensus or correspondence. For further details see R Poscher, 'Wahrheit und Recht. Wahrheitsfragen des Rechts im Lichte deflationärer Wahrheitstheorie' [2003] *Archiv für Rechts- und Sozialphilosophie* 200.

[19] Damaška, n 4 above, at 296.

[20] W Hassemer, 'Das Selbstverständnis der Strafrechtswissenschaft gegenüber den Herausforderungen ihrer Zeit' in A Eser, W Hassemer and B Burkhardt (eds), *Die Deutsche Strafrechtswissenschaft vor der Jahrtausendwende* (München, Beck, 2000) 34ff, speaks of a 'false promise'.

relate instead to Habermas' discourse theory.[21] In its original version discourse theory presupposes that normative consensus (ie truth) is reached by way of exchanging arguments in a setting that is free from repression.[22] That said, we immediately sense the inherent restrictions of a consensus model in criminal procedure because of the question of power. This question has two sides. On the one hand, it implies the balancing of inequalities, and the establishment of legal safeguards and so on. On the other hand, we cannot disregard the fact that criminal law, if need be, will be executed by force. Thus, in most instances, 'procedural consensus' will at best be acceptance on the part of the 'underdog'.

The Anglo-American and Scottish approach to fact-finding in procedure is not in contradiction with the correspondence model. Rather it starts out from the assumption, perhaps the illusion, that the existence of rival parties with their selfish interests, in short the adversarial principle, guarantees an optimal output of valid information.[23] Of course, Anglo-American lawyers do occasionally give the impression that they believe in adversarialism, and not truth, as the basic theme of criminal procedure, as the refinement of the adversarial method becomes an end in itself. The detrimental side-effects of this endeavour may jeopardise the credibility of the criminal justice system in general.[24]

4 PATHS TO TRUTH

The contribution of John Jackson and Sean Doran to the Jerusalem colloquium on 'Rights of the Accused, Crime Control and Protection of Victims' was entitled 'Addressing the Adversarial Deficit in Non-Jury Criminal Trials'.[25] Admittedly, this title is not without a provocative touch for me as a continental European lawyer who is always tempted rather to address the inquisitorial deficits in jury trials. However, I hesitate to take sides in the contest between rival procedural models, or to be more precise, I opt for compromise solutions. Let me illustrate this by way of personal experience. My position when discussing adversarial versus inquisitorial models of criminal procedure depends on where I am. In an Anglo-American and Scottish context I insist on the short-comings of an adversarial procedure with a more or less passive judge, whereas in a German or French context I plead for the strengthening of participatory elements. A visit to the ex-Yugoslavia Court at the Hague taught me a

---

[21] For a recent appraisal of discourse theories and criminal procedure, see H Radtke, 'Das Strafverfahren als Diskurs' in *Festschrift für H.L. Schreiber* (Heidelberg, C F Müller, 2003) 375.

[22] For further details, see G Ellscheid's critical account 'Zur Kritik der diskurstheoretischen Begründung von Demokratie' in *Il diritto e la differenza. Scritti in onore di Alessandro Baratta* (Lecce, Pensa, 2002) 75.

[23] Weigend, n 13 above, at 159ff.

[24] Cf W T Pizzi, *Trials without Truth* (New York and London, NYU Press, 1999). This does not mean that I endorse Pizzi's critical account of the American trial system, since I do not share his basic assumption that truth would profit from the curtailing of defendants' rights.

[25] (1997) 31 *Israel Law Review* 645.

lesson about the inefficiency of a trial structure which does not allow for judicial intervention in the truth-finding process.[26] After an hour of patient and attentive listening to the defence, I only realised what the whole thing was about thanks to Presiding Judge Schomburg's intervention from the bench. This type of trial shows that the judge should not remain behind a veil of ignorance. Of course, as a judge of a court of first instance I never looked at the file, but in this situation I was not the presiding judge and I did not have to cope with cases that dragged on for months—in which case even the most experienced judge will be lost at the beginning, and thus perhaps throughout, without some advance knowledge.

You need not be afraid, as I am not going to rehearse the whole debate about adversarial versus inquisitorial models of fact-finding.[27] I can summarise my own position as follows.

First, the antagonism is overrated. Here I follow Goldstein:

> The operation of any model and of the procedure reflecting it will depend upon the interaction of many factors: the normative content of the standards to be applied in making decisions, how the participants are perceived and trained, the controls introduced at strategic points, and the resources assigned to implement policies and controls.[28]

Above all, 'the end result of the search for the truth in inquisitorial systems will often be strikingly similar to that of the adversarial process—a half-truth based on what the defendant and more or less interested third parties are willing to disclose.'[29] Thus, theorising about procedural structures cannot be restricted to a rehearsal of the debate about inquisitorial versus adversarial procedure. On the one hand we have to reach beyond this popular dichotomy in order to get a more complete, and perhaps a more meaningful, picture of the convergence and diversity of procedure. The structural problems do not necessarily follow such superficial classifications, but rather run along the line of such meta-principles and meta-conflicts as fairness, checks and balances, procedural transparency, democracy versus professionalism and so on.[30] On the other hand, meticulous

---

[26] For a closer view of the structure of international criminal procedure, see K Ambos, 'International Criminal Procedure: "Adversarial", "Inquisitorial" or Mixed?' (2003) 3 *International Criminal Law Review* 1.

[27] See inter alia A Goldstein, 'Reflections on Two Models. Inquisitorial Themes in American Criminal Procedure' (1971) 26 *Stanford Law Review* 1009; A Goldstein and M Marcus, 'The Myth of Judicial Supervision in Three "Inquisitorial" Systems: France, Italy and Germany' (1977) 87 *Yale Law Journal* 240; J Herrmann, 'Various Models of Criminal Proceedings' [1978] *S African Journal of Criminal Law and Criminology* 3; M Damaška, 'Models of Criminal Procedure' (2002) 51 *Zbornik (collected papers of Zagreb Law School)* 477.

[28] Goldstein, n 27 above, at 1021.

[29] Weigend, n 13 above, at 161.

[30] H Jung, 'Der Strafprozeß: Konzepte, Modelle und Grundannahmen' in *Festschrift für Waltoś* (Warzaw, Wydawnictwa Prwnicze PWN, 2001) 27; D Krauß, 'Rechtsstaat und Strafprozeß im Vergleich' in *Festgabe zum Schweizerischen Juristentag* (Basel, Helbing & Lichtenhain, 1985) 171.

comparative research at the level of the practical implementation of criminal procedure will help to overcome this stage of mere name-calling.[31]

Secondly, in addition to this, the debate is somewhat obfuscated by mutual misunderstandings as to what is meant by the terms inquisitorial and adversarial. Even at the level of a theoretical debate it is no longer possible to come forward with a pure model of inquisitorial or adversarial procedure, which makes me doubt, contrary to Gane,[32] whether the terms remain useful analytical tools. Nobody, I presume, wants to return to the historical situation where the roles of judge, prosecutor and defence are confused or where torture is routinely used to extract confessions. Indeed, I cannot imagine any procedure which does not allow 'moves for evidence' by either party. Section 244(3) of the German Code of Criminal Procedure (*StPO*), for example, allows for special motions which can only be rejected under certain enumerated conditions, so that this 'right to move for evidence' (*Beweisantragsrecht*) is considered to be a very powerful weapon in the hands of the defence.[33] Equally, it is popular to associate adversarial trials with the autonomy and dignity of the accused, values which supposedly cannot be guaranteed by the inquisitorial trial.[34] However, this argument overlooks the fact that the idea of the accused as an object of procedure was abandoned a long time ago. It is more useful to take note of the fact that a human rights oriented perspective has led to a 'conceptual overhaul' of (inquisitorial) procedural systems, than to battle with an outdated version of a particular model.

Thirdly, it is of course relevant to consider your starting point. I take the view that participatory elements in evidentiary procedure should be optimised. However, forms of adversarial procedure which do not provide for self-restraint by the prosecution or compensatory mechanisms for the court to balance inefficiencies on the side of the defence may fail to meet the standard of fairness.

Fourthly, often enough the case is already 'settled' before the trial starts. Wolter has argued that, in the German context, the phase of preliminary

[31] For further insight, see H Jung (ed), *Der Strafprozeß im Spiegel ausländischer Verfahrensordnungen* (Berlin and New York, de Gruyter, 1990); C Van den Wyngaert in *Criminal Procedure Systems in the European Community* (London, Butterworths, 1993); M Delmas-Marty (ed), *Procédures pénales d'Europe*, (Paris, Presses Universitaires de France, 1995); P Fennell, C Harding, N Jörg and B Swart(eds), *Criminal Justice in Europe. A Comparative Study* (Oxford, Clarendon, 1995); J Hatchard, B Huber and R Vogler, *Comparative Criminal Procedure* (London, BIICL, 1996); C M Bradley (ed), *Criminal Procedure. A Worldwide View* (Durham NC, Carolina Academic Press, 1999).

[32] C Gane, 'Classifying Scottish Criminal Procedure' in P Duff and N Hutton (eds), *Criminal Justice in Scotland* (Dartmouth/Aldershot, Ashgate, 1999) 56.

[33] For a general rehearsal of the issue of control of the fact finding process, see H Jung, 'Appellate Review of Judicial Fact-Finding Processes and Decisions' (1997) 31 *Israel Law Review* 690.

[34] The deeply rooted procedural cliché of the juxtaposition of adversarial and inquisitorial is also revealed in the reasons for the decision of the Trial Chamber of the ICTY in the Milošević case to refuse to assign a defence counsel against the will of the accused. The Trial Chamber was wrong to base its decision on the concept of adversarialism. It should rather have invoked the principle of fairness: *Prosecutor v Slobodan Milošević* , Case No IT-02-54. Reasons for decision on the prosecution motion concerning assignment of counsel (4 April 2003).

investigation is the central part and high point of the process.[35] The current German debate is about introducing more participatory elements at this early stage of proceedings since it is clear that the preliminary investigations leave their indelible mark on the hearing.[36] In any case, greater attention should be paid to the pre-trial phase and its role in shaping the truth.

Finally, it may be that the confusion of models is linked to the reciprocal intrusions that have taken place in recent years, stimulated by the fact that in Europe we are operating under the auspices of the European Convention on Human Rights. It makes more sense to distil elements of a common standard from the Strasbourg court's ample case material than to cling to historical myths.[37] Instead of perpetuating the traditional divide we should take note of the fact that the concept of fairness, or its functional equivalent the '*Rechtsstaat*', provide an uncontested common platform for discussion. In the light of the ongoing Europeanisation of criminal law and procedure the development is programmed towards convergence rather than the traditional divide.

5 IMPOSSIBILIUM NULLA EST OBLIGATIO

Legal proceedings are not a simple recapitulation of a past occurrence. It is never possible simply to reconstruct the exact actions or utterances that gave rise to the case at hand. No witness can precisely remember what was once said, heard or seen, and even the videotape of an undisputed crime cannot reveal the state of mind of the accused. Faced with such uncertainties any legal system must cope with the problem of defining as well as discovering facts.[38] Vico goes even further with his fundamental distinction between '*verum et certum*'. Here *verum* denotes the area of a priori knowledge which can only extend to what the knower himself has created. In his own words: 'the criterion and the rule of truth is to have made it.'[39] Historians, to whom we might turn for help, since they are constantly engaged in finding the truth about past events, disillusion us even further. Johannes Fried, the Frankfurt historian, not only questions the reliability of memory but also the reliability of documents. According to him we can never be sure that they are a true chronicle of past events.[40]

---

[35] J Wolter, *Aspekte einer Strafprozeßreform bis 2007* (München, Beck, 1991) 35.

[36] B Bannenberg et al, *Alternativ-Entwurf Reform des Ermittlungsverfahrens (AE-EV)* (München, Beck, 2002).

[37] Eg R Esser, *Auf dem Weg zu einem europäischen Strafverfahrensrecht* (Berlin, de Gruyter, 2001).

[38] Rosen, n 9 above, at 20.

[39] Quoted in Isaiah Berlin, 'Against the Current' in H Hardy (ed), *Vico's Concept of Knowledge* (London, Pimlico, 1997) 111.

[40] See the illuminating case study by J Fried, 'Recht und Verfassung im Spannungsfeld von Mündlichkeit und kollektiver Erinnerung. Eheschluss und Königserhebung Heinrichs I' in *Festschrift für Dilcher* (Berlin, Erich Schmidt, 2003).

'Memory is pure presence! The remembered past is nothing but contemporary time though in the mode of the past . . .'.[41] Whatever we are looking for will be tainted by the presuppositions of the particular era in which we live. The trial against Galileo Galilei and its revision centuries later shows that sometimes society is not yet ready for the truth. Even today, criminologists argue about the question of whether and to what extent it may be permissible to hide the truth from the public at large. Truth will have to be accepted as such, an idea which fits better with the concept of '*auctoritas*' than that of '*veritas*'.

Moreover, there are situations in which we readily acknowledge that there are good reasons not to bother with a too thorough investigation of the truth. Criminal trials are costly endeavours. They lead to intrusions into the private life of many people. In Germany for example, only twenty per cent of all indictable cases end up in a court trial.[42] Likewise in the USA fully-fledged jury trials are rare events. Of course, yielding to expediency does not mean that we are no longer interested in the truth. However, anyone who tells me that charge or plea bargaining is a process which has to do with truth risks no longer being taken seriously. Thus, the whole concept of plea bargaining has dealt a devastating blow to the idea that we should be aiming for the truth. All we can say instead is that it can be called in support of procedural efficiency—or perhaps for the case of the consensus theory provided the partners have really negotiated on an equal footing.[43]

6 RECONSTRUCTION AFTER DECONSTRUCTION

The synthesis that follows this exercise in disillusionment is not very original. To begin with, we need more cross-cultural research into decision-making processes in criminal matters and their role in their respective societies.[44] This kind of research will confirm the relevance of the institutional component of truth, that is to say the way that the role and task of decision-makers oscillates between discovery and construction.[45] This institutional aspect favours a constructionist approach. Such an approach receives further support for pragmatic reasons: litigation cannot drag on endlessly, resources are limited, witnesses are fallible, confessions can be false, documents can be forged and so on. In these

[41] 'Erinnerung ist pure Gegenwart! Erinnerte Vergangenheit ist stets gegenwärtige Zeit, wenn auch im Modus der Vergangenheit . . .' (my translation): Fried, ibid, at 301.
[42] See W Heinz, 'Der Strafbefehl in der Rechtswirklichkeit' in *Festschrift für Müller-Dietz* (München, Beck, 2001) 271.
[43] For a more detailed account see H Jung, 'Plea Bargaining and its Repercussions on the Theory of Criminal Procedure' (1997) 5 *European Journal of Crime, Criminal Law & Criminal Justice* 112.
[44] Such as Rosen, n 9 above; H Jung, 'Zur Kadijustiz' in *Festschrift für Rolinski* (Baden-Baden, Nomos, 2002) 209.
[45] Cf W Ohler, 'Wahrheit als Geschichte. Eine prozessuale Alternative zum Aufschrei des Richters Wildermuth', in H Jung (ed), *Das Recht und die Schönen Künste* (Baden-Baden, Nomos, 1998) 63, putting the emphasis on '*erfinden*' (creation/construction) instead of '*finden*' (discovery).

circumstances it is hard to stick to a correspondence model. Or, as Lagarde has put it, the idea of truth barely survives the treatment it is subjected to in the course of the legal process.[46] However, it does not help to change sides and switch over to a consensus model, since this also suffers from deficiencies—though of a different kind.[47] The matter is complicated by the fact that both models form part of the internal world of doctrinal thought as well as of the external world of justification. From the point of view of justification a strong case can be made for the correspondence model: nobody will surely accept a system which starts out from the assumption that striving for the 'real' truth is immaterial.[48] This does not exclude, however, that the structure of the fact-finding process should be guided by the visions of discourse or consensus, though it is difficult to use this term in the 'shadow of the Leviathan'. In the end, procedures operate according to a set of normative aspirations for the settlement of conflicts and these put truth into perspective. It is not a value in itself, but is modulated by legal principles which include particular human rights standards and above all the principle of fairness.

[46] X Lagarde, 'Vérité et légitimité dans le droit de la preuve' (1996) *Droits* 31, at 32.

[47] Eg A Kaufmann, 'Läßt sich die Hauptverhandlung in Strafsachen als rationaler Diskurs auf-fassen?' in H Jung and H Müller-Dietz (eds), *Dogmatik und Praxis des Strafverfahrens* (Köln, Heymanns, 1989) 15.

[48] For an account upholding this vision of objective truth as a '*Leitbild*' (concept/model), see T Weigend, 'Unverzichtbares im Strafverfahrensrecht' (2001) 113 *Zeitschrift für die gesamte Strafrechtswissenschaft* 271, at 303ff.

9

The Distinctiveness of Trial Narrative

ROBERT P BURNS

1 INTRODUCTION:
DESCRIPTION, INTERPRETATION, AND EVALUATION

WITTGENSTEIN'S INJUNCTION TO 'Don't think, look!' gives us the first step to an adequate understanding of the trial, but only the first. As I have recently argued at length,[1] much more is afoot in the trial than our received philosophies of law would suggest. Indeed, an adequate understanding of the trial, 'the central institution of law as we know it,'[2] cannot but enrich our understanding of 'what law is.' I believe that the common law trial is one of our great cultural achievements, but that we need first to describe, then interpret, and finally 'think what we do,' as Hannah Arendt liked to put it, in order to fully appreciate it. Finally, the most adequate interpretation of the account of the 'consciously structured hybrid of languages' that make up the trial will have an idealising quality. It will be 'partly evaluative, since it consists in the identification of the principles which both best "fit" or cohere with the settled law and practices of a legal system *and also provide the best moral justification for them, thus showing the law "in its best light."* '[3] These principles will turn out to be situated ideals, ideals already implicit in the practices that constitute the trial. And so the best account can be justified only in the same way that the best judgment can be achieved at trial, hermeneutically, 'by the mutual support of many considerations of everything fitting together into one coherent whole.'[4] The method for an adequate interpretation of the trial must involve 'a continuous dialectical tacking between the most local of local detail and the most global of global structures in such a way as to bring both into view

[1] R Burns, *A Theory of the Trial* (Princeton, Princeton University Press, 1999).

[2] J White, *From Expectation to Experience: Essays on Law and Legal Education* (Ann Arbor, University of Michigan Press, 1999) 108.

[3] H L A Hart, *The Concept of Law* (2nd ed, Oxford, Oxford University Press, 1994) 239–41, quoting R Dworkin, *Law's Empire* (Cambridge, Belknap Press, 1986) 90.

[4] J Rawls, *A Theory of Justice* (Cambridge, Mass, Harvard University Press, 1971) 579.

simultaneously.'[5] Such an account is reflexive, an interpretation of an interpretation. The criteria for the adequacy of both interpretations are the same, and both interpretations have an idealising element. Primarily insofar as actual trials fall away from that ideal, is there call for explanation, rather than interpretation, for efficient causes or correlations, rather than final or formal causes. And, though I will say almost nothing about this here, the best way to understand those deviations from the ideal is by examining the formal and often bureaucratic framework within which practices of the trial go forward, to understand how practices can be distorted by the institutions within which they are encased. But this, too, is a delicate business, because the formal rules of the trial—the rules of discovery, evidence, professional responsibility, and procedure—are enabling as well as distorting. And the discriminations here have to be as careful and context-specific as are the discriminations made at trial.

I have spoken of the common law trial. There is no doubt that my own experience of the common law trial is in its American incarnation. My knowledge of the English and Scottish versions is through reading and conversation. There are significant differences in trial practices within the common law tradition, though they are relatively less significant than the differences between common law trials and 'inquisitorial' procedures. Although the trial is an important institution in all common law countries, one may argue about whether the history and subsequent 'spirit of the laws' of one or other country makes the trial more or less central. One can also imagine a continuum with the American trial at one extreme, British trial procedure near it, and continental versions further along. Though the greater availability of the jury, especially in civil cases, in America is a feature of these differences, it is not itself the focus of my argument. I focus on the trial's linguistic practices and the constitutive rules that surround them. Though I am wary asking what is 'essential' to the common law trial, let me mention some important features. Common law trials involve a relatively greater control by the parties over what evidence is presented and perhaps more importantly, *how* it is presented, and thus, implicitly, greater control over the range of social norms and common sense judgments which the party may invoke. Common law trials create a tension between the parties' 'theories of the case,' narratives designed to embody powerful social norms, including those not explicitly appearing in the law as written, and the almost obsessively detailed presentation of evidence of events in question. In the American version, this 'theory of the case' is explicitly presented in opening statement, but it is also present implicitly, as I understand it, even in the Scottish version (which does not employ opening statement) where it appears incrementally in the parties' witness examinations, both direct and cross, and then explicitly in summation. Though the 'law of rules' is important to the structure of the common law trial in a number of ways, it does not provide the only social norms at play in the trial.

[5] C Geertz, 'From the Native's Point of View: On the Nature of Anthropological Understanding' in P Rabinow and W Sullivan (eds), *Interpretive Social Science: A Reader* (Berkeley and Los Angeles, University of California Press, 1979) 239.

Depending on one's perspective, one can describe the whole range of common law trials as more individualist, more political, more democratic, more empiricist, more egalitarian, more dramatic or theatrical, and more adversarial than their continental cousins. Likewise they can be described as less authoritarian, less statist, less rationalist, less normatively coherent, and less professional. Which form of trial is better? In a recent exchange with Lindsay Farmer,[6] I argued that one can begin to compare the relative strengths of trials only in relation to the societies in which they have their places. The 'right' trial for a more traditional, hierarchical, and organic society will be different from the 'right' trial for a more market-based, egalitarian, and individualist society. With the exception of features of the trial that are responsive to fully universal norms,[7] judgments about relative superiority of this or that procedural feature can only be evaluated in the context of all the procedural features of the trial and from within a particular political tradition. It is only because procedure X in tradition A solves a problem in tradition B that its own procedure Y cannot solve that one may say that procedure X is superior to Y for B.[8]

One final, related, and perhaps controversial point. The most adequate account of the trial will require a 'style of "attentiveness to reality" that is more the mark of the political actor than a scholar because political understanding relates more closely to political action than to political science . . .'[9] The most adequate knowledge of the trial is that which an experienced participant—say a trial lawyer or a judge—has in his or her reflective moments. It involves 'finding a footing' (Heidegger) or 'finding one's way around' (Wittgenstein). This is what occurs at trial, I will argue. If an account of the trial is successful, it is what begins to occur in the reader of that account.

2 AN INTERPRETATION OF THE COMMON LAW TRIAL

Let me state rather baldly a set of conclusions that seem to me to constitute the core of the best interpretation of the common law trial. I will devote most of my efforts here to describing the place of the narrative structure of the trial within this interpretation. Though the received view expresses only a partial truth, the languages and performances of the trial are highly structured. This structure, about which more shortly, is what imposes the discipline on the largely tacit response to an engrossing situation that determines the jury verdict. The more engrossing that structure—and a well-tried case can be enormously engrossing—

---

[6] L Farmer, 'Whose Trial? Comments on *A Theory of the Trial*' (2003) 28 *Law and Social Inquiry* 547; R Burns, 'A Response to Four Readings of *A Theory of the Trial*' (2003) 28 *Law and Social Inquiry* 553.

[7] Whether there are such and what they are is, of course, an enormous inquiry that I avoid here for reasons of space.

[8] See A MacIntyre, *Whose Justice? Which Rationality?* (Notre Dame, University of Notre Dame Press, 1988) 349–69.

[9] D Luban, *Legal Modernism* (Ann Arbor, University of Michigan Press, 1994) 206.

the better will be the judgment the jury renders. The judgment is better because the jury has 'dwelled' within the tensions created by that structure. The effect of the trial's hybrid of languages is to create an almost unbearable tension of opposites. Some of those tensions are among roles (judge, lawyer, witness, jury), but many are among forms of language. Those tensions reflect the tensions among the conflicting forms of life, norms, and mode of social ordering that exist within the society as a whole. It is within those tensions, created in part by the constitutive rules of the trial, that the jury can get it right, can decide what is the most important aspect of the case in front of them, not in general, but in the context of a level of knowledge about a concrete situation that they will almost never have in ordinary experience. This experience allows the trial to function as a kind of critique of both common sense and of the law. The jury's final form of understanding is a literally indescribable[10] grasp of facts, norms, and possibilities for action. Its implicit mode of social ordering is not formalistic and is anti-bureaucratic and so the trial is an important bulwark for us against the often bureaucratic 'onslaught of modernity.'[11] What the common law trial allows is a practical judgment of the relative importance of the moral, political, and formal legal aspects of the case, again, not generally, but in the very specific context of the facts of the individual case. One of the tensions within which the mind of the jury dwells is the tension between formal legality—'closeness of fit' with the legal rules—and the other dimensions of the case. The importance of that tension is, more narrowly, that it keeps the law from ossifying into a rigid ballet of bloodless categories. More broadly, it allows us moderns to renew our society after the passing away of any Archimedian point from which the entire society may be criticised at once—whether Absolute Knowledge, a politically dispositive Categorical Imperative or Divine Revelation, or a 'scientific' understanding of the interests of the Universal Class. Instead, the common law trial is one of the places we moderns can do what we need to do, 'less to create constantly new

---

[10] This phrase occasioned quite a bit of consternation and discussion at the Stirling conference. This was understandable in that I have gone on for hundreds of pages about trial decision-making. What is 'indescribable', I think, is the subjective 'grasp' (note the physicalist metaphor) in the individual case of the right way to go forward. One can identify all the elements of the rules and practices of the trial, what I call the objective side of the trial event, to which the jury responds. One can identify the cognitive operations of which the jury would have be capable in order to get it right. One can give increasingly adequate philosophical accounts of those operations. In an individual case, one can provide reasons defending the chosen resolution of the factual and normative issues. But this subjective grasp seems to require an integration of incommensurable factual, legal, moral, and political considerations unique to the case, 'too fine to avail separately, too circuitous to be convertible into syllogisms.' If the trier of fact can 'get it right,' it will not be because the result *necessarily or deductively* flows from any inevitably general descriptions of features of the case. The philosophical tradition contains many attempts to explain the 'practical holism' that this account suggests. Those attempts are *themselves* inevitably hermeneutical in that they rely on 'the mutual support of many considerations, of everything filling together into one coherent view' that does not *compel* assent. See Burns, n 1 above, at 4–5, 201–19. See also P Steinberger, *The Concept of Political Judgment* (Chicago, University of Chicago Press, 1993).

[11] H Arendt, *On Revolution* (New York, Viking, 1965) 196.

forms of life than to creatively renew actual forms by taking advantage of their internal multiplicity and tensions with one another.'[12]

These are enormous claims, and I will not be able to provide all the evidence for all of them here. What I will do, however, is to show how the narrative structure of the trial is of a piece with the interpretation of the trial I have offered. The general structure of the trial is familiar. The common law trial begins not with the evidence, but with opening statement. Here the lawyers are permitted to tell the jury what the evidence will *show*, not merely provide a preview of what the actual evidence will *be*. Significantly, he may narrate, but he may not argue. The party with the burden of proof then will present his evidence, mainly in the form of a series of direct examinations of his witnesses. The direct examinations will require the witness to answer non-leading questions and testify 'in the language of perception,' that is, in the main, recount what he did and what he saw. They will typically be structured in the form of description followed by chronological narration and will force the mind of the jury down to the details of the events recounted. Witnesses will be limited to the 'representative' function of language: they will typically not be permitted to make promises (not to do it again), give advice (how to rule in the case), or provide overt interpretations of the behaviour they recount (what was on the perpetrator's mind when he acted). Each witness will be subject to cross-examination, which will interrupt the flow of direct examinations and force the jury to see the evidence from a contrary point of view. When the party with the burden of proof rests, then the opposing party will present its evidence, itself interrupted by cross-examination. The party with the burden of proof may offer rebuttal testimony. The parties will offer closing argument, the jury instructions will be read, and the case will be submitted to the jury.

3 THE ORTHODOX INTERPRETATION: THE RECEIVED VIEW OF THE TRIAL

Let me present first the outlines of what I take to be an orthodox understanding of the trial, what I call the 'received view of the trial.' Within this view, which I take not so much to be wrong as to be woefully partial, the trial is the institutional device for realising the rule of law where there are disputes of fact. The goal of trial procedure, including the law of evidence, is to allow the jury[13] to engage in a three-step process: (1) to construct an accurate, value-free account of what occurred; (2) to engage in an act of what might be called 'fair categorisation', by which it determines whether the value free account previously

---

[12] D Kolb, *The Critique of Pure Modernity: Hegel, Heidegger and After* (Chicago, University of Chicago Press, 1986).

[13] For ease of reference, I will refer to 'the trier of fact' as the 'jury'. The social scientific literature suggests that judges and juries reach the same conclusions in the significant majority of cases. Not much turns on the distinction for purposes of the account I provide.

constructed fairly fits within the categories defined by the substantive law and found concretely in the jury instructions, and finally (3) announce a verdict that emerges solely from the inspection of the conclusions reached at stage (2) to determine whether the party with the burden of proof has established by the legally defined standard ('preponderance of the evidence' or 'clear and convincing evidence' or 'beyond a reasonable doubt') each of the elements of the crime, claim, or affirmative defence. In this view, the construction of a value-free and accurate account of what happened is the result of common-sense reasoning, common sense being conceived as a 'web of belief' containing value-free empirical generalisations about probabilities connecting bits of circumstantial evidence to 'material' factual conclusions. It is important that this account be value-free so that the only source of norms to enter the trial flow from the law embedded in the jury instructions, itself legitimised somewhat differently in natural law and positivist traditions. The rule of law should be the law of rules.[14] Put less charitably, it is a form of 'mechanical jurisprudence' at the trial level.

The received view has power. It explains a good deal of what actually goes on in common law trials, their most distinctive features. In particular, it explains the central evidentiary doctrine of 'materiality', a doctrine that requires that each bit of evidence has a pedigree, or 'warrant', that connects it up though an empirical generalisation found usually in common sense, though sometimes in science, with a fact that is 'of consequence', that is, which the substantive law declares to be of significance. It also in part explains the pervasive preference of the common law of evidence for testimony in the language of perception by witnesses who themselves have had perceptual experience of the matter to which they would testify. The received view is also connected with important political ideals, specifically with justice as regularity, the notion that legal decisions should be based on rules announced ahead of time and that similar cases be similarly decided. The former fosters autonomy of the citizen in that it allows him to avoid the State's intrusion into his freely planned affairs by his staying clear of the lines drawn by the pre-announced rules. The latter assumes that there are constant and legally salient aspects of inevitably different situations whose presence or absence can be made the criterion for decision in different cases.

It is also connected up with notions supporting the normative superiority of the substantive law to the contextual moral intuition that would likely prevail in the absence of legal doctrine. In natural law traditions, such as that represented by Blackstone, the slow development of common law rules provides a deeper appreciation of the demands of right reason in particular contexts than could ever be expected from the immediate intuitions of a particular judge or jury. In positivist traditions, this normative superiority usually is derived from the source of law in the statutes passed by democratically elected bodies and so expresses the will of the people. (Of course, there are many varieties of each tradition and the lines between them can be blurred).

---

[14]   A Scalia, 'The Rule of Law as Law of Rules' (1989) 56 *University of Chicago Law Review* 1175.

I have argued that this model of trial decision making fails to take account of a large range of the practices in which we are actually engaged, and that those practices, and even the legal rules that structure them, reflect a different ideal of trial decision-making. This is largely a descriptive matter and I have argued at length that the received view does not fairly capture central aspects of what our actual practices are. Description, however, cannot here be wholly separated from evaluation. It is always open to a defender of the received view to argue that all the aspects of trial practices that are inconsistent with the received view are simply appropriate targets for reform. But this is simply to emphasise the point made earlier about the inevitably hermeneutical or circular nature of justification in this context. Each theorist must argue that the descriptive details he emphasises are, as Rawls puts it, 'considered judgments' of justice, and so deserving of normative weight in the process of achieving reflective equilibrium on these matters, and also that they are consistent with broader political ideals which we accept and which we can defend. In other words, justification comes 'by the mutual support of many considerations of everything fitting together into one coherent whole' that requires 'a continuous dialectical tacking between the most local of local detail and the most global of global structures in such a way as to bring both into view simultaneously.'

During and after the Stirling conference, philosopher Sandra Marshall raised a series of questions concerning the status of the received view and my view that it expresses a 'partial' view of the trial. The orthodox view is partial in a number of ways. It captures some trials more than others. I argued in *A Theory of the Trial* that common law trials are ultimately about what dimension of the situation is most important. Thus, in some cases, cases which have relatively little moral or political importance, the jury may well decide that 'fairness of fit' with the legal categories is the most important question that the case presents and will decide the case like the received view would expect. The received view is also an important aspect of all contemporary common law trials, even in American jury trials, because, I argue, the political values implicit in the 'rule of law as the law of rules' are important for our mode of self-governance, though not the only values of importance. And so, for us, the received view does not present a unitary or dominant ideal to which we ought to aspire; it does not offer an appropriate form of adjudication for us. Are the features identified by the received view necessary, if not sufficient, conditions of a proceeding to be a 'trial'. For me, this is not a conceptual question, but a normative one. We meaningfully use phrases like, 'trial by combat' and 'trial by ordeal.' At the other extreme, there exist in some places what are, by common law standards, extremely unstructured forms of dispute resolution. I am not sure what we are asking when we ask whether such procedures are 'really trials.' For us, the fluid tension among formal-legal, moral, and political modes of decision making that the common law trial expresses, I have argued, is a 'considered judgment' of justice, to use Rawlsian language, a structure that reflects judgments made over a long period of time under favourable conditions by those in a position to know what they are doing. Justification of this mode of decision making has both descriptive and normative elements. The task of understanding the trial is an interpretive task and it 'is partly evaluative, since it consists in the identification of the principles which both best "fit" or cohere with the settled law *and legal practices* of a legal system *and also provide the best moral justification for them*, thus showing the law "in its best light".'[15] So yes, for us, the best form of trial is one where the values that the received view of the trial celebrates are represented, but are in a harsh and demanding tension with other important values.

4 THE RHETORICAL DIMENSION OF THE TRIAL

My focus here will be on the narrative structure of the trial, how it proceeds by the construction and deconstruction of narrative, of different sorts of narratives. That is itself a partial perspective. To appreciate the trial fully, it is also necessary to appreciate a range of other characteristics that are so basic that their significance can easily be missed. The trial is spoken; it proceeds through time; it is a sort of drama; it is a rhetorical situation. Each of these features has significance.[16] 'The aspects of things that are most important for us are hidden because of their simplicity and familiarity. . . . [W]e fail to be struck by what, once seen, is most striking and most powerful.'[17] Because it is a partial antidote to the received view, I want now to give a very compressed account of the ways in which the trial is a *rhetorical* event.[18]

In a rhetorical situation, someone says something to somebody. Persuasiveness to an audience is the primary criterion for judging the performance. Rhetoric rules where a practical resolution of a concrete situation is necessary. In such a practical context, the jury's common sense is inevitably a source of norms, not simply a depository of empirical generalisations. Rhetoric is in play where action is necessary under uncertainty, and persuasion must occur through the 'cumulative force of minute considerations,' rather than by any direct comparison between what is said and the thing itself. Such a comparison is impossible. As Gadamer put it with regard to artistic works,

> works of art are not reproductions of a reality that can be identified independently of the work of art and used to judge the adequacy of its representation; rather the features of the objects works of art represent . . . are illuminated only by means of the representation itself; . . . Hence the representation does not provide a mirror of reality that exactly reflects it. . . .'[19]

---

[15] Hart, n 3 above, at 239–41 (emphasis added), describing Dworkin's jurisprudential method.

[16] Burns, n 1 above, at 124–54.

[17] L Wittgenstein, *Philosophical Investigations*, trans G E M Anscombe (New York, Macmillan, 1953) 50.

[18] For a fuller account, see R Burns, 'Law and Rhetoric', in W Jost and W Olmstead (eds), *A Companion to Rhetoric and Rhetorical Criticism* (Oxford, Blackwell, 2004).

[19] G Warnke, *Gadamer: Hermeneutics, Tradition and Reason* (Stanford, Stanford University Press, 1987) 58.

The whole and the parts are mutually determining and the entire position is likely accepted or rejected at once. This only suggests what we will see later—that understanding the trial's linguistic practices is the key to understanding the kind of truth that is allowed to emerge within them. Rhetoricians' 'commonplaces'— multiple sources for arguments—have always understood the multiplicity of the sources of 'persuasives'. We don't only 'use' rhetoric to achieve goals instrumentally, our norms and so our identity are *constituted* rhetorically, in disputing the relative importance of multiple norms for a highly specific situation—that is how we decide 'who we are.' Negatively, this suggests the limitations of the received view, especially when one considers, for example, an engrossing two-week trial, followed by the reading for twenty minutes of (often unintelligible) jury instructions. Decision in rhetorical situations stems from a tacit response to a situation in which one is engrossed. This engrossing rhetorical situation is the trial itself, a 'consciously structured hybrid of languages' which determines the kind of truth that can emerge under uncertainty for a practical purpose.

Now, to the ears of a certain sort of analytic philosopher, the 'rhetorical' nature of the trial may suggest the conclusion that the mode of thought at work at trial is irrational, or worse. After all, doesn't rhetoric have 'savage roots,' doesn't it inhabit the 'world of the lie,' isn't it 'a weapon called upon to gain victory in battles where the decision hung on the spoken word,' isn't it always 'possible for the art of "saying it well" to lay aside all concern for "speaking the truth"'?[20] At the very least, doesn't the rhetorical dimension of the trial suggest that decisions made there are 'emotional' or based on 'sentiment'? Though I cannot make the argument here at length, the constitutive rules of the trial, the rules of court procedure, evidence, and professional responsibility, seek to maintain the energy that comes from rhetoric's primitive roots (and so protect us from the dead weight of bureaucratic lethargy) while structuring that energy to a productive tension of opposites. I will say more about that in a moment. For now, the rhetorical nature of the trial should make us suspect that the received view of the trial cannot quite be true, that there is more in play than accurate fact-finding followed by fair categorisation. In fact, rhetoric does call forth a larger range of human responses than the received view's notion of judgment suggests.[21] My view is that this broader range of responses allows the juror to capture more of the human truth of the situation before him:

> Emotions can sometimes mislead and distort judgment; Aristotle is aware of this. But they can also . . . give us access to a truer and deeper level of ourselves, to values and commitments that have been concealed by defensive ambition or rationalization.
>
> But even this is, so far, too Platonic a line to take: for it suggests that emotion is valuable only as an instrumental means to a purely intellectual state. We know, however,

[20] P Ricoeur, *The Rule of Metaphor: Multidisciplinary Studies of the Creation of Meaning in Language*, trans Robert Czerny (Toronto, University of Toronto Press, 1975) 10–11.

[21] The received view operates on what Peter Steinberger has called the 'tripartite model of judgment', a process of categorisation of particulars within universals: *The Concept of Political Judgment* above n 10, at 91. Steinberger argues that this is an impoverished account of the range of performances embedded in quite ordinary human judgment.

that for Aristotle appropriate responses . . . can, like good intellectual responses, help to constitute the refined 'perception' which is the best sort of human judgment.[22]

The perception that is created by the trial's 'consciously structured hybrid of languages' relies[23] not only on feeling, but on what one theorist has called political wisdom:

> Taken as a whole, this composite type of knowledge represents a contrast with the scientific type. Its mode of activity is not so much the style of the search as of reflection. It is mindful of logic, but more so of the incoherence and contradictoriness of experience. And for the same reason, it is distrustful of rigor. Political life does not yield its significance to terse hypotheses but is elusive, and hence meaningful statements about it often have to be allusive and imitative. Context becomes supremely important, for actions and events occur in no other setting. Knowledge of this type tends, therefore, to be suggestive and illuminative rather than explicit and determinate.[24]

5 THE CENTRALITY OF NARRATIVE AT TRIAL: A PRELIMINARY SUMMARY

We will see shortly that the kind of narrative that is available in opening statement is quite different from the kinds of narrative that pervade the evidentiary phase of the trial. But first, I want to consider briefly the significance of narrative in general as it operates at trial As my title suggests, this is the least interesting aspect of the narrative quality of the trial, and so easy deductions from the conclusions of the burgeoning field of 'narratology' to the nature of the trial are thus far misplaced. The full sequence of considerations goes about like this. First, we should consider the narrative quality of the trial in general. Then we should consider the significance of the fact that the jury faces almost immediately two competing narratives in a context where an 'either-or' choice will have to be made. We should consider the criteria that are likely to control what may be called an 'initial' theory choice between the two 'factual theories of the case' embedded in the opening statements. (This will prove important, though not always decisive, because of the inevitably circular or interpretive nature of trial decisions making: the meaning and truth of the whole (the theory of the case) is determined by parts (the circumstantial evidence), but the meaning and truth of the parts (the circumstantial evidence) is determined by the whole (the theory in which they are embedded and give them both significance and relative plausibility).) Then we should consider the meaning of the tensions between the form of narrative that prevails in opening and that which occurs during the presentation of evidence. Ultimately one would ask how the entire consciously struc-

---

[22] M Nussbaum, *The Fragility of Goodness: Luck and Ethics in Greek Tragedy and Philosophy* (Cambridge, Cambridge University Press, 1986) 390.

[23] More precisely, the trial's languages not only rely on these capacities, but, in a strong sense, realise them.

[24] S Wolin, 'Political Theory as a Vocation' in M Fleischer (ed), *Machiavelli and the Nature of Political Thought* (New York, Atheneum, 1972) 44–45.

tured hybrid of languages creates the situation in which the jury is immersed and to which it responds. Though this is beyond the scope of this essay, one should then show how that determination among the incommensurable values made by the jury was within its capacities, and identify the forms of understanding that is consistent with the trial's consciously structured hybrid of languages and performances. Finally, one ought to provide an understanding of the place of this mode of social ordering within the range of orderings available to us.

6 EPISTEMOLOGICAL INTERLUDE: WHY THE CHARACTERISTICS OF TRIAL NARRATIVES MATTER

I don't think that the trial has come to have the structure it does for exclusively epistemological reasons. The trial is a practical enterprise, not a theoretical inquiry. Political and moral considerations outweigh strictly epistemological considerations. Nonetheless, accuracy has political and moral significance. (And epistemological concerns have been in the recent past of particular interest to British and American philosophers.) From a political point of view, the values implicit in the rule of law, including democratic governance and the control of political officials, could not be realised if officials simply *could* not find facts with some degree of reliability or could easily manipulate evidence to justify their own preferences. From a moral point of view, we should remember the words of Iris Murdoch, 'What looks like mere accuracy at one end looks more like justice or courage or even love at the other.'[25]

An attempt to think of the trial in much the way that the received view understands it will show why the reasoning that occurs there is inevitably circular or interpretive, and so why the received view cannot be quite right. It also shows why, insofar as an understanding of the evidence is possible at all, one pole of this circular movement will inevitably be a narrative. This is true because 'the characterization of actions allegedly prior to any narrative form being imposed upon them will always turn out to be the presentation of . . . the disjointed parts of some possible narrative.'[26] This means, of course, that characteristics of narrative are necessary characteristics of trial understanding.

One may distinguish provisionally (1) circumstantial evidence[27] from (2) a 'bare' or 'purely perceptual' account of events[28] constructed from such evidence

---

[25] I Murdoch, *The Sovereignty of Good* (London, Routledge, 1970) 89.

[26] A MacIntyre, *After Virtue* (2nd edn, Notre Dame, Notre Dame University Press, 1984) 215.

[27] The law of evidence distinguishes circumstantial evidence from direct evidence. Circumstantial evidence requires a number of intermediate inferences to establish a 'material' fact. Direct evidence, such as eyewitness testimony, requires only a determination with regard to the credibility of the witness. But since the credibility of witnesses is always determined circumstantially, it is fair to say that the probative value of all evidence is circumstantial.

[28] I do not suggest that this 'bare narrative' is in any way more concrete or basic or foundational than the interpreted narratives. See H Pitkin, *Wittgenstein and Justice* (Berkeley and Los Angeles, University of California Press, 1972).

from (3) a fully characterised, or interpreted narrative of events, such as the kind of story told in opening statements. In the common law trial, the jury starts with the third and then moves to the first and second in order to decide between the two narratives presented. The notion of a 'bare narrative' is derived from one sort of *question* the jury will naturally ask in deciding which of the opening statements proves to be the more adequate. That question is basically, 'What would you have seen had you been there?' But even in the best prepared cases even the bare narrative will be underdetermined by the circumstantial evidence presented. Often common sense will not be able to reliably assign relative probabilities to the episodes contained in the proposed and conflicting bare narratives. Often there will be no circumstantial evidence at all to adjudicate the *potentially significant* details of the bare narrative. The *existence* of this or that bit of circumstantial evidence is likely to be hotly contested, a contest often made fiercer by the relative lack of evidence one way or the other. (Could a police officer accused of manslaughter for the shooting death of a motorcyclist bearing down on him have stepped out of the way? Where *exactly* was his car parked? What *exactly* did he say before shooting? How far *exactly* was the cycle when he first saw it and when he fired)? These bits of circumstantial evidence come to the jury 'under a description.' The description or *characterisation* of the circumstantial evidence may be hotly contested. (Were the defendant's words an 'accusation' or a 'threat')? Since, as we will see, the plausibility of the overall narrative is determined in part by its overall likelihood or probability as a factual matter, its consistency with the empirical generalisations are contained by common sense, these underdetermined factual issues of disputed characterisation may be decided in part by their consistency or coherence with the more likely 'bare narrative'. The lines of implication between the part and the whole run both ways, and those lines are lines both of meaning and of factual plausibility.

That is, however, only the first of the inevitably circular cognitive movements even at the most basic factual level. Even when the nature of the circumstantial evidence is both complete and uncontested (almost never), that evidence is always linked to the episodes in the bare narrative by a commonsense generalisation[29] that provides its 'logical relevance'.

The jury will necessarily ask implicitly, 'How universal is the commonsense generalization that links the circumstantial evidence to the episode in the bare narrative for which it is offered as proof?' Since the structure of the commonsense generalizations that provide those links is always, 'Generally and for the most part . . .' the next question is always 'Are all the particular additional facts in this case (F1 . . . Fn) such as to make the generalization more or less powerful than it would be, all other things being equal?' But the existence of these latter facts (F1 . . . Fn) and their proper characterizations will themselves be in dispute just as is F1. And the strength of the commonsense

---

[29] I am considering common sense here as a treasury of purely empirical generalisations. In fact, it is in large part practical, in that it provides modes of coping with situations rather than descriptions or explanations of them.

generalizations that link those facts to what the proponent seeks to show is also caught in another web of mutually determining probabilities.[30]

This suggests a kind of coherence theory of truth for the trial and even suggests that the general criteria for the acceptability of one narrative over the other ('the best story') can overwhelm the evidence in a particular case. Trial lawyers like to say, 'Every fact has two faces.' Almost every fact can be interpreted to support either theory. In a murder case, does the fact that the defendant drank a number of pints before the shooting make it more likely that he was the perpetrator, because of lowered inhibitions, or less likely, because his drinking would have deprived him of the physical co-ordination that this particular shot seems to have required. The senses in which I am a 'realist' about what the trial achieves are complex. Evidence is not infinitely plastic to reinterpretation and some forms of evidence, such as admissions of party opponents, much prized by trial lawyers, are likely to provide *relatively* more secure anchors in these generally holistic processes. To borrow from Henry James, trial evidence is a kind of pudding, but it is a lumpy pudding.

More importantly, the stories that lawyers may tell in opening statement are highly *constrained* narratives, as we will see at greater length below. But this is not my main point here. The only point I want to make here is that the existence, proper description, and meaning of even the most basic of circumstantial evidence at trial is partly determined by its place in different levels of narrative. They will thus be partially determined, 'coloured' if you wish, by whatever renders those narratives more acceptable to the jury. In the end, I argue that the jury is not simply making a theoretical or historical[31] judgment about what more likely happened. Its final cognitive state is not a mental screening of the events that it determined to have occurred. It is, again, a literally indescribable grasp of facts, norms, and possibilities for action. The devices of the trial take it beyond story telling. The story, or rather the tensions among stories, are merely the scaffolding that allows for the integrative and practical grasp that occasions the verdict.

7 THE GENERAL SIGNIFICANCE OF THE NARRATIVE STRUCTURE OF THE TRIAL

Narrative provides the 'systematic means of storing, bringing up to date, rearranging, comparing, testing, and interpreting available information about social behavior.'[32] Cognitive psychologists tell us that 'what does not get structured

---

[30] Burns, n 1 above, at 190.

[31] I am begging the important question of whether historical judgments are themselves theoretical or are themselves inevitably normative.

[32] W Bennett and M Feldman, *Reconstructing Reality in the Courtroom: Justice and Judgment in American Culture* (New Brunswick, Rutgers University Press, 1981) 5.

narratively suffers loss in memory.'[33] Empirical investigators tell us that narrative is 'how jurors actually organize and analyze the vast amounts of information involved in making a legal judgment.'[34] It is through narrative that we remember (re-member), and the internal characteristics of narrative, such as presence of extraneous details, can affect its plausibility even before any evidence is offered. We seem to have a natural 'predisposition to organize experience into a narrative form into plot structures and the rest.'[35] And, mercifully, this spontaneous tendency seems not to be a mere consoling artifice imposed on a featureless substrate, because narratives are 'found . . . in the midst of experience and action, not in some higher level linguistic construction or reconstructions in the experiences and actions involved.'[36] In short, stories 'are told in being lived, and lived in being told.'[37] Narrative structure demands of the story-teller a judgment of relative importance that eliminates the inessential. It is often through a well-crafted story that one can show 'things that cannot be put into words. They make themselves manifest.'[38] The internal morality of stories is highly contextual. Although any retelling of a human action will involve some evaluation of it, that evaluation will not be through what Stuart Hampshire called 'an abstract computational morality,' in the imposition of a single-ruled standard on that action. Rather, the narrative form allows the story-teller to invoke all the subtleties for the understanding of human action that the culture's common sense can provide. Narrative seems internally related to questions of justice, and an important story schema—legitimate status quo, disruption of the status quo, and its often difficult restoration[39]—places the jury *within* the context of what Aristotle called commutative justice. The jury is thus reminded of its practical task, to take part in the action that will restore justice to the community.

8   THE DISTINCTIVENESS OF TRIAL NARRATIVES: THEORY, THEME, AND WITNESS EXAMINATION

Trial narratives have distinctive features. The received view's understanding of opening statement is that it is a preview of the evidence that will be presented. It is in fact much more. In *A Theory of the Trial*, I presented an edited version

---

[33] J Mandler, *Stories, Scripts, and Scenes: Aspects of Schema Theory* (Hillsdale, Lawrence Erlbaum Associates, 1984).

[34] H Kalven and H Zeisel, *The American Jury* (Boston, Little Brown, 1966) 6–7.

[35] J Bruner, *Acts of Meaning* (Cambridge, Mass, Harvard University Press, 1990) 47.

[36] D Carr, *Time, Narrative, and History* (Bloomington, Indiana University Press, 1986) 50.

[37] Ibid, 61.

[38] L Wittgenstein, *Tractatus Logico-Philosophicus*, trans D F Pears and B F McGuinness (London, Routledge, 1961) 6.522. David Luban argues that Wittgenstein did not abandon this view, even in his later philosophy and himself argues that '[w]e narrate stories in order to make manifest whatever unsayable meaning resides in them': D Luban, at 201.

[39] Bruner, n 35 above, at 39–40.

of an actual opening statement in a criminal case. I offered a running interpretation of what the lawyers were doing and how the openings functioned in
the case. Each opening statement provided, indeed 'performed' the mode of
social ordering that it recommended, in that case, one of bureaucratic processing, the other of a combination of moral judgment and psychiatric explanation.
'What is to be done' determined and was determined by 'What happened?' Facts
were, to a limited extent, purposes. Much in the way that Kuhn argued that
proponents of rival scientific theories often 'talk past each other,'[40] so did the
advocates here. (It is also true at trial that it is 'difficult, or, more likely, impossible for an individual to hold both theories in mind together and compare them
point by point with each other and with nature,' or, in the case of the trial, with
the evidence that would be presented). Each *way* of telling the story had a
bite: the prosecutor presented a sequence of the stages of the legal process and
placed the judge within this 'processing' of the defendant, while the defendant's
more 'omniscient' narrator could order all of the details of the story to suggest
a single meaning for the event. Each lawyer was aware of the rhetorical dimension of what he was doing, and each opening was a product of what trial lawyers
call a 'factual theory of the case,' an inevitably simplifying narrative interpretation of what had occurred: much would be omitted by each party because it did
not contribute to his theory. The 'political truths', assumptions that could not
realistically be challenged in this forum in front of this judge, were respected by
the parties. Both parties knew what the anthropologist Clifford Geertz wryly
observed, that whatever the law is after, it is not the whole truth. The legal ter-
rain the parties were moving on contained what evidence scholars sometimes
call 'codified inferences', apparently factual inferences that had been mandated
'as a matter of law.' Thus, appellate courts had sanctioned the notion that prior
child abuse was evidence that the abuser acted in the specific instance before the
court with the knowledge that great bodily harm was likely to result from his
actions (even though no such great bodily harm resulted on the previous occasions). This was actually a moral judgment impersonating a factual inference.
Both advocates used language that appeared nowhere in the criminal code—
words like 'child' or 'victim' or 'madness'—but which had enormous power to
define the meaning of the event being tried.[41] The ability of counsel to tell a fully
characterised story in opening inevitably brings to play all the normative

---

[40] T Kuhn, 'Objectivity, Value Judgment, and Theory Choice' in T Kuhn, *The Essential Tension:
Selected Studies in Scientific Tradition and Change* (Chicago, University of Chicago Press, 1977).

[41] 'A sentence always means more. Even a single word, within the weave of incommensurable
connotation, can, and usually does. The informing matrix or context of even a rudimentary, literal
proposition—and just what does *literal* mean?—moves outward from specific utterance or notation
in every-widening concentric and overlapping circles. These comprise the individual, subcon-
sciously quickened language habits and associative field-mappings of the particular speaker or
writer. . . . No formalization is of an order adequate to the semantic mass and motion of a culture,
to the wealth of denotation, connotation, implicit reference, elision and tonal register which envelop
saying what one means, meaning what one says, or neither . . .': G Steiner, *Real Presences* (Chicago,
University of Chicago Press, 1989) 82–83.

resources embedded in the common sense of the community, its life-world. Aspects of the situation could be shown that could never in this context be said. The legal categories were not ignored, indeed had to be respected, but there was much more at work in these apparently simple stories.

At trial there is not, of course, one opening statement, but two. As Hampshire[42] has shown, this two-story schema is a feature of ordinary moral experience in which we oscillate between two different ways of describing our actions, one of which approves what we are considering, while the other condemns it. Although there is often no neutral way of describing the alternatives, some of us seem to have the ability to engage in a 'theory choice' that is fairer or wiser. As I noted above the two opening statements often talk by each other, since each is urging and, in a sense, 'performing' the adequacy of the understanding that it urges, as well as the eligibility of the mode of social ordering appropriate to the interpretation of events it provides. Unlike standard narrative historiography, where there exists a single account of events that purports to be congruent with the single course of events it recounts, the duality of opening statements is democratic. It leaves it to the jury to provide what coherence there is to the well-represented perspectives presented at trial. The duality of trial openings begins the process of relativising the easy moralising that narrative allows and alerts the jury to the always present danger of a gap between events and the retelling of them. They invite the jury to look *through* the stories. It begins the process by which a well-tried case can achieve some limited transcendence of the norms that are embedded in the common sense scripts of the jury's life world.

What are the normative criteria for what we can call a preliminary choice between the stories offered in opening statements? Because the trial is largely a battle for the imagination of the jury, and because of the interpretive nature of reasoning at trial, the initial attraction of opening statements is important. Trial lawyers are taught that the opening statement should make the jury *want* to rule for you. (Although now largely debunked, there was even an attempt to argue that juries decide most cases after opening statements and before the presentation of evidence.)[43]

First, the jury will be comparing the opening statements to assess their relative factual plausibility. This has two aspects. The internal coherence and completeness of the narrative presented can affect its plausibility. 'The inadequate development of setting, character, means, or motive, as any literature student knows, render a story's actions ambiguous . . . In a trial it is grounds for reasonable doubt.'[44] Even here one of the constraints on opening statement is apparent. The opening is a story, but it also has another performative feature—

[42] S Hampshire, 'Public and Private Morality' in S Hampshire (ed), *Public and Private Morality* (Cambridge, Cambridge University Press, 1978).

[43] W Burke, R Poulson, and M Brondino, 'Fact or Fiction: The Effect of Opening Statement' (1992) 18 *Journal of Contemporary Law* 195.

[44] Bennett and Feldman, n 32 above, at 10.

it is a *promise*. It promises that there will actually be evidence to support what are actually conclusions, factual and normative, in the story offered. (One of the standard rhetorical commonplaces of closing argument is to suggest that counsel has 'broken his promise' by failing to present evidence to support the assertions made.) Secondly, unlike the kinds of stories told in most imaginative literature, the story told in opening is about a specific event that occurred in the past, a *definite* event. Each thing is what it is and no other. This forces the storyteller in general to make relatively more specific factual assertions than he or she might choose for purely 'internal' rhetorical purposes. But factual plausibility will also be initially assessed by what we may call 'external' factual plausibility, the extent to which the story offered is consistent with the generalisations implicit in the jury's common sense, what trial lawyer Louis Nizer, called the 'rule of probability'. Each advocate relies on the kind of generalisations that in part constitute common sense, that say, 'Generally and for the most part . . .' (for example, generally and for the most part, close relatives have affection for their kin). But the opposing party will be telling a story (and presenting evidence to suggest) that says implicitly '. . . but not when . . .' Ultimately, a 'triable case'[45] will present a level of even purely factual complexity that all previous commonsense factual generalisations do not conclusively adjudicate. Each case requires a 'new' level of insight even on the factual level, well beyond Kant's warning that there are no rules for the correct application of rules.

So far I have recounted the ways in which opening statements may be more or less persuasive based on their 'factual' plausibility. But trial lawyers, in presenting a case, choose not only a factual theory of the case, but what they call a 'theme'. A theme is the moral claim that the case makes and, in a well-tried case, pervades the choice, characterisation, and sequencing of all the details in the opening statement and, later, in the evidence. For, as Paul Ricoeur puts it, narrative is 'based on an experience of an *ethics already realized*' in a context in which 'there is no action that does not give rise to approbation or reprobation, to however small a degree, as a function of a hierarchy of values for which goodness and wickedness are the poles.'[46] For good or ill, 'every historical narrative has as its latent or manifest purpose the desire to *moralize* the events of which it treats.'[47] This morality is what Hegel called *Sittlichkeit*, the norms implicit in the practices and institutions of the society. 'And this suggests that narrativity, certainly in factual storytelling, and probably in fictional storytelling as well, is intimately related to, if not a function of, the impulse to moralise reality, that is, to identify it with the social system that is the source of any morality that we can imagine.'[48] 'In this sense, narrative already belongs to the ethical field in virtue

---

[45] Trial lawyers call a case 'triable' when it contains some aspect that is fairly debatable.

[46] P Kemp, 'Ethics and Narrativity', in L E Hahn (ed), *The Philosophy of Paul Ricoeur* (Chicago, Open Court, 1995) 371, 376.

[47] H White, 'The Value of Narrativity in the Representation of Reality' in W Mitchell (ed), *On Narrative* (Chicago, University of Chicago Press, 1981) 13–14.

[48] Ibid.

174   *Robert P Burns*

of its claim—inseparable from its narration—to ethical justice.'[49] In the *Rhetoric,* Aristotle identified forensic rhetoric as concerned specifically with praise and blame, and argued that narrative was its distinctive medium.[50]

Thus, each of the opening statements tells a story in which there is an implicit moral evaluation of persons and actions. The opening that presents the 'more powerful norm' will offer the theme that is most likely to begin to win the battle for the jury's imagination, and to provide the central organising principle for the interpretation of the levels of disputable fact that will appear in the evidentiary phase of the trial.[51] But the trial is not only about a judgement of personal morality. It is a public practice carried out within public institutions. Not only will the jury be making a moral judgment and defining its moral identity,[52] it will be making a political judgment and defining the community's political identity. 'Stories tell us how each one finds or loses his just place in relation to others in the world. And the communication of the story is confirmed when justice has been recognized.'[53] By exercising the power that they have collectively, the jurors decide what they will do, based on what evidence, at what level of uncertainty. Especially in criminal cases, which always involve the executive or police power of the State, the jury will decide whether the exercise of that power is consistent with their own political self-understanding. The opening statements thus have another performative function, a 'signalling' as well as a 'labelling' function. Each tries implicitly to offer to the jury a political self-understanding about the exercise of public authority to which she can give her public allegiance. As de Tocqueville put it in his classic statement:

> The jury, and more especially the civil jury, serves to communicate the spirit of the judges to the minds of all the citizens; and this spirit with the habits which attend it, is the soundest preparation for free institutions. It imbues all classes with a respect for the thing judged and with the notion of right. If these two elements be removed the love of independence becomes a mere destructive passion. It teaches men to practice equity; every man learns to judge his neighbor as he would himself be judged. . . . The jury teaches every man not to recoil before the responsibility of his own actions and impresses him with that manly confidence without which no political virtue can exist. It invests each citizen with a kind of magistracy; it makes them all feel the duties which they are bound to discharge towards society and the party which they take in its government. By obliging men to turn their attention to other affairs than their own, it rubs off that private selfishness which is the rust of society.[54]

[49] P Ricoeur, *Time and Narrative* (Chicago, University of Chicago Press, 1988) 249.
[50] Aristotle, *Rhetoric* 1414a–b.
[51] Kalven and Zeisel called this the 'liberation hypothesis', the way in which unavoidable factual ambiguity 'liberates' the jury from a rigid application of the legal norms: at 166.
[52] C Taylor, *Sources of the Self: The Making of the Modern Identity* (Cambridge, Mass, Harvard University Press, 1989). Taylor argues that identity is always intertwined with moral evaluation. What I judge good and bad defines who I am. 'By his manner of judging the person discloses to an extent also himself, what kind of person he is and this disclosure is involuntary': R Beiner, *Political Judgment* (Chicago, University of Chicago Press, 1983) 18.
[53] M Hill, 'The Fictions of Mankind and the Stories of Men' in M Hill (ed), *Hannah Arendt: The Recovery of the Public World* (New York, St. Martin's Press, 1979).
[54] A de Tocqueville, *Democracy in America*, trans H Reeve (New York, Vintage Books, 1945) I: 295.

An effective opening suggests that to reject the proponent's case is to diminish the public identity of the juror and the way of life with which it is intertwined. And so the trial will inevitably involve an act of public self-interpretation.

Of course, the trial does not end after opening statement.[55] The opening's strength, its ability to offer the full range of considerations and norms relevant to the *meaning* of the case can also be, from the perspective of justice, its weakness. Some of the internal features of narratives that render them persuasive may be indifferent to the *truth* of what is said. 'That is to say the *sense* and the *reference* of a story bear an anomalous relationship to each other.'[56] Now the adversary context of competing narratives and the constraints on opening statements already take this into account. But so do the tensions created by the very different sorts of narratives offered by the witnesses on their direct examinations. These chaste narratives require physical description followed by a chronological account in the language of perception. Openings try to be fair to all the values implicit in the community's common sense. That is why trial advocacy is sometimes called 'trial diplomacy'. Mercifully, the witnesses at trial are rarely diplomats. They provide a much more personal account of a specific event. Those accounts are a challenge to the universality of all the norms implicit in common sense. Their accounts are not written by the author of the entire story, as are fiction, drama, and at least some historiography. The witnesses are, to a large extent, really on their own, and their accounts can create a tension between the proposed *meaning* of the case offered in opening and the *truth* of what occurred in this case. Although we often see what we want to see, we are able to see what may shock or disappoint us. Accuracy is of high moral value. The accounts provided by witnesses provide a critique of the inevitably overgeneralised principles that inhabit the common sense and the law of the community. Finally, the 'brutally elemental data' that the direct examinations offer provides the ideal crucible for the determination of the central questions of the relative important *in the specific context of this case* of all the competing factual and normative dimensions of the situation. If 'justice is conflict'[57] the harsh tension of opposites created by the trial provides the ideal forum within which justice can be done.

To show that these linguistic tensions can actually be the occasion of a genuine form of understanding would require us to provide an account of human understanding that was, in a sense, the subjective side of the trial. I believe that such an account can be given, that there exist philosophical resources that provide the main lines of an account of such understanding.[58] I believe as well that

---

[55] Even where court procedures do not include an opening statement, an effective advocate will still have a theme and factual theory of the case in order to organise the evidence he presents. In such a system, the theme and theory of the case will likely appear explicitly in closing argument, where both the factual theory and theme are (re)presented and the factual and normative arguments in favor of them are marshalled.

[56] Bruner, note 35 above, at 44.

[57] S Hampshire, *Justice is Conflict* (Princeton, Princeton University Press, 2000).

[58] Burns, n 1 above, at 211–19.

sensitive observers of what actually occurs at trial provide evidence of these sorts of nondeductive cognitive processes. Holmes opined that 'many honest and sensible judgments . . . express an intuition of experience which outruns analysis and sums up many unnamed and tangled impressions—impressions which may be beneath consciousness without losing their worth.'[59] Judge Jack Weinstein, a very prominent American trial judge and evidence scholar, put it this way, 'The jury's evaluation of the evidence relevant to a material proposition requires a gestalt or synthesis of evidence which seldom needs to be analysed precisely. Any item of evidence must be interpreted in the context of all the evidence. . . .' In sum:

> The capacity which leads courts so consistently to get it right is, I suggest, a specialization of a general cognitive ability that functions in somewhat different ways in both factual and normative investigations, and somewhat differently still in the combined normative-factual inquiry that is the trial. It is holistic and interpretive. It can grasp 'the cumulations of probabilities . . . too fine to avail separately, too subtle and circuitous to be convertible into syllogisms.' It is likely to 'trust rather in the multitude and variety of its arguments than to the conclusiveness of any one. Its reasoning should not form a chain which is no stronger than its weakest link, but a cable whose fibers may be ever so slender, provided they are sufficiently numerous and intimately connected.' The devices of the trial both supply innumerable such fibers and dramatize their possible connections in ways directly relevant to courts' tasks.[60]

9   CONCLUSION

What is distinctive about the narratives at trial is the way in which they are constrained and counterposed to increase the level of intellectual tension. The story-teller must anticipate his opponent's case. He must anticipate the evidence that will be presented, both because the opening statement is a promise, but also because of ethical rules that generally forbid assertion of fact for which there will be no evidence. All conspire to prevent the advocate from telling the most persuasive story regardless of its truth. The opening statement is made in the context of what the jury knows to be a determinate past event and in a legal context that usually requires an either-or judgment of liability. This demands a lower level of 'subjunctivity' or indeterminacy of the key narrative elements— details are blurred in opening only if uncertainty about the evidence forces the advocate into that rhetorically unattractive posture. Each lawyer must respect the political truths and legally codified inferences that operate within the legal order. Each lawyer has the motive to emphasise precisely those facts and norms that the other cannot easily integrate into his factual theory and theme. The advocate must be concerned as well about the moral force of the jury

---

[59] *Chicago, B & Q Railway Co v Babcock*, 204 US 585, 598 (1907).
[60] Burns, n 1 above, at 210–11. The first quote is from John Henry Newman, the second from Charles Saunders Peirce.

instructions and, in civil cases, the possibility of a directed verdict or a new trial. These constraints pull the accounts towards each other, since they must anticipate the opponent's most powerful evidence and arguments; towards the evidence, because of the performative aspect of opening statement; and towards the written law. The factual theories of the case are themselves in tension with the narratives offered by the witnesses during their direct examinations, narratives that are, in their particularity, unlikely to be wholly subsumed by the factual theory and theme of even the most accomplished advocate. Cross-examination can be used to tell a 'counter-story' to the one offered by the witness, to the factual elements of which the witness must agree, which can by contrasting selection, characterisation, and sequencing of facts, offer a starkly different interpretation of events. And both cross and final arguments can be used in purely negative attack on the credibility of a witness and the persuasiveness of the interference that the opponent offers.

This is as it should be. The trial proceeds by the construction and deconstruction of narrative. It is the crucible of democracy. A well-tried case can refine the community's common sense to the point where it can achieve a truth beyond story-telling.

10

The Objection that Cannot be Heard: Communication and Legitimacy in the Courtroom

EMILIOS CHRISTODOULIDIS[1]

1 THE UNSEEN

I N 1981, NANNI Ballestrini wrote a book-homage to the lost generation of the 'years of lead', the 1970s, in Italy. It retraces an itinerary from early university political activism in the *Lotta Continua*, through the days of revolutionary activism, of armed struggle in the Red Brigades, of prosecution and incarceration. The account does not follow a temporal sequence as two narratives run parallel: on the one hand the narrative of revolutionary action, manifestos, committee meetings and militancy, and on the other the narrative of interrogation, trial and solitude. Both narratives are run together *in tension* in a text that is unpunctuated, continuous and consists of 'phrases murmurées, ressassées.'[2] It is a stunning testimony, impertinent and subversive, full of emotion and bereft of hope. But more than anything else, it is the account of the encounter with the State that remains most memorable: the author's discourse, fluid and undisciplined, moves beyond and below the official language of law remaining ultimately unintelligible to the latter and unengaged-with. The unhappy co-existence of legal and revolutionary idiom comes into sharp relief as the contrast is fed into the text itself and revealed in incoherences, lacunae, the breakdown of the narrative continuum. And it is to the credit of this literary work as art form that the tension between the discourses is built into the text in this way, *Les Invisibles* not an account of an impossible dialogue but a testimony of one:

---

[1] Many thanks to Antony Duff, Victor Tadros and Scott Veitch for valuable comments on earlier drafts.
[2] M Fusco, 'Introduction' in N Ballestrini, *Les Invisibles* (Paris, POL Editeur, 1987, (original in Italian 1981)).

j'ai fait oui de la tête pour dire que je voulais répondre et tout de suite le président sans même me regarder me demande si je plaide coupable ou non coupable . . . je réussis à dire avant que je réponde il faut nous mettre d'accord sur la signification de ces mots car ce n'est pas sûr que pour vous et pour moi ces mots coupable ou innocent ont le même sens avant tout il faut éclaircir ce point comprendre j'étais en train de dire plus ou moins une chose de ce genre et j'ai entendu un hurlement du procureur qui me coupait la parole disant que je devais repondre aux questions et ne pas faire des jeux de mots inutiles.³

Activist and judge inhabit 'universes' closed off to intertraffic of meanings. Note the activist's effort to shake the naturalness of the signifiers 'coupable' and 'innocent'. Note the judge's invitation to the activist to stop the 'jeux des mots inutiles' and to join the universe where these equivocals are fixed to concepts. And note that the judge attributes to the opponent the strategy of delaying discussion of the facts through discursive manoeuvres. He denounces this avoidance tactic and at the same time proclaims the law's innocence in the urgency of his appeal to discuss acts as 'brute' events:

vous m'accusez vous dites bande armée que j'ai été que j'ai participé a une bande armée que je suis un subversif là le président me coupe non non minute ce n'est pas moi qui dit ça et il tape de la paume de la main sur la pile de dossiers qui est devant lui ce n'est pas moi qui dit ça ce sont les actes et il tape encore de la main sur les dossiers et c'est sur ces actes que le code pénal se fonde pour établir contre vous le délit de bande armée c'est a partir de ces actes qu'il faut discuter et que vous devez répondre parce que c'est sur ces actes que nous sommes en train de faire ce proces.⁴

J G A Pocock writes this:

Language is referential and has a variety of subjects. It alludes to those elements out of which it has come and with which it offers to deal, and a language current in the public speech of an institutional and political society may be expected to allude to those institutions, authorities, value symbols, and recollected events that it presents as part of that society's politics and from which it derives much of its own character. A 'language' in our specialised sense, then, is not only a prescribed way of speaking, but also a prescribed matter for political speech . . . [The latter] obliges one to acknow-

---

³ Ibid, 289. 'I indicated with a nod that I would like to respond and immediately the judge without even glancing at me asks me if I plead guilty or innocent . . . I managed to say that before I respond we must agree on the meaning of the words because it is not at all certain that for you and for me the words innocent and guilty have the same meaning above all we must clarify this point I was in the process of saying more or less something of this sort and I heard the howl of the prosecutor who cut me short saying that I should answer the question and stop playing games with words' (my translation).

⁴ Ibid, 290. 'you accuse me you say armed group that I was that I participated in an armed group that I am a subversive there the judge interrupted me no just a minute it is not me who says that and he tapped the palm of his hand on the files before him it is not me who says that it is the acts and he continued to tap his hand on the files it is on the basis of these acts that the penal code establishes the delict of belonging to an armed group and it is these acts that are the departure of our discussion and to which you must speak because it is for these acts that we are conducting this process' (my translation).

ledge that each language to some degree selects and prescribes the context within which it is to be recognised.[5]

We will return to this, though not to Pocock, because our concern is narrower than his, and because our claim is stronger. 'The objection that cannot be raised' is not merely one that is side-lined in official discourse; rather, it will be argued, the very possibility of raising it, in the courtroom, is structurally removed. But for now, before that argument is made, let us keep in mind the testimony only of how the language of the judge imposes itself as exclusive register. The judicial utterance makes available the context that situates the communicative offers of the parties, and the other side of this supposed opening up of possibility concerns the mutations it imposes on the utterance of the activist, collapsing *political* speech and a *political* understanding of revolutionary action into expressions of hatred pure and simple, in turn identified with the subversion of politics:

> en essayant de plonger dans le chaos les institutions fondamentales de notre démocratie ce ne sont pas des révolutionnaires que vous avez devant vous mais des hommes et des femmes transformés en bêtes féroces par leur haine de la société et les têtes des jurés se tournent toutes ensemble vers la cage sans aucun idéal sinon la destruction et la mort chez eux aucune vraie culture seulement le culte de la violence écoutez-moi bien en semant la haine dans les esprits immatures et naïfs des jeunes générations en profitant lâchement des libertés que notre democratie offre à tous sans aucune distinction pour réaliser leurs desseins subversifs visant à jeter à bas les fondements de notre société civilisée et pacifique.[6]

Note how there is an ambiguity as to whom the phrase 'aucune vraie culture [chez eux] seulement le culte de la violence' is attributed. In the continuum of the narrative it could be part of the prosecutor's speech and therefore attributed to the radicals, and equally it could be attributed by the narrator to the jury. The ambiguity works to underline the reciprocal and simultaneous denunciation by both sides of the politics of the other as violence *simpliciter*. But, more important, note that the discourse of the revolutionary is carried in the official discourse through a nonsense-language, a 'paralanguage', that results as the judge uproots the revolutionary utterance from its context and realigns it to conditions of the legal context.

---

[5] J G A Pocock, *Virtue, Commerce and History* (Cambridge, Cambridge University Press, 1985) 12.

[6] Above n 2, at 292. 'in trying to throw into chaos the fundamental institutions of our democracy it is not revolutionaries you have before you but men and women transformed into ferocious beasts through their hate for society and the members of the jury all together turned their heads to the cage without any ideal except destruction and death in their minds without any culture except the cult of violence listen to me carefully in cultivating hatred in the immature and naïve minds of the young generations in taking advantage of the liberties that our democracy offers to all without distinction to realise their subversive plans aiming to overthrow the very foundations of our civilised and peaceful society' (my translation).

It is this latent, and thus ideological, displacement that I will take issue with in what follows. Ballestrini's text has served to introduce this displacement from the activist's perspective, manifested in a confrontation that never quite becomes one, a series of elisions, non sequiturs and failures to register any of the protestations or objections. At the same time, the judge is forever reinstating the supremacy of the legal idiom, forever realigning the activist's idiom to the prescriptions of a second order language. By controlling the criteria of what counts as political speech at the meta-level, his is a move that circumscribes politics to constitutional democracy ('des institutions et lois de la démocratie') and short-circuits political speech to support for existing arrangements. The allusion to democratic values by the judge serves to set up a context that can accommodate the judicial *but not* the revolutionary utterance as political. In the process the political radical is deprived of the means to articulate a political claim other than as violence. The judge's 'invitation' to Ballestrini to declare guilt or innocence is rebutted: 'pour ma part je ne comprends pas ce que signifie pour moi déclarer que je suis coupable ou innocent car il n'est pas question pour moi de nier ou plutôt de renier ce que j'ai fait et ce que j'ai été.'[7] The point is that in effacing the opposition over the construction of meaning as a stake in the struggle, the judge establishes the innocence of the legal idiom, so that in positing the idiom as universal, the interchangeability of addressor and addressee can of course be assumed, removing the asymmetry and subsuming both the 'I' and the 'you' under a posited 'we'. By obliterating the incompatibility of the two languages the rest becomes easy and obvious: the judge can envisage the autonomy of the addressee who can now also become the sender of prescriptions since the asymmetry between them is obliterated. The experience of the political is *thus* universalised in law. Ballestrini's book is about the flipside of the universalisation, the experience of effacement, and that is why its title is *Gli Invisibili*. The revolutionary's utterance is a lost utterance, every objection countered by the law before it can be raised, a silencing that is in Lyotard's words 'a challenge to the occurrence,' and with it 'a contempt of being.'[8]

This is what Lyotard writes in *The Differend*:

> Un destinateur survient, dont je suis le destinataire, et dont je ne sais rien, si ce n'est qu'il me situe sur l'instance destinataire. . . . Elle est le scandale d'un moi déplacé sur l'instance toi. . . . Une autre phrase se forme, où il revient en situation de destinateur, pour légitimer ou rejeter, peu importe, le scandale de la phrase de l'autre et sa propre

---

[7] Above n 2, at 291. 'For my part I do not understand what it means to declare myself innocent or guilty because it is not in question for me to deny or moreover to renounce that which I have done and that which I have been' (my translation).

[8] With Scott Veitch I have explored the applicability of the concept of the 'différend' in the context of legal discourse in a series of papers. The most recent among them: 'The Ignominy of Unredeemed Politics: Revolutionary Speech as différend' (1997) 29 *International Journal of the Semiotics of Law* 141.

dépossession. . . . Mais elle ne peut pas annuler l'évenement, seulement l'apprivoiser et le maîtriser . . .⁹

2 THE SPECTRE OF SEDITION

I do not for a moment assume that any of the above has yet been established or proven. Against the background of Ballestrini's account of lack of engagement I want to inquire into the legitimacy of the courtroom as a forum that provides the procedural means to accommodate and resolve disputes and to judge wrong-doing. The kind of claim (and counter-claim) that is presented to that forum and that I will treat here as a test case is the kind raised again and again in Ballestrini's account: 'You are exercising class justice' or 'your ideology is that of State violence.' But it can be expanded to include others: 'the Crown has no jurisdiction in Ireland'; 'your jurisprudence is but the will of your class trans-formed into law for all'; 'The Prosecutor General is a terrorist'; etc, etc. That these all involve limit situations of a kind is not in doubt. But test cases in limit situations are not exceptions that can be ignored because of the rarity of their occurrence. Instead, in an important way, they show up characteristics of the observed institution or context that ordinary cases leave unnoticed and untouched.

These 'communicative offers' in courtroom interaction customarily do not register at all; when they do, they register as offences that can be loosely grouped under the category of sedition. I should say that it makes little difference to my argument whether the radical's speech act is criminalised or ignored (although sedition, of course concerns what is criminalised), since what I want to argue is that in neither case does it register in its own terms. Also, despite my focus on the trial, it is part of my argument that no significant distinction exists between fora, sedition applying to speech acts performed both in the political sphere proper and in the adjudicative sphere, and therefore that certain communicative offers are deemed inappropriate according to the same rationale whether they are per-formed in the constitutional sphere of democratic politics or in the courtroom.

'Sedition', as I employ the term here, covers the category of offences where what is punishable is the subversion of the constitutional process, and where this subversion is carried out by rhetorical means. Both premises are inscribed in the *actus reus* of seditious offences

---

⁹ J-F Lyotard, *Le Différend* (Paris, Seuil, 1981) 163–64: 'A sender [of prescriptions] appears whose addressee I am and about whom I know nothing beyond the fact that he situates me in the instance of addressee . . . It is the scandal [violence] of a me displaced onto the instance of the you . . . Another sentence forms, in which the me comes back into position of sender in order to legitimate or reject, little matter, the scandal of the sentence of the other, and its own dispossession. . . . . But it cannot annul the event, only tame it and master it' (my translation).

(i)   the offence is of a rhetorical nature—ie it pertains to speech, discourse, the propagation of ideas,
(ii) the offence being punished is the attempt to disrupt the constitutionally-sanctioned processes of norm-creation or norm-application.

Speech is excluded from protection if it endangers or is aimed at endangering, if it offends or aims to offend, the political system as laid out and sanctioned by the Constitution. The precise aim of sedition laws is to remove the conflict in a way that leaves the political process intact, when the conflict is alleged to have arisen at the level of the rules of the game. The rationale behind the criminalisation of utterances is the disruption of the political life of the society at the level of respect for the rules of the political process. Notice how what is prohibited is a form of behaviour—speech—that is generally permitted, particularly in the public domain where it occupies a 'preferred position'.[10]

Sedition laws extend to both the public sphere and the trial. As regards the public sphere, the common law still 'draws a distinction between the expression of political opinion and the advocacy or incitement of violent political action,'[11] a distinction resorted to less infrequently than one might have assumed. In dealing with the threat of terrorism in Northern Ireland the UK government has consistently relied on anti-sedition legislation, with both major pieces of anti-terrorist legislation in recent years, the Terrorism Act 2000 and the Anti-terrorism, Crime and Security Act 2001 containing an explicit abrogation from the European Convention on Human Rights that is law in the UK under the Human Rights Act 1998.[12] In American law, the question of subversive advo-

---

[10] First encountered in the famous fourth footnote by Chief Justice Stone to *US v Carolene Products Ltd* 304 US 144 (1938).

[11] E Barendt, *Freedom of Speech* (Oxford, Clarendon, 1985) 155. 'The common law of sedition sets the bounds for general political discourse' (S H Bailey, D J Harris and B L Jones, *Civil Liberties: Cases and Materials* (London, Butterworths 1991) 291. In his *Digest of the Criminal Law*, Fitzjames Stephen provided the following wide definition for the common law offence of sedition in England '[a] seditious intention is an intention to bring into hatred or contempt, or to excite disaffection against the person of Her Majesty . . . or the government and constitution of the United kingdom, . . . or to excite Her Majesty's subjects to attempt otherwise than by lawful means the alteration of any matter in Church or State by law established' (56, art 93; 8th ed, art 114). Brazier adds that this could 'encompass any forceful criticism of the existing structure of authority within the state' (S A de Smith and R Brazier, *Constitutional and Administrative Law* (8th edn, Harmondsworth, Penguin Books, 1998) 462). 'We should not consider it decisive that sedition is hardly ever taken down from the armory in which it hangs,' remarked the judge in *R v Aldred* [1909] 22 Cox CC 1. 'In time of crisis an uncertain executive might resort to it again, as it has done in modern times in areas of British colonial rule' (I Brownlie, *Principles of Public International Law* (4th edn, Oxford, Clarendon, 1990) 239). It is, for example, significant (if 'paradoxical' according to Barendt) that although there have been no reported decisions on sedition in Ireland since 1922, the Irish Constitution preserves the offence of seditious libel in the very article that guarantees citizens' freedom of expression, Art 40.6 of the Constitution of Eire.

[12] Art 15 of the ECHR allows derogation (as a matter of international law) 'in time or war of other public emergency threatening the life of the nation' but even then 'only to the extent strictly required by the exigencies of the situation.' The UK's violation of the prohibition of detention without trial was challenged before the ECtHR in *Brogan v UK* (1991) 13 EHRR 439; the UK responded to the Court's decision in *Brogan* by an Art 15 derogation from ECHR Article 5(3). The validity of this derogation was subsequently upheld by the ECtHR in *Brannigan and McBride v UK* (1994) 17 EHRR 539.

cacy, ie the incitement to violence as a means of effecting political change, returned to again and again from the sedition trials under the Smith Act, to the Civil Rights cases in the late 1960s and 1970s testing the limits of 'symbolic speech', later the 'flag-burning' cases, etc, has been a consistent preoccupation of American constitutional courts and of course of American constitutional scholarship.[13] The clamping down on 'sedition' has recently made a spectacular return with the Patriot Act. Neither the US nor the UK legal systems are alone among liberal democratic states to punish subversive advocacy.[14]

When it comes to seditious offences that apply to trials,[15] by far the most important instances of 'sedition' in this context involve direct confrontations in court that carry an overtly political denunciation of the system. With the cases *sub judice*, contempt here is mainly dealt with at the level of rules of criminal procedure, in the form of refusals to all petitions, withdrawal of the right to

---

[13] For an overview, see C E Baker, *Human Liberty and Freedom of Speech* (New York, Oxford University Press, 1989). The long and fierce debate centres on whether the damage inflicted through the censorship of subversive political statements ought to be seen as a contradiction of democratic founding principles. For an overview of the history of the debate in the American Supreme Court and the succession of 'tests' devised, see K Greenawalt, *Speech, Crime and the Uses of Language* (New York, Oxford University Press, 1989). In this book Greenawalt suggests a distinction drawn from linguistic philosophy, namely that between (prima facie) subversive statements that carry locutionary and those that carry illocutionary force.

[14] Seditious offences against the State and the 'free democratic order' abound in a number of other Western jurisdictions. At the height of the terrorist threat in West Germany, for example, the government introduced a number of amendments to the criminal law, including the anti-Constitutional Advocacy Act of 1976. S 88a of the Penal Code provided that offences 'against the Constitution' could be punished with imprisonment for up to three years. The seditious element was designated here as 'capable of encouraging the willingness of other persons to commit offences against the existence or safety of the FRG.' The legislation was not seen as contradicting the Constitution which requires fidelity to the free democratic order and thus arguably excludes forms of militant democracy and direct action. S 88a was finally repealed in 1981, but other parts of the Penal Code designating offences like that of 'Endangering the Democratic Rule of Law' (Title III), and punishing the defamation of the federation (ss 90, 90a, 90b) in conjunction with provisions against criminal association (ss 129, 129a) may be used to punish sedition. Generally see J E Finn, *Constitutions in Crisis* (New York, Oxford University Press, 1991).

[15] Two categories can be distinguished here, depending on whether the contemptuous statement is in fact made sub judice (category b, below) or not (category a). Category (a) covers common law offences like 'scandalising the Court' ('murmuring judges' in Scotland). The bodies protected are only Courts of Justice properly so called. It is of paramount importance that the attack is directed at the judge *qua* judge, at the judicial office itself and not the personal reputation of the judge. The *degree of harm* required to constitute 'scandalising' sets a low threshold to the offence: that of creating a real, albeit small, risk of prejudice to the administration of justice. But the requirement of 'substantial risk' of the Contempt of Court Act has been interpreted restrictively, and in effect any undermining of public confidence in the administration of justice can fairly be described as a serious impediment to justice. The *offending conduct* is the publication of material that either constitutes 'scurrilous abuse' or imputes a political motive and thus challenges or compromises the assumed impartiality of the judicial office. The mens rea in scandalising through imputation of political motive includes a requirement of 'ulterior' intent. The intention to subvert the legal system rather than incidentally subverting it, is inscribed in the offence of scandalising the court in a way that is not in direct contempt. *The confrontation between scandaliser and judge is total and pre-meditated.* It is significant that scandalising the court is not tied to a case *sub judice*. It is aimed at justice as a continuing process. Category (b) covers direct confrontations in court that carry an overtly political denunciation of the system.

speak, expulsion from the proceedings, penal custody, etc.[16] The silencing of contemptuous statements in court is a central case of sedition. The notion of independent justice underpins and legitimates constitutionalism. Courts are to be seen as agents of justice above politics and also as guarantors of the political process itself, primarily by securing that political action in the form of rights is not impeded. What brings courts into disrepute, in our case the accusation that they are complicit within a certain logic of rule, erodes these assumptions and is clearly seditious. It is significant in this respect that the derogations from the ECHR introduced in the recent UK anti-terrorist Acts are derogations from the article guaranteeing the right to a fair trial.[17]

So what we encounter throughout this broad spectrum is a banning of statements. Under sedition statements are banned that contest jurisdiction and impute a political bias to the administration of justice. From the 'treason trials' of South Africa to the criminalising of statements 'in support of terrorism', from the trials of the urban guerrillas in Italy and Germany to the silencing of those un*patriotic* enough to officially question the US's response to '9/11', *whether* the banning concerns statements in the public sphere or in the courtroom, and *whether* the statements are punished or ignored in the latter forum, what is repeated in each case is a common pattern of *non-engagement*, of an impossible dialogue. I will say more on the effect of this non-engagement as an expression of precisely what I want to argue is the fundamental elision that allows a silencing that finds no representation in law.

3 WHAT NORMATIVE UNDERPINNING FOR THE TRIAL? INTERNAL AND EXTERNAL JUSTIFICATIONS AND DISCOURSE THEORY

I will argue that the only response that is able to provide a normative justification for the passing of a sentence on a citizen is one that includes the citizen in the *creation* of the norm (from which the sentence stems) and gives him a voice during the processes of deliberation as to whether the norm *applies* to him. This 'democratic' legitimation of the trial presupposes and insists upon a certain continuity between legislation and adjudication. The trial is the moment in which we apply to ourselves the norms we have given ourselves. Habermas puts it unequivocally: '[T]he modern legal order can draw its legitimacy only

---

[16] Such examples of *political confrontation in law* were at their most dramatic during the trials of terrorists in the days of urban guerrilla warfare that succeeded the big social upheavals of the late 1960s and early 1970s. The crack-down on the Red Brigades in Italy and the Baader-Meinhof group in Germany provide some of the most spectacular examples. Here is one of many: Baader: 'What Federal Prosecutor General Buback is doing is by exact definition terrorism, state terrorism. And so the terrorist Buback . . . Judge Prinzing: 'Herr Baader I am withdrawing your permission to speak. If you are trying to accuse the Federal Prosecutor General of pursuing a course of state terrorism, that goes beyond what we will tolerate' (5/8/75, 23rd day of the Baader-Meinhof trial). All extracts of the Baader-Meinhof trial from S Aust, *The Baader-Meinhof Group* (trans Anthea Bell; London, Bodley Head, 1987).

[17] See above, n 12, and sch 3 of the Anti-terrorism, Crime and Security Act 2001.

from the idea of self-determination: citizens should always be able to understand themselves also as authors of the law to which they are subject as addressees.'[18] In that sense Klaus Günther too speaks of the trial as a 'mirror' of our self-understanding as autonomous citizens: '[t]he deliberative concept of personhood that informs the notion of citizen finds its mirror image in the concept of the legal person as addressee of norms.'[19] He adds: 'The democratic process is distinguished from all other forms of legitimisation of norms in unifying the notion of citizen and the notion of legal person in the concept of the deliberative person.'[20] Addressor and addressee of norm here are perfectly commutable and a perfect symmetry establishes itself between legislation and adjudication, both pivoting on deliberation, both engaging the citizen in a form of rational self-binding. No discourse-theorist, it seems to me, can stray away from this central premise without compromising the foundational principle of discourse theory itself.

I take this premise both to provide the only credible normative underpinning to the trial and at the same time to be one that inevitably yields under its own ambition. This, I will argue, leaves us with no normative underpinning of the trial across the board, and consequently, with no defence against the charge that this silencing of political claims is simply the preferred option of a 'we' who have usurped the position to speak for 'us'. 'Juris-diction' thus involves a 'we' speaking the law to 'us'. Those who level political/jurisdictional challenges, of the kinds we have looked at, logically break the coincidence of 'we' and 'us'; they are consequently displaced onto the instance of a 'them' who are spoken *about*. But the first person plural of jurisdiction cannot account for this displacement. It insists on a projection of commonality, continues to invoke those who are spoken about, in their absence, usurping the right to speak *in the name of* those whose speaking position has been withdrawn.

The structure of my argument is as follows. For the remainder of this section I will explain, and defend against possible objections, my claim that the commitment to a discursive rational self-binding, as put forward by discourse theory and outlined above, is the only legitimate response for a society that is willing to punish some of its members for violating its norms. Then, in the remaining sections, I will undertake to show, in three gradual steps, how this legitimation collapses under the weight of its own demands.

Why do inclusion, reflexivity, and self-binding furnish the normative underpinning of the trial? Why not other justifications too? Justifications, for example, that assert that fascists and communists, racists, anti-Semites and other fanatics need to be silenced because what they say is wrong, dangerous or unpleasant? Still, of course, the imposition (of the silencing) would have to

---

[18] J Habermas, *Between Facts and Norms* (Cambridge, Polity, 1997) 449.
[19] K Günther, 'The Criminal Law of "Guilt" as Subject of a Politics of Remembrance in Democracies' in E Christodoulidis and S Veitch (eds), *Lethe's Law* (Oxford, Hart Publishing, 2001) 10.
[20] Ibid, 11.

redeem itself through a *convincing* rationale. But then rationales abound: the protection of liberty, of society, of rightfully acquired property, of order. Why look to discourse and inclusion and not to one of these other rationales? I think the answer lies in the term 'convincing', which again imports a requirement of rational redemption: convincing to whom? Surely not to those who already stand in a position to gain from the silencing. If the symmetry between addressor and addressee of norms is not assumed at *some* level, the imposition of a norm on a citizen who isn't its addressor needs to seek an *external* justification and this externality instantly imports a certain arbitrariness into the political context, a question-begging premise. This applies to most kinds of arguments that are called upon to provide such external justifications, whether natural law arguments, arguments from authority, or whatever. Remember, the justification for silencing assumes the form 'We will not tolerate these kinds of statements' (because they are fundamentalist, subversive, etc). If this intolerance doesn't call upon agreement to justify it, then it should be in turn premised on a higher-order reason 'x' (my authority to decide this matter is justified) which must again turn on the argument about why 'x' is a good reason, where this defence, too, would have to seek its basis on something *other* than that we consented to it. I do not intend to turn this into a discussion over the foundations of normative statements. I want simply to warn that 'external' reasons for silencing statements (rather than democratic/consensual ones) are only binding to those who find them convincing and thus carry uncertain justificatory weight; and that while those of us here discussing this issue may all agree that there are good reasons to silence racists and anti-Semites, it is harder to decide on what statements should be banned as 'subversive' or 'fundamentalist'. But then perhaps even the first concession is too high. A cursory look at what passes as 'anti-Semitic hate speech' in the American academy these days[21]—I have in mind the banning of any statement questioning Israel's insidious genocidal practices[22]—suffices to make one wary about the confident drawing of boundaries here.

[21] The following statement comes from Lawrence Summers, President of Harvard University: 'Profoundly anti-Israel views are increasingly finding support in progressive intellectual communities. Serious and thoughtful people are advocating and taking actions that are antisemitic . . .'. Quoted in J Butler: 'No, it's not Anti-semitic' (2001) 25 (16) *London Review of Books*, 19.

[22] A controversial characterisation perhaps. I use 'genocide' in a sense compatible with the definition of the term in international law as involving the deprivation inflicted on a people of its ability to exist *as a people* by denying them the possibility to gain their means of subsistence or reproduce their culture, where this denial is perpetrated through a *systematic* destruction of their means of education and livelihood. One of the most eloquent indictments comes from Rachel Corrie, the American peace activist who was crushed to death by an Israeli army bulldozer in March 2003, in the published e-mails to her mother. She says: 'All of the situation that I tried to describe, . . . constitutes a sometimes gradual—often hidden but nevertheless massive—removal and destruction of the ability of a particular group of people to survive. . . . So I think that when all means of survival is cut off in a pen (Gaza) which people can't get out of, I think that qualifies as genocide. Even if they could get out, I think it would still qualify as genocide. . . . I don't like to use those charged words. I think you know this about me. I really value words . . . . I spent a lot of time writing about the disappointment of discovering the degree of evil of which we are still capable' (*The Guardian*, 18 March 2003).

Let me return then to what is banned *justifiably*, and why discourse theorists may be offering us the best available reason here. According to Habermas's famous formulation of the discourse principle, only those norms are valid to which all possibly affected persons could agree as participants in rational discourse. The terms 'all possibly affected persons' refer to the position of addressee. The counter-factual 'could agree' situates any of us, and all of us, as addressor. This coincidence of the speaking positions does away with any need for external justifications (from authority, natural law etc,) and premises the bindingness of our law, including our test cases where statements are disallowed, on a rational, self-reflexive move.

The obvious weakness of a theory that attempts to ground the correctness of normative statements on consensus is that the latter remains forever only potential: the agreement of all is practically unattainable. To counter this, Habermas replaces the criterion of actual consensus with that of 'well-grounded' consensus as criterion of truth:

> The meaning of truth lies not in the circumstance that some consensus is actually achieved, but rather in this: that at any time and in any place if we but enter into discourse, a consensus can be achieved under certain conditions which prove this to be a well grounded consensus.[23]

The criteria of what counts as 'well-grounded' are tied to the framework of a logic of discourse (the 'ideal speech situation') in which 'communication is neither hampered by external contingent factors, nor by constraints which are internal to the structure of communication itself.'[24] The solution thus becomes dependent on the integrity of procedures. Klaus Günther stresses this too: '[l]egal norms are valid even for those persons who did not, or not exhaustively, participate in the democratic process. Legal norms demand respect if the correct procedures have been followed, even if the factual agreement of all concerned is missing.'[25] That is why the 'well grounded', procedurally correctly enacted norm binds us as addressees whether we did *in fact* agree with it or not. The fact that we *could* or *would* agree under conditions that would make our consensus rational (the terms 'would' and 'could' are interchangeable here, given that the emphasis is on what counts as 'rational' participation), ie, under conditions of unfettered communication, make it binding for internal not external reasons, because it establishes the coincidence of addressor and addressee.

But how convincing is this? Let us return to our comrades of the Red Army faction and their injunction to the judge: 'The state machine [is what] you sit here to represent, and as whose representative you sadistically act.'[26] Remember that under the rationale of sedition what is being condemned by the Court is the

---

[23] J Habermas, 'Wahrheitstheorien' at 239, quoted in R Alexy, *A Theory of Legal Argumentation* (Oxford, Oxford University Press, 1989) 111.

[24] Ibid, 255.

[25] K Günther, n 19 above, at 10.

[26] Gudrun Ensslin, on 5 August 1975, during the Baader-Meinhof trial.

activist's 'jurisdictional/political' injunction. It is the speech act of refusing to play the game that is being criminalised. In discourse terms the claim now must become something like this: '*We do not allow **ourselves** these kinds of claim.*' There is something deeply suspect in this formula. Not because self-censorship needs to be seen as irrational at all times. But what begins to surface in this improbable construction is the suspicion that the collective 'self' of discursive self-censorship is a self that becomes rather difficult to 'rationally' contain. Because either it is a silencing that *we* impose on *us*—and isn't imposition as the very curtailment of reflexivity inimical to discourse theory?—or it begs the question of the constituency of the 'us'.

What follows is an elaboration of this point. I have argued that the discourse-theoretical, 'democratic' or 'internal', identification of addressors with addressees of norms provides the best available justification for our courtroom practices, and yet, I will now argue, in those test cases I have been discussing, where courts either ignore or actually criminalise[27] the giving of counter-reasons in the form of jurisdictional/political objections, *discourse theory collapses on the very thing on which it pivots*. Against the purported 'reflexivity', 'accommodation' and 'rationality' of discourse-theory, I will argue that the trial depends, in the last instance, on the institutionalised power of those who speak in our name, and its redemption in terms of 'rational self-binding' is ideological, ideological in the sense propounded by Marxists whereby a system of signification sustains relations of domination via a move at the level of representation.

4 ALTERA PARS AUDIATUR

The inclusionary logic of discourse theory that underlies the justification of the imposition of sanctions—as sanctions that 'we' impose on 'us'—can be stated also as a continuity or symmetry in 'giving' the law and 'receiving' the law in the trial. Both processes are deliberative through and through. At neither point—of the creation or application of the law—is the free flow of communication stemmed, the giving of reasons curtailed: for if it were, the conditions of discourse would not obtain and furthermore, were communication to be curbed at one of the two points, the symmetry of creation and application would be broken.

I want to argue that the symmetry is indeed broken on two grounds, and that whatever the applicability of discourse theory to legal discourse in general (which again is contestable) it certainly fails as a normative theory of the trial.

My first argument against the discourse-theoretical solution addresses this symmetry on an issue that has divided discourse theorists. The question, in a

---

[27] I will explain below why I don't treat this distinction as significant in this context. The 'silencing', I argue, occurs irrespective of the choice the court makes to ignore or to banish the subversive statements.

nutshell, is this: are the procedural rules and constraints that are introduced in the courtroom too 'thick' or 'confining' to meet the conditions of uncoerced communication as envisaged by discourse theory? The asymmetry in the distribution of roles in the courtroom, the restraints governing the admissibility of statements and the uses of evidence, the 'strategic' rather than 'communicative' nature of the contributions of participants, are these not obstructive rather than facilitative of communication? And if that is the case, does that not introduce an *a*symmetry between the free flow of reasons in legislation, and their restriction in adjudication?

Against this critique of 'thickness', associated mainly with Ulfrid Neumann,[28] Robert Alexy has defended the applicability of discourse theory to courtroom interaction, by arguing, chiefly, that the 'strategic' motivations of participants (to win the case) do *not* cancel out the communicative nature of the exchange (geared to persuading rather than defeating). This is because the parties must raise a *claim to correctness* if their arguments are to convince the judge, and this introduces a communicative rationality that works all the way up, since the court in turn must justify its decision before the participants, the legal public and the general public. The layers of demands work as filters to establish the correctness and rationality of any decision; the institutionalisation of the procedure along these lines, argues Alexy, guarantees the rationality of adjudicative outcomes, as part of the broader operation of law as a 'special case' of rational practical discourse.[29] Alexy thus claims—and this is the meaning of the special case thesis (*Sonderfallthese*) in this context—that decisions over the just application of the law can raise a claim to correctness within the constraints of the prevailing legal order, where these constraints do not compromise the rationality of those decisions.

Now there is much of value in Alexy's elegant defence, especially given that the operability of the discursive solution depends on there being a 'well-grounded' consensus and, arguably, that is all that Alexy is aspiring to establish at the level of the communicative requirements of the trial. However, if a certain 'thickness' of procedural requirements does in fact stand in the way of what participants may deem vital to their arguments, does this not import a certain 'rationality-deficit' into the courtroom, and with it a certain asymmetry to 'giving and receiving' the law?

The question turns on the purported openness of the process of adjudication to unfettered communication against law's drive to reduce contingency, in that context too, in radical ways. Against discourse-theorists it can be argued that the institutionalisation of proceedings in the courtroom imports a 'mundane' sort of violence to the effect that not everything can be contested, not everything finds its way through filters and procedures. The ambit of all that could be

---

[28] U Neumann, *Juristische Argumentationslehre* (Darmstadt, Wissenschaftliche Buchgesellschaft, 1986).

[29] See R Alexy, n 23 above.

contested is delimited by institutional categories that determine the who, the how and the when of courtroom interaction.

To anticipate this kind of objection Alexy says this:

> Legal discourse can be distinguished from general practical discourse in that the former is, in short, restricted in its scope by statute, precedent, legal dogmatics, and—in the case of actual legal proceedings—by procedural legislation and regulations.[30]

He will accept that in contrast to the (general) model of communicative rationality, interaction in the trial may, for example, often include the right of the accused to remain silent, often involve involuntary participation in the proceedings, often rule out statements on grounds of admissibility, etc. [31] The concession that Alexy is willing to make is that legal claims,

> are not concerned with the *absolute* rationality of the normative statement in question, but only with showing that it can be rationally justified within the framework of the validly prevailing legal order.'[32]

But why the concession? Alexy tells us that it is about remedying a 'weakness':

> The need for legal discourse arises out of the weakness of the rules and forms of general practical discourse. This weakness consists in the fact that these rules and forms define a decision-making procedure which in many cases leads to no result at all.[33]

Therefore, for Alexy, what 'rationally justifies' the structural constraints imposed at the level of the trial against discourse theory's commitment to 'unfettered communication' is the need to redress the latter's 'weakness' which is its (occasional) inability to yield consensus and thus outcomes.

But is this 'rational justification' *rational in terms of discourse theory*? Is it not instead, argues Scott Veitch, that rationality here is 'a requirement being placed *externally* on the legal system?'[34] And the crux of the matter, he argues, is this:

> Legal forms are required to 'reduce the range of discursive possibilities' since 'all things considered' will not produce a result. . . . In the end the court must decide and must produce a winner, and must do so by reference to norms that can produce determinate answers. My question is, in what sense is it rational to do this? . . . Issues recur concerning: how and on what terms radical disagreement has to be homogenised to make a solution reachable? What does it mean to 'reduce the range of discursive possibilities' and what effects does this have? etc.[35]

I think that there is nothing that Alexy can say to redress the rationality deficit at this point. Instead it might be that discourse theorists may have something to learn from their most feared adversary here. For when Niklas Luhmann

---

[30] Ibid, 18–19.
[31] Ibid, 212–20.
[32] Ibid, 22.
[33] Ibid, 287.
[34] S Veitch, *Moral Conflict and Legal Reasoning* (Oxford, Hart Publishing, 1999) 161.
[35] Ibid, 163.

describes the law as a 'reduction achievement' he means that the institutive rules that map out and contain the world of legal meaning enable a form of communication (here: in the courtroom) that would have otherwise been impossible. Law's 'reductions' allow conflicts to be disciplined in the sense of enabling the staking out of joint boundaries for conflicts, which is the minimum condition for anything to be disputed rationally, let alone resolved. Law is important because it allows the casting of conflicts as resolvable and gives us norms and procedures to do just that. After all as the Romans put it, *lites finiri oportet.*

But of course every single aspect of the institutional achievement carries a serious cost in terms of what can be contested in the courtroom, and if Alexy is to justify 'reducing the range of discursive possibilities' he cannot do it on the back of the conditions of practical discourse but only in the name of an *instrumental* (for Veitch: external) function: that disputes *must be* resolved. This is not an imperative of rationality itself (there may be every reason to leave 'well grounded' dissensus unresolved) but of the decisionism of legal, adjudicative procedures. But further, for our purposes, look how different the modalities and effects of that principle appear in the instances of adjudication and legislation respectively. Discourse theory cannot but embrace the decisionist imperative in adjudication—law's need to reach and enforce decisions—*at the expense* of the ideal situation of communicative openness and the infinite openness of the truth to potential challenge, that at the level of legislation may leave some issues unresolved, for now, and all issues open to repeal. What appear as revocable general statements at the level of norm-creation, irrevocably enact violence through their enforcement in the here and now at the level of norm-application, where decisions *must* be reached and thus discussion over any issue is finite, because subject to the constraint of a final decision. As we saw, Alexy's 'Sonderfallthese' for law allows him to say that of course, like practical statements, legal statements too raise a claim to correctness *albeit* (given the nature of law) within the constraints of the prevailing legal order rather than in absolute terms. But what Alexy does not address is that there is a crucial deficit at the level of adjudication that cannot be remedied. Law's decisionist imperative, a *sine qua non* for adjudication, is an abrupt curtailment of processes of reflection and dialogue. To say that *enough* time should be allowed to make the decision *sufficiently rational* either begs the criterion of 'sufficient' or (if true to itself) must remain infinitely open to the determination of 'sufficient', or leads to a *petitio principii*: those who deem it sufficiently rational deem it sufficiently rational to have set the threshold at that point. In the case of each of these solutions the *reflexivity*— and in the way discourse-theorists have laid the cards, inevitably, the *rationality* also—of the process is severely undermined.

'Judgement cannot be delayed,' wrote Derrida. But for him, with the admission of the urgency of this imperative comes a double realisation. First, that this 'structural urgency' for a decision, what he calls the 'overflowing of the performative' 'always maintains within itself some irruptive violence [and thus] no longer responds to the demands of theoretical rationality,' . . . 'marking the

interruption of the juridico-, politico- or ethico-cognitive deliberation that precedes it.'[36] Secondly, and paradoxically, that this declaration, in judgment, of
what is just is in fact the opposite of justice, 'that remains, is yet to come, à venir
. . .,'[37] in fact incalculable in the here and now. 'To say "this is just" or "I am
just" immediately betrays justice.'[38] Derrida's argument about the incalculabil-
ity of justice is tied to deconstruction's bearing witness to what every exercise of
judgment elides, to what finds no adequate register in judgment. With it comes
the modesty of the admission that judgment does not involve the progressive
realisation of justice in the here and now but an 'aporia', an act that is both
urgent (because justice must be done) yet impossible to perform (because justice
is yet to come.) What is striking in this context is that discourse theorists, also
committed to an openness to communicative offers across the board—to what
has remained suppressed, silenced or ignored—are nonetheless happy to cele-
brate legal reason as the 'instantiation', somehow, of the openness of debate, the
adjudicative act as a moment of practical Reason, and thus, in the way rationality dovetails with truth, also as a moment of moral truth.

Let me introduce, very briefly, the second ground on which the symmetry
between giving and receiving the law breaks down. It concerns a distinction
between the justification of a rule and its application; otherwise put, the
distinction between the justification for having a rule and the justification
for applying it in any particular case. If this distinction is seen as presupposing
different reasons, if there is a disjunction between the discourse of justification
and the discourse of application, then the coincidence between those who create
norms and those who are addressees of particular decisions can no longer be
simply assumed.

The justification of general norms as products of deliberation requires that
they apply to all particulars that are subsumable under them. But no norm is
self-applying: it always requires a decision that in some sense 'activates' it.
Because, of course, no norm ever 'reaches down' to claim its instantiations; subsumption is an *active* intervention in the world. Justification, to recall Saussure's
terms, resembles 'langue' while application resembles 'parole'. The application
of the law thus always depends on the structures of the justification of norms but
remains an independent moment. Justifications *under*determine applications. If
I have understood Klaus Günther's thesis correctly,[39] application calls for a separate moment of judgment over the appropriateness of the application of a
norm to a specific set of particulars. As *determinatio* an application instantiates
a rule with reference to a concrete configuration of events. But a *determinatio* is
an active intervention akin, for Günther, to the exercise of Aristotelian *phronesis*. The exercise of *phronesis* entails reasons that are context-sensitive, and

---

[36] J Derrida 'The Force of Law', in D Cornell, M Rosenfeld and DG Carlson, *Deconstruction and
the Possibility of Justice* (London, Routledge 1992) 26, 27.

[37] Ibid, 27.

[38] Ibid, 10.

[39] K Günther, *A Sense of Appropriateness* (Albany, SUNY Press, 1993).

what is crucial here is that the relevant context is that of application.[40] Günther's analysis of how a certain 'Kantian' logic of the justification of norms and an Aristotelian one of the justification of their application diverge, is complex and nuanced and I cannot begin to do it justice here. But if *with* him we assume that a consideration of appropriateness must intervene between the justification of a norm and the justification of its application then *against* him, perhaps, we must query whether the perfect commutability of creator and addressee of norm is at least qualified with the appearance of reasons specific to application in a fresh judgment over appropriateness, reasons that cannot and *could not* be rationally settled at the level of legislation. So much more so if one adds to this the former injunction, that rationality in terms of justification concerns an unfettered 'giving of reasons', whereas application is driven by the decisionist imperative to reach a decision and enforce it. In this 'fresh' judgment over enforceability, the structure of justification 'unfolds' to call up an event, to invoke a concrete instance as instance of a rule. And it is this 'surplus', inherent in application, that my initial statement was meant to capture: a norm requires a decision in order to claim its instances. And in this differentiation of justification and application, of norm and decision, the simple coincidence of addressor and addressee is undone.

5 *PETITIO PRINCIPII*: SELF-REFERENCE *AS* JUSTIFICATION

What I have argued in the previous section is that the discursive redemption of the trial, the inclusive move that legitimates the trial as the moment in which *we* sanction the law *we* have given ourselves, breaks down on two fronts. It breaks down because the application of the law, the instance of adjudication, cannot be communicatively redeemed as an instance of uncoerced communication, due to its inherent structural constraints. And it also breaks down because the coincidence of addressor and addressee of norms comes undone if we see the giving of norms and the receiving of norms as moments subject to their own different logics, of norm and decision, justification and application, universalisability and appropriateness, respectively.

Could it be, though, that this disjunction between creating the law and receiving it is not in fact that problematic *if it is the case* that communication in the courtroom is in fact justifiably hedged in, structurally constrained and subject to a different logic, *because* the proper forum for raising objections is other? It is only natural, this argument goes, that the kinds of objection we have been discussing are silenced or ignored in trials because the public democratic sphere is where they ought to have been raised. The response to the seditious objector is thus that she has failed to distinguish between fora.

---

[40] Michael Detmold had also argued that there exists a difference between what is reasonable in law and what is reasonable to apply in law in *The Unity of Law and Morality: A Refutation of Legal Positivism* (London, Routledge, 1984).

Of course, this argument continues, the conditions for levelling challenges to the system may be absent in the public sphere too. That merely implies that that forum isn't properly functional. Imagine the statement 'you are a pawn of the terrorist State' addressed in this precise form, identical, by Andreas Baader to the judge as representative of a capitalist oligarchy, and by Nelson Mandela to the judge as representative of the apartheid regime. We would probably say, then, that the anti-apartheid activist is unjustly silenced because there was no public forum where he could properly put his objection.[41] One would perhaps need to pause to reflect more about what 'proper functioning' dictates when it comes to the urban guerrilla who wants to overthrow the institutions of bourgeois democracy, the anti-globalisation protestor who ignores 'proper' political transactions and engages in direct action, or the IRA sympathiser who challenges the right of the Crown to administer justice in Northern Ireland. But however one solves *that*, it has no impact on the delineation of what properly belongs to the public sphere and what to the courtroom. What cannot be contested is that statements like this one of Ulrike Meinhoff's cannot count as part of communication proper to the courtroom:

> This is the first political trial in the FRG since 1945. The Federal Prosecutor's Office and this Court are not intelligent enough to see that the object of their destructive means is also a victim. All that the Federal Prosecutor and the court see is an enemy they want to defeat. This also shows the difference in the definition of our struggle. We are able to see, in a Fascist, the product of his circumstances and the state machine. We ourselves do not need fanaticism; the Federal Prosecutor and the court are the fanatics. They have never come to understand the content of the arguments put forward by Andreas [Baader] and the rest of us. They are merely observing the formalities.

> (30/7/75. Petition submitted by Meinhoff to challenge the Court's jurisdiction)

This is a powerful argument but ultimately it fails. It fails because it depends in the last instance solely on the determination of what counts as proper forum, and this criterion cannot be determined independently of the fora in which it is discussed. There cannot, that is, be any meta-criterion for what is properly 'proper'. The determination of appropriate boundaries, arguments and reasons has to occur within discourse that takes place within certain institutional parameters, albeit the constitutional-democratic sphere or the courtroom. The institutional parameters in each case set the contours of possible debate and those contours cannot be transcended for the question of whether they are proper to be raised. To go back to the difficulty with the dialectic method that Lukács grappled with,[42] the distinction between what *is* (proper) and what *ought to be* (proper) is not transcended and cannot be transcended in the sphere in which it is enacted. Context-bound activity cannot at the same time be context-

---

[41] Similarly perhaps for the American academic who challenges the Patriot Act.

[42] G Lukács, *Die Theorie des Romans*, quoted in I Meszaros, *Lukács' Concept of Dialectic* (London, The Merlin Press, 1972) 52.

transcending activity. And thus no meta-level argument over 'proper limits' is possible at the first-order level of constitutional politics or court procedure. Instead every determination of 'proper' occurs within the givenness of those parameters. I will have something to say too, at the end of the section, about the meta-theorist who ignores both of these contexts.

To argue this point I need to look at how the logic of self-reference 'unfolds', because ultimately it is self-reference on which this argument stumbles. It is the self-reference of the argument that those who deem it proper, deem it proper to have determined it thus. And on the back of that, the self-reference that any attempt to understand or scrutinise a challenge to those limits and those determinations involves re-instating those limits and determinations, unable to break through the circularity.

Let us return to sedition to see this logic enacted. The seditious challenge to the court that we have called political/jurisdictional ('Your courts are instruments of class justice') is rebutted on the grounds that it is not proper for the courts to address those issues. The seditious challenge to the constitutional *public sphere* ('Your jurisprudence is the will of your class made into law for all') is rebutted on the grounds that it is not a permissible constitutional challenge. Regarding the latter, in fact, in delimiting the sphere of public participation constitutions regularly remove from political negotiation and dialogue questions over the protection of economic freedoms and the security of property rights on which turn the operation of the capitalist system, by entrenching them at a level beyond challenge. Admittedly not all such protection is 'rigid', and not all challenges are always excluded from constitutional amendment under *any* majority, but let's accept the modest claim that that is often enough the case, to universalise this assumption. What is happening in both these cases that turns a *political* claim seditious or irrelevant?

Confronted with the denunciation of judges as class enemies or the appeal to overthrow the constitutional order, the law asks the following question: should this utterance be protected under the freedom of speech principle as the exercise of a political right or is it seditious? The exercise of the freedom of speech is protected activity, therefore legal, except where the intention is to subvert the constitutional order, where it becomes illegal. Caught in the specific cluster of the exclusive alternatives *a* and *not-a*, the identity of the instance can only be asserted in the mirror of its negation (each is what the other is not) that brackets out and suspends latent what it is not.[43] Law's 'observation' is clearly structuralist here, the identity of a concept identified, in Saussure's words, 'purement differentiel'.[44] Due to the fact that free speech and sedition are coded together in

---

[43] On the idea of the non-indicated value as 'Reflexionswert' see N Luhmann, 'Distinctions Directrices: Über Codierung von Semantiken und Systems' (1986) 27 *Kolner Zeitschrift für Soziologie und Sozialpsychologie* 145, and on the function of negation generally, Luhmann, *Soziale Systeme* (Frankfurt, Suhrkamp, 1984).

[44] N Luhmann, 'Distinctions Directrices: Über Codierung von Semantiken und Systems', n 43 above, at 148.

the distinction, the right (free speech) acquires its meaning in the 'mirror' of its counter-value (sedition). In that structural articulation, then, law brings the existence of the institutional process to bear on the possibility of political truth. Why? Because law reflects its criterion of what counts as political activity in the mirror of negating activity that subverts the constitutional process. In the process the possibility of politics becomes negated sedition, 'negated' subversion of the institutional process. The inherently *political* questions whether judges are instruments of class justice, whether terrorism is political, whether political action can and should be directed against the State and its law, are read by the law as answering the question whether they contribute to the constitutional political process, a question that the law of course solves for itself, as a question of sedition, contempt of court, criminal advocacy, 'incitement to disaffection', and the rest. The question of what is politics—and what it means for the political actor to be free and sovereign—is asked in law through an internal distinction that makes sedition—as negated other—the significant criterion in the definition of what it means to act politically. It is in this sense that the system finds itself in an environment of politics that it has re-enacted, a re-enactment premised upon a specific rationality of *politics* that relies on *legally* projected means, limits and possibilities. And it is only a natural consequence of this setting itself in context that the positive side of our distinction free speech/sedition becomes not just the hallmark of 'proper' politics but the sign of politics as such, a realm that cannot be transcended because there is nowhere to go beyond this self-produced boundary. And sedition now becomes observed as the breaking off point of political action itself. The radical hypothesis that our political actors are politically disempowered when perceived as constitutional players cannot be voiced within a system that circumscribes the political within the constitutional sanctioning of the public sphere, with its attendant prescriptions regarding jurisdiction and the mode of exercise of political and economic power.

I have employed the language of systems-theory, to argue in this context a certain legal 'domestication' of politics, a certain recasting of politics in law's own image. I have argued that if law criminalises sedition it is because it sees it, in the final instance, as speech directed against politics. Sedition marks the threshold beyond which law cannot accept speech as political. At this threshold the legal demarcation of what counts as political speech is closed off self-referentially. While I have argued at greater length elsewhere how law's reference to politics is mediated by its own self-descriptions,[45] for present purposes enough has been said, I hope, to establish that any reference to 'proper fora' is ineluctably caught up in an 'internal' determination of 'proper', one that carries into that self-determination the limitations of the context. That the evaluation of appropriateness cannot escape this self-reference repeats the logic of the *petitio principii:* the agent that delimits what is proper deems it proper to have thus delimited it. Moreover, sedition, as it straddles both public sphere and courtroom inter-

---

[45] E Christodoulidis, *Law and Reflexive Politics* (Dordrecht, Kluwer, 1998) ch 12.

action, establishes a continuity of the interdiction of all that is 'improper' to challenge 'politically'.

6 'WE, LAWGIVERS, SUBJECTS': METONYMIES OF THE FIRST PERSON PLURAL

Throughout this chapter I have insisted on the difference between those who give and those who receive the law, between those who speak the law and the particular person who is spoken about in the law. I argued, *with* discourse theorists, that without the coincidence of addressors and addressees of norms, the externality of any justification of silencing statements in the trial means that it cannot be assumed to bind those who find it wanting. But then, *against* discourse-theory, I argued that this coincidence first falters on a disjunction between the 'logic' of norm-creation and that of norm application, then stumbles on the self-reference of a constitutional language that, at both levels, remains radically *un*-accommodating of certain political voices and thus falls radically short of an 'unfettered' consensus. I will conclude by arguing that this exclusion—more than that: the irrepresentability of dissensus—remains hidden behind a certain homogenising logic in the invocation of the 'we', both at the level of democratic politics of 'we the people' and that of pronouncing 'our' law in the courtroom. It is an invocation that assumes too much because it enacts a 'we' through transgression.

A long tradition in democratic thinking makes the legitimacy of political arrangements dependent on rulers and ruled—addressors and addressees—being *co-referential* terms. This, for Carl Schmitt, was the identity that constantly recurred in democratic life.[46] All democratic arguments, claimed Schmitt, rest logically on a series of identities: of governed and governing, of sovereign and subject, of subject and object of state activity. This 'Jacobin' logic, he argued, guarantees that the subsumption of the individual to the general will occurs as a matter of conceptual necessity. It is precisely this conceptual necessity that we have encountered underlying the inclusionist logic of discourse theory too. Legislation, paradigmatically (in Rousseau) occurs as a speech act in the first person plural. The 'we' is staged as endorsing a shared intention, where this staging, in Habermas's theory of the public sphere now, is underwritten as a counterfactual norm of discourse.

But then, as the German philosopher Waldenfels puts it,

it is impossible for a we to say we. . . . Linguistically speaking, this means that the 'we' of the utterance content does not coincide with the 'we' of the utterance process that speaks the we or with the 'I' that speaks for the we.[47]

---

[46] C Schmitt, *Verfassungslehre* (Berlin, Duncker & Humblot, 1993 [1928]).

[47] B Waldenfels, *Topographie des Fremden* (Frankfurt, Suhrkamp, 1997) 149; this translation by Hans Lindahl, 'Acquiring a Community' (2003) 9 *European Law Journal* 433, at 449. I have much benefited from reading Lindahl's paper on this.

The 'we' is thus announced by those authorised to speak it, or as Bert van Roermund puts it 'what we encounter [in such utterances] is a web of various metonymies accounting for membership of the term speaker.'[48] The 'we' cannot announce itself because there is no first-person-plural *speaker*. This is a serious conceptual point. The argument here (I should add: considerably simplified) is that there is always inevitably a performative element in any invocation of the 'we'. This absence cannot be redeemed by invoking a counterfactual norm of discourse or pragmatic opportunities to contest the invocation. The important point, I think, is that at the moment of the invocation of the 'we' by another, the speaking position of she who was silent was usurped, and this appropriation cannot be countered except *after the event*, after the invocation has already been effected. (Assuming, that is, that the opportunity is there; and often, as in Ballestrini's case, it wasn't). Then it is the temporal gap (between the invocation and its possible rebuttal) that points to the conceptual point. The invocation *at the moment of its occurrence* usurps and overdetermines, and in that carries the performative element. It is the performative element that allowed the 'founding fathers' to legislate for the American people, when at the time of the invocation of 'we the people' there were neither 'people' not legislators as such, and when the risk was very real that that 'we' could be rebutted and the founding fathers relegated to outlaws rather than legislators.

What is crucial here is how the operation of the 'we', by the legislator and the judge, invokes and projects a commonality: 'We, citizens, subjects'. This context of mutuality cannot be taken as given at the moment of its utterance, only ex post facto. What in fact allows this move is that institutions, like the trial, offer default settings to regularise and customise these kinds of invocations. The democratic principle of adjudication that we have been talking about (the principle that the addressees of a norm should be capable of regarding themselves as its addressors) amounts to little more than this kind of institutional self-inclusion that isn't, and couldn't be, *self*-inclusion at the time when it is performed.

It only begs the question, albeit in a most illuminating way, to object that the invocation of the 'we' is nonetheless proper in settings where it is properly instituted (where there is prior agreement for example, as to what 'we' agree on or what 'we' stand for). The point is that the invocation of the 'we' only stands to the extent that he who has not spoken it consents to what was uttered in his name. This reflexivity—'am I really represented in the "we"?'—becomes one that is impossible to pre-contain. Consent to inclusion can only be certified after the event, that is, *after* the invocation of the 'we' has been effected. It is this temporal economy that makes it *'impossible* for a we to say "we".' If this is the case, it is a fortiori so when the invocation relies on a prior institutionalisation of a

---

[48] B van Roermund, 'First Person Plural Legislature: Political Reflexivity and Representation' (2003) 6 *Philosophical Explorations* 235, at 238. This paper is a profound philosophical attempt to 'scrutinise the canonical form of a first-person legislative speech act.'

relationship; and this, in turn, becomes even more problematical when the 'we' has not been entered into through actual but only virtual, if '*well-grounded*', consensus. Typical examples of this unwarranted invocation have been those we have visited: 'we citizens', 'we subjects of the Crown', 'we, economic- and property-right holders', 'we, US patriots, committed to the war against terrorism', or 'the security of the state of Israel', etc, etc. And it is precisely the arbitrariness of *that* invocation and inclusion in a first person plural that surfaces in that most improbable formulation of the discourse principle that we saw addressed to the subversives : '*We* do not allow *ourselves* these kinds of statement.'

And the problem, going back to our silenced comrades, is this: theirs is an objection to the invocation of the 'we': 'We have been robbed' began the ANC manifesto during the struggle, and whether that 'we' is the 'we' of the new South Africa remains a deeply political question. Or more poignantly in the Baader/Meinhof trial: 'I find it hard to say anything at all here. It is my view that we ought not to talk to you or about you any more. Action is called for to deal with the antagonism of the state machine towards humanity, . . .'.[49] Each injunction is one against the invocation of a commonality that includes them in order to efface their claim: that in the very moment when a tribunal invites them—as one of 'us'—to litigate their claim they have already been robbed of their claim, because their conflict is so fundamental that it cannot survive the passage into a first-person-plural. Baader's refusal to join as interlocutor—'we ought not to talk to you or about you any more'—is impossible to make heard since the dialogue includes him anyway. And the objection against the inclusion cannot be raised at any level, since the heroic theorists that raised it to the point where they might make a difference found to their cost that they had joined those on the side of sedition, from the RAF defence lawyer, Croissant, convicted for complicity with his 'clients', to those American academics who protest against government practices and find their unpatriotic stance consigns them to post-'9/11' blacklists, with very real effects on their lives and livelihoods. Caught out by the inclusionist move, which makes it impossible to envisage how 'we' could be anything else except both addressors and addressees of norms, it is no longer possible for an addressee of the norm to step back and object not to the norm but to being addressed it in the first place. That is ideology operating at the deep level where the possibility of raising an objection is always-already undercut, the dissident of law *invisible* except as an outlaw.

With the objection that cannot be heard we have come to a crucial threshold, to the limits of legal possibility: to challenge the jurisdiction of the court challenges its ability to pronounce judgment and thus to say anything at all about the challenge itself, in the same way that to challenge the constitutional processes challenges the capacity of the system to express the 'will of the people' since that will is bound—constitutively—to the processes that yield it. It is this

---

[49] Baader, 5 August 1975, 23rd day of the Baader-Meinhof trial.

line of reasoning that led Kant to put it so bluntly in the *Metaphysical Elements of Justice*: 'there is no right of sedition, much less a right of revolution.'[50] That is because, for Kant, there could be no general will outwith the legal processes for ascertaining it as contained in the Constitution. And sedition (and revolution) aim to undermine those legal processes and with it the 'juridical condition' itself of the constitution of the will.

And yet doesn't our heroic meta-theorist, surveyor of proper delineations and proper limits, have a duty to account for the truth of those who oppose the processes that yield well-grounded consensus and with it moral truth? To put it the other way around, if political action can only be action contained in and prescribed by constitutional processes, how are the politics of those who defy or oppose these processes to be expressed? If political truth is the outcome of those processes how is the truth of those who contest them to register? No recourse to aspirations of communicative openness and well-groundedness, no recourse to proper fora can save the day. I think, instead, that this question, addressed to the theorist, should be approached as a question of moral responsibility, but that it leaves her, as it left Derrida, on the precipice of silence.

To try to unpack this, we can take the lead again from Kant. Because it was Kant who also said of the French Revolution that 'this revolution, nonetheless finds in the hearts of all spectators (who are not engaged in the game themselves) a wishful participation which borders on enthusiasm, . . . this sympathy can have no other cause than a moral disposition in the human race.'[51] The problem for Kant is of course that while he claims that this 'sympathy' to the revolution testifies to our moral nature, his own theory denies him the revolutionary's justifications. Christine Koorsgaard places Kant, brilliantly I think, on a precipice of a moral vacuum at this point. She says that 'a kind of gap opens up in the moral world in which the moral agent must stand alone.'[52] 'The moral life can contain moments when responsibility is so deep that even a justification is denied us.'[53] At moments like this one may find that one must 'take even the moral law into his own hands.'

In all this the decoupling of the question of *just* action from the integrity of *legal* procedures returns it to us in purely *political* terms and as a matter of *ethics*. Let us return for the last time to the political radicals of the *Lotta Continua*, and to their most famous member. This is now Antonio Negri, in *The Politics of Subversion*,[54] on the definitions, justifications and proper limits of political action: when we return to these questions, he says, we shall be involved, and can only be involved, in a discussion about ethics.

[50] Kant, *The Metaphysical Elements of Justice* (trans John Ladd; New York, Macmillan, 1965) 320.
[51] Quoted in C Korsgaard, 'Taking the Law Into Our Own Hands: Kant on the Right to Revolution' in A Reath, B Herman and C M Korsgaard (eds), *Reclaiming the History of Ethics: Essays for John Rawls* (Cambridge, Cambridge University Press, 1997) 299.
[52] Ibid, 319.
[53] Ibid, 322.
[54] A Negri, *The Politics of Subversion: A Manifesto for the Twenty-first Century* (trans J Newell) (Collingdale PA, Diane Publishing Co, 1989).

Index